D0921606

PHILOSOPHY FOR BEGINNERS

PHILOSOPHY FOR
BEGINNERS

By

HILAIRE MORRIS, O.S.M., D.D., Ph.D.

Consultor of the Sacred Congregation
of Sacraments.
Apostolic Examiner of the Clergy of Rome.

THE   NEWMAN   PRESS
WESTMINSTER,   MARYLAND

First published 1960

M832.

Nihil obstat :
    Fr. Antoninus M. Basso, O.S.M.,
                Censor deputatus.
    Vicetiae, die 20 Septembris, 1958.

Imprimi potest :
    Fr. Gabriel M. Roschini, O.S.M.
                Vicarius Generalis.
    Romae, die 25 Septembris, 1958.

Nihil obstat :
    Jacobus Canonicus Bastible,
                Censor deputatus.

Imprimatur :
    ✠ Cornelius,
    Episcopus Corcagiensis et Rossensis,
                7 . 12 . 59.

© THE MERCIER PRESS LTD.

PRINTED   IN   THE   REPUBLIC   OF
IRELAND BY CAHILL AND CO., LTD.,
PARKGATE PRINTING WORKS, DUBLIN

CONTENTS

v

Part IV.
COSMOLOGY

CHAP.   PAGE

INTRODUCTION TO COSMOLOGY 111
1. HYLOMORPHISM 112
2. MATTER AND FORM 115
3. QUANTITY 119
4. QUANTITY AND THE SUPERNATURAL 122
5. THE PRINCIPLE OF INDIVIDUATION 126
6. NUMBER 128
7. PLACE AND SPACE 131
8. MOTION 135
9. TIME 139

Part V.
PSYCHOLOGY

INTRODUCTION TO PSYCHOLOGY 145
1. LIFE 146
2. THE ORIGIN OF LIFE 149
3. THE SOUL IN GENERAL 152
4. ANIMAL LIFE 156
5. COGNITION 159
6. FACULTIES AND SENSES 161
7. CONSCIOUSNESS AND PERCEPTION 165
8. IMAGINATION 168
9. MEMORY 172
10. INSTINCT 175
11. EMOTIONS AND REFLEXES 178
12. THE INTELLECT 182
13. THE AGENT INTELLECT 186
14. THE INTELLECTUAL SPECIES 189
15. DIRECT AND REFLEX KNOWLEDGE 194
16. THE INDIVIDUAL CONCEPT 197
17. PARTICULAR REASON 200
18. THE HUMAN SOUL 202
19. INDEPENDENCE OF THE HUMAN SOUL 206
20. IMMORTALITY OF THE HUMAN SOUL 210
21. THE WILL 214
22. FREE-WILL 218
23. THE INTENTION OF THE WILL 222
24. THE WILL-ACT 226
25. THE ANGELS 229

VOCABULARY AND INDEX 231
BIBLIOGRAPHY 245

PREFACE

This Philosophy for beginners is an attempt to show that the terms and distinctions, the definitions and arguments of Scholastic Philosophy are not quite so obscure and obsolete as they are generally thought to be.

It is written in plain English for the special benefit of students who are grappling with the perplexities and difficulties of Scholastic phraseology.

It is essentially a beginner's reference manual, dealing exclusively with Scholastic Philosophy, with no reference to other philosophical systems, and as little as possible to debated questions. It is not meant for the advanced philosopher, and has not the pretension to be a complete treatise of philosophy or a new contribution to the field of philosophical research. Its sole aim is to foster the study of the old traditional philosophy.

Servite Monastery,

S. Marcello, Rome.

PHILOSOPHY IN GENERAL

Philosophy is the knowledge of the supreme and universal causes, says St. Thomas. Descartes calls it the pursuit of wisdom or the knowledge of truth by the first causes. Its object is the rational explanation of the general principles which are taken for granted by all other branches of knowledge. This conception of philosophy is that of practically all ancient and modern philosophers. The definition of philosophy as the science of principles, says the Encyclopedia Britannica, is perhaps the most usual definition, and one of the least misleading.

Until the end of the Middle Ages, the scope of knowledge was rather limited and was confined to what was known as the seven sciences. Experimental science was practically unknown, and no sharp boundaries existed between philosophy and other branches of knowledge; these were all included in the study of philosophy which was the *Science* of the Ancient World. Thus science, knowledge and philosophy were synonymous, and represented all that was taught in those days.

But the experimental discoveries of subsequent years gave a new impulse and orientation to the pursuit of knowledge. A division into separate channels soon became an absolute necessity. And so the word *science*, which formerly meant the knowledge of abstract causes and was synonymous with philosophy, came to be used as a short term for natural science, namely for the ordered knowledge of natural phenomena and of the relations between them. Science, thus understood, has entirely severed itself from, and even usurped, the unchallenged supremacy of the philosophy of the Ancient and of the Middle Ages. Little time is left for the study of abstract truth and first principles to-day, and although philosophy still figures in the curriculum of modern studies, for many people it consists merely in the survey of the various systems put forward by philosophers of all ages, a survey which is bound to be superficial by reason of the multiplicity of systems it endeavours to examine and criticize.

Metaphysics, which above all other branches of philosophy consists in the search for the final causes of things, figures no longer in

the curriculum of modern philosophical studies. Rational Psychology
is also ignored and has given way to mere experimental psychology.
Likewise Cosmology has become a mere experimental research into
the phenomena of the Universe, and is no longer concerned with
the abstract analysis of the nature and properties of material things.
Logic is the only branch of philosophy which is sometimes taught
in modern schools; the rest of the time is given to reading and
criticizing what other people have said on philosophy : a sort of
encyclopedic knowledge.

Philosophy is divided into three parts, Rational, Natural and
Moral Philosophy.

Rational Philosophy or Logic is concerned with the laws of
correct reasoning. It also deals with the objectivity of our knowledge;
this forms a separate part of Logic called Criteriology. Epistemology
is the critical examination of various philosophical systems and
opinions; for practical purposes we can consider Criteriology and
Epistemology as synonyms.

Natural Philosophy investigates the nature of things. It is
divided into three parts: Metaphysics, Cosmology and Psychology.
Metaphysics, also called Ontology, is the study of abstract being,
namely of the abstract nature and of the abstract properties both
of material and immaterial beings. Cosmology on the contrary deals
exclusively with problems concerning the material things of this
world. Psychology is the study of living beings and of their activities.

Moral Philosophy or Ethics deals with the principles which
guide man towards the acquisition of his ultimate end by the right
use of his free-will.

First Philosophers. Thales of Miletus, 620-546 B.C., founder
of the Ionian school of Asia Minor, is commonly considered the
first real philosopher. Until then no system of philosophy had
been attempted, although a certain amount of philosophy had been
incorporated in the ancient oriental religions. The word philosophy
is said to have been used for the first time by Pythagoras of Samos,
who lived about 530 B.C.; he pointed out that however much
men learned, they never really acquired wisdom, and so suggested
that they should be called lovers of wisdom, from two Greek
words meaning *friend* and *wisdom*.

The real time of philosophical glory was the Aristotelian period.
First Plato (427-347 B.C.), and then Aristotle, sometimes called the
Stagirite, from Stagira in Macedonia where he was born in 384 B.C.,

had numerous followers. When teaching, Aristotle liked to stroll up and down the shady walks round the gymnasium of the Lyceum he had founded at Athens; hence his disciples were called Peripatetics, from the Greek meaning " to walk around ". Aristotle died in Chalcis in Euboea in 322 B.C.

The vogue of Aristotle's works reached its height in the 13th century. They were first translated into Latin from an Arabian text, and later on from the original Greek. The initial reception was cold ; Gregory IX in 1231 and Urban IV in 1263 went so far as to forbid their being used as text-books in the University of Paris. This was largely due to the many doctrinal inexactitudes which had crept into the very faulty Arabian translation. Later on his works were translated directly from the Greek, and Aristotle then became the only recognized authority taught in ' the Schools. His works were immortalized by the commentaries made upon them by St. Albert the Great (1193-1280), and especially by his illustrious disciple St. Thomas of Aquinas (1227-1274). From this time onwards, the Peripatetics were called Scholastics.

In spite of its decline in the 16th century, Scholasticism has always held its own and has emerged victorious from countless assaults. It had a magnificent revival after the Encyclical of Pope Leo XIII *Aeterni Patris,* and to-day it is gradually returning to its place of honour even in non-Catholic circles.

Scholastic Philosophy alone is in perfect harmony with revealed truth and Catholic dogma ; no other system can disentangle supernatural truth from apparent contradiction. Its neglect is at the root of almost all the errors which in the course of time have clashed with the teaching of the Church. As regards the unfamiliar terminology to which it has recourse, we must remember that philosophy, like any other science, is compelled to create words and expressions of its own, not in general use, because it deals with things which are not the subject of general conversation ; they are however quite easy to understand when explained. To explain them is precisely the scope of the present work.

PART I

FORMAL LOGIC

INTRODUCTION TO LOGIC

Logic, also called Dialectics or Analytics, is both a science and an art, which enables us to think clearly and to reason correctly and consistently. Formal or minor Logic enquires into the relations existing between thoughts and the words by which we express them, and thus deals with terms; it shows how to join them in propositions, and how to unite propositions to form arguments or syllogisms. Material or major Logic enquires into the relations existing between thought and the objects we think about, and thus deals with questions such as the Universals and the criterion of truth. Material Logic is also called Criteriology or Epistemology.

Logic is a science because it establishes the general principles upon which right thinking is based; it is an art because it gives practical rules which guide the mind in the enquiry for, and in the expression of, truth.

To sum up the nature of Logic, it can be said to be the art of arguing correctly. To argue means to infer one assertion from another one. Now there is a certain natural logic known as common sense, which enables us to reason and argue correctly in all ordinary circumstances, without any preliminary study of the laws that govern our rational acts; we can rely upon this common sense quite as safely as we can trust our sight, for example, without knowing Optics. But in difficult and intricate problems, we are subject to error. Common sense proves inadequate in unravelling the truth and assessing the value of obscure conclusions. It would therefore be a great mistake to approach the study of philosophy without the help of Logic. Logic is of the greatest importance and necessity in the study of philosophical problems.

This art of arts was unknown as such before Aristotle. By hard thinking, without the help we generally obtain from books and masters, this great genius built the whole edifice of human reasoning and argument. He may have made mistakes in natural Science, but he made none in Logic. His work is at the basis of practically every book written on the subject. His Logic is not dead as some would have it. Many strange words coined exclusively for this great work of his are still of current usage amongst people who have not the

3

faintest knowledge of Logic, although the meaning of these words
has changed, as for example, the words *predicate*, *predicament*,
category, *comprehension*, *genus*, *species*, and so forth.

Formal Logic is the art of constructing a proper argument called
a Syllogism. A syllogism consists of three propositions, each of which
contains two terms. We must therefore deal firstly with terms, then
with propositions and syllogisms.

CHAPTER I

TERMS IN GENERAL

1. *Terms* are words used in a proposition as subject and predicate. Mere sounds which have no particular meaning, or are just expressions of a feeling, are not words, and therefore cannot be used as terms.

2. *Syncategorematic signs* are words which have a meaning, but not a complete one, such as the words *all, every, no, many, some, a few.* Their purpose in Logic is to modify the meaning of the terms to which they are joined, and to help determine the degree of logical extension of these terms. Hence they are also called signs of distribution.

3. *Abstract terms* are those which represent something considered without its concrete individuality. Thus for example, we can speak of heat or darkness without referring to any hot or dark object. But we have no words to express *man, flower, stone,* or any other exterior object in the abstract; this is why it is so difficult to form an abstract concept as distinct from the picture our imagination draws of a particular man, of particular flowers or stones, and so forth.

4. *Concrete terms* represent individual objects. They are also used to represent the nature of a thing in the abstract, since there are no abstract words to express it; thus we say that a lion is a species of the genus *animal.* In order to know whether a term is taken in a concrete or an abstract meaning, definite rules are given when dealing with the Supposition of terms.

5. *Proper* and *Singular terms* are those which apply to one definite individual, such as *Plato, Dickens, my terrier, that house. Common terms* apply to several individuals, such as *a plate, a tree. Collective terms* apply to several things united in, or conceived as forming, a whole, such as *an army* or *a nation.*

6. *Indivisible terms* are those which designate things which are unique of their kind such as *fire, sun, ink, honour, greatness,* or else a whole class or species such as *man, trees.*

7. *Relative terms* are those which imply each other such as *father* and *son*. *Privative terms* are those which represent something deprived of a quality or an attribute usually found in it, like *blind* or *lame*.

8. *Categorical* or *Predicamental terms* represent things which belong to one of the ten categories. *Ex.: substance, colour*. *Transcendental terms* are those which designate things not confined to any single category. *Ex.: being, unity, truth.*

9. *Distributive* or *Universal terms* are those which are used in a sentence to designate each and every one of the individual objects to which they could apply, *for ex.: roses*, in *roses are flowers*, meaning all roses are flowers. They are called distributive because all the things to which they apply partake equally of their meaning, and they are called universal because they are common to those things.

Non-distributive or *Particular terms,* on the contrary, refer to some only of the individuals which they could be used for. *Ex.: roses*, in *some roses are white*. There are definite rules which enable us to determine whether a term is universal or particular.

10. *Equivocal terms* are ambiguous words used in a sentence without a clearly defined meaning. *For ex.: I don't like that type* could refer to a type of person or to printed type. *Univocal terms* are those used in several sentences in exactly the same meaning, as *for ex. man*, in *Peter is a man*, and *man is a living being. Analogous terms* are those used in several sentences in different, but somewhat connected, meanings. *For ex.* the term *rent* used to signify the rent in a coat, the rent of a hired house, or that in a political party.

CHAPTER 2

SUPPOSITION OF TERMS

11. As the number of words is necessarily inferior to the unlimited number of our thoughts, it often happens that the same words have to be used with different meanings. We call supposition of a term

the special meaning given to it by the context. There are various kinds of supposition.

Equivocal supposition is that of a term which could be used in two or more different meanings, and is actually used without any reference to the exact meaning in which it is taken. Thus if we say that *Smith is a doctor*, it is not specified whether he is a doctor in medicine, theology or law.

Univocal supposition is that of a term which is used in two or more sentences in exactly the same meaning, as when we say that *stones are hard* and that *diamonds are stones*.

Analogous supposition is that of a term used in different but connected meanings, as has been said above.

12. Supposition of the *first intention* is that of a term which expresses a direct concept, namely a concept abstracted directly from the outside world, such as that of the term *animal* in *there are many kinds of animals*, or in *animals are useful to man*.

Supposition of the *second intention* is that of a term which represents a reflex concept, namely a concept of one of the predicables. Thus the term *animal* is used in the second intention in the sentence *the comprehension of animal is greater than that of its extension*.

13. *Formal supposition.* Concrete words represent two things: the hidden nature of a being, and the concrete subject to which that nature belongs. When we use a concrete word in a sentence, stress can be placed on either one or the other of these two meanings. If it is the nature of the thing that is principally taken into consideration, we have what we call *a formal* or *simple* supposition. In this case the sentence will be true only when we bear in mind that we are talking of the nature of the thing expressed by the term. Thus if I say that *Peter is a man*, *man* has a formal supposition; I mean that Peter has a human nature, in contradistinction to those things that are not human. *A concrete term used as predicate of a proposition has always a formal supposition.* It is evident that all abstract words, whether used as subject or predicate, must have a formal supposition.

14. *Personal supposition.* If on the contrary we stress the other meaning of a concrete word, and primarily intend to consider the concrete individual or subject, that subject being none other than the suppositum or person, we have what is called a *personal* or *material* supposition. I say that *man can walk* or *speak*, I am taking into consideration a particular individual that happens to have a

human nature. These attributes *walk* and *speak* do not belong to the
abstract nature of man but to his concrete individuality or person.
In fact it is not the nature of man that walks or speaks, although his
nature is the root and remote principle of these actions; it is the
individual called *man* that really does those actions. On the contrary
when I say that *Peter is a man*, it would be a mere tautology if I
meant that Peter is an individual.

*A concrete term used as the subject of a proposition always has a
personal supposition.* That is why we can truly say that God died for
us; the subject *God* has a personal supposition and denotes the
individual or person of Christ who was God because he had a divine
nature, but could act and suffer in a human way because he also had
a human nature.

15. *Universal supposition,* also called *distributive,* is that of a
term used to denote all the individuals to which it could possibly
apply, such as *men* in *all men are rational animals.*

Particular or *non-distributive* supposition is that of a term used
to denote some only of the individuals to which it could be applied,
as *for ex. men* in *some men are cruel.*

CHAPTER 3

THE PREDICABLES OR UNIVERSALS

16. *Predicables* are the names of the five general ways in which
one term can be affirmed of another one. They are the *Genus,* the
logical *Species,* the specific *Difference,* logical *Property* and logical
Accident. A predicable term is one which is actually considered as
belonging to one of these headings, and consequently as being apt
to become the predicate of a proposition. The grammatical term
predicate means *attribute* of a proposition, and is used in Logic in
the same sense. Now the predicate is nothing else than a predicable
which is actually attributed to, asserted or predicated of, a subject.
Thus *man* is a predicable because it can be asserted of Peter; it
becomes a predicate when we actually assert that Peter is a man.

The beginner who tackles the study of Logic is usually greatly puzzled by the question of predicables. The difficulty arises from not realising that a predicable is only a mental quality, a point of view, which our mind discovers when it relates one term or one concept to another. If we had to adjust some pieces of machinery, we would say that they were, or were not, adjustable; to be adjustable does not change them, but makes them appear to us in a different light. An adjustable piece is one in which we discover a relation to the other pieces of the machine. In a similar manner, when we discover that a term can be affirmed of another one, we say that it is predicable. A predicable therefore really means a *predicable term*, and it can be defined as a term or concept that can be predicated or affirmed of another one in a proposition. When a predicable is actually predicated in a proposition, it is called a predicate.

The usefulness of the present question lies in the fact that the object of any kind of knowledge, and particularly the study of Logic, is to know things as they really are, that is to say, to give the right attribute to the right subject; if we always did this, we should never make a mistake. But in order to assert one concept of another, this concept must have something in common with the other, and there are five ways only in which this can happen. Whenever we make an affirmation, the attribute must necessarily come under one of these headings, otherwise the affirmation will be false. In other words, the attribute of a proposition must be *attributable* or *predicable* of the subject. Thus we can say that *man is an animal*, because *animal* is the genus of man, but we cannot say that *an animal is a plant*, because *plant* is not one of the five predicables in relation to *animal*.

17. *Species*. Before explaining the meaning of these predicables, it is necessary to explain the term *essence*. The popular meaning of this word is an extract, something in a concentrated form. Philosophically, essence means the inner nature which makes a thing exactly what it is; it is a sort of concentration of all that is essential to a thing. Thus *rational animal* or *man* represents the essence of Peter or Jack. Now the term *species* designates purely and merely the essence of several individual objects considered as having that common essence, without any reference to any of the differences which exist between them. Thus species is a synonym or an essence, considered as being attributable or predicable of many individuals.

18. *Genus*. The Genus represents the common nature or essence of several species considered, not only without any of the individual

and numerical differences which make one lion, let us say, distinct
from another one, but also without any of the differences which exist
between a lion, a cat, a fish, a bird, or any other animal. Genus is
thus a term common to any individuals or different species. *Animal*
for example, is the genus of lion, cat, fish, bird and so forth; *material*
is the common genus of inanimate and organic beings.

19. *Specific Difference.* This term represents that by which the
individuals of one particular species resemble each other and differ
from those of other species. Thus *rational* is the specific difference of
man.

Both genus and difference are logical components of the species;
thus man contains the genus *animal* and the difference *rational*. But
we must be careful not to say that the genus represents only a part of
the species, otherwise we could not affirm that *man is an animal,* since
no part of a thing is equivalent to the whole. Therefore the genus
represents the whole essence of man, but in a more abstracted and
universal manner than the species which only abstracts from
individual features, whilst the genus abstracts also from specific
differences. It is a question of a point of view; the genus *animal* represents man from the point of view of the features he has in common
with beasts; the species represents the same man from the point of
view of his distinctive characteristics. Therefore although it is true
that the genus is contained in the comprehension of the species as
we shall see later on, it is only contained as a logical part, that is to
say, that the mind thinks of a united and indivisible whole as having
parts into which, however, it cannot actually be divided. It is something like saying that iron is a constituent part of a key, or that a
window contains glass.

We must also beware of thinking that the genus contains the
several species into which it can be divided. We can logically divide
animal for example into *man* and *beast,* by thinking of *animal* as a
man or as a beast; but these species are not real parts of the genus;
on the contrary the genus is a logical part of the species.

20. It would be useful to give some examples to illustrate these
rather obscure notions of essence, species, genus and difference.
Unfortunately we have no abstract nouns to represent the abstract
nature of things as expressed by these concepts. We have to be
content to talk about the *nature* or the *essence* of man, the *essence* of
stone, whatsoever it may be. Things have, besides their exterior

qualities which are sense-perceived, a hidden nature or essence, which makes them what they are, something by which a metal for example is metal and not a liquid, and which makes gold what it is, and not brass; this hidden nature is the essence expressed by the term species. Specific difference is the name of the distinctive feature of the essence, whilst genus is a term that denotes the common feature of several essences. Thus the genus of gold, iron or brass, would be the *nature* of mineral; their specific difference, *that by which* we distinguish gold from brass and so forth. But we do not really know what that nature is, neither do we know what distinguishes gold for example from brass; all we know are the properties which a thing manifests, not its internal nature. It is something real, but we have no words to denominate it.

21. *Property* is a quality which, although no part of the essence, is inseparable from it to such an extent that it is always found in all the individuals of that species, and in no individual of any other. It is said to be *in all, only,* and *always.* Logical property is the term which expresses the concept of this essential property of a thing.

22. *Accident.* Logical accident is the name given to the concept of any quality which is common to individuals of several species, such as *blackness* or *height.* We must be especially careful to distinguish between logical accident which is a predicable term or concept, and metaphysical accident which is the real existent quality expressed by the logical term. Logical accident therefore, which is a mental concept opposed to that of logical property, is always a logical accident and is unique in its species, namely that of being the fifth predicable. Metaphysical accident on the contrary, is an extra-mental reality opposed to substance, one of the nine metaphysical or predicamental accidents, and can be considered either as a logical accident, such as for example the *whiteness* of a rose, or as a logical property such as the *barking* of a dog.

23. *Logical Universals.* We have seen that each of the five predicables is common to all those things which come under its heading. Now in Logic we often use the word *universal* instead of common. It therefore follows that predicables are also called *Universals,* and are often referred to as *Logical Universals.* A metaphysical Universal on the contrary is not the name of a mere concept, but that of the very nature or essence represented by the concept, and considered as actually belonging to each and every one of the individual things

from which the mind has abstracted it. Therefore the Species, the specific Difference and logical Property are called logical Universals because they represent concepts that are common to, and predicable of, all the individuals having an identical nature; Genus and logical Accident are logical Universals because they represent concepts common to things of different kinds.

CHAPTER 4

COMPREHENSION AND EXTENSION OF TERMS

24. *Comprehension.* By comprehension of a term we mean the sum total of all the essential elements of its definition. It is sometimes called Connotation or Intension. A definition in fact makes us *comprehend* or understand what a thing is. For example, the logical comprehension of *table* would be all that which is connected with a piece of furniture with a flat surface raised on legs; that of *dog* is all the essential characteristics which make it a species of the canine race.

To understand what is meant by the comprehension of a term, we must remember that words represent not simple, but compound things, things composed of various constituent elements; even those physical elements which are known as simple ones, are composed of parts, because no one has so far, and probably never will, discover the ultimate simple constituent of matter. Anyhow, however simple it might prove to be, there would still be many metaphysical elements to be taken into consideration. To enumerate these elements is to analyse a term. The contents of this analysis are expressed by the definition and constitute the term's comprehension. Now a complete analysis would take much time and study; a full knowledge for example of the term *tree*, would require complete mastery of many branches of botany and of other kindred sciences. We therefore use terms as a kind of shorthand sign, an abbreviation of many things, some of which we do not know, and all of which are summed up by what we call comprehension.

25. *Extension.* Here we are not dealing with physical extension which is a divisible magnitude. We are concerned with the logical extension of terms. This kind of extension consists in the relation between a term and the greater or smaller number of individuals to which this term can be applied. If we except people, pet animals, and a few other things, we do not give a special name to each individual thing, but call all those things which have the same characteristics by the same name, and distinguish them by the words *this* or *that*. Thus the word table is a common name applicable to hundreds of tables, the word *dog* can apply to many dogs. We say that these things are contained in the extension of that word, which is therefore common to them all.

Extension, sometimes also called Denotation, is therefore the fact of a term being common to several things of the same genus or species. Now since the word *universal* in Logic is often used as a synonym for common, we can say that logical extension consists in the universality of a term, and consequently that it makes a term predicable. Thus for example, *animal* is universal on account of its extension, because it is the common genus of man and beast of which it is predicable.

26. There are different *degrees of extension* or universality, according to the number of objects to which a term is common. Some terms have a greater extension than others. Species, for example, namely a nature abstracted merely from the individual characteristics of matter, although truly universal, only possesses a universality of the most inferior kind; it is the lowest universal in the Porphyrian Tree, viz., in the scale of Universals. But many terms have a far greater universality than that of the species. Indeed we can continue the process of abstraction so far that we at last arrive at what we do not call any more a universal, but a transcendental, which is a concept so abstract that it bears only an analogy with the things from which it is abstracted. By abstracting the concept of a species from, or so to say by divesting it mentally of, that by which it differs from other species, namely from its specific difference, we arrive at the concept of a nature common to several species. We call this concept that of a genus.

By a succession of abstractions we obtain what are known as the inferior, intermediate and supreme genus of a thing. *Matter* for example, applies to many more things than *tree*, since it includes not only trees, but all mineral, vegetal and animal matter.

Plant has more extension than *rose,* because it applies to all kinds of trees, vegetables and flowers, including roses. Terms which represent concepts having more extension than others, are called *superior* universals. Less extended ones are called *inferior* universals, because they are contained under the superior ones. Thus *rose* is contained under the heading *plant,* and *tree* under that of *matter;* therefore rose and tree are inferior universals. *Plant* and *matter* are superior universals in this case, but they are *intermediate* universals between rose and substance.

27. Terms that have the highest degree of universality are called *Supreme* universals; those of intermediate degree, *Intermediate* ones, and those that have the smallest degree, are called the *Lowest* universals. A supreme genus is not a species of anything else; a lowest species is not a genus, because it has no inferior species. But intermediate genera and species can be both species and genera according to the point of view from which they are considered. Thus if we consider *animal* as a term common to men and beasts, it will be a genus. But if we consider this same term *animal* as the distinctive name of those living beings which are not plants, we will say that it is a species of living beings.

28. *Comprehension is in inverse ratio to extension.* This means that as comprehension increases, extension decreases, and vice-versa. All concepts have not the same degree of comprehension; some have little, such as *substance* in general, which excludes all the characteristics contained in the comprehension of particular substances; if it did not exclude them, it would no longer be substance in general, but a particular substance. Thus also *plant* is more simple and has less comprehension than *rose,* because if we say that a certain flower is a plant, we imply much less than by saying that it is a rose.

But at the same time all concepts, and the terms which express them, have not the same extension. Thus *plant* is common to many more things than *rose,* and consequently has a greater extension, precisely because it has less comprehension. Indeed the more simple a concept is, that is to say, the less comprehension it has, the greater is the number of things to which it is common, or in other words, the greater is its extension, and vice-versa. As an example, although a skeleton-key will open many more doors than a special key, yet it is much more simple and has less detail; in fact, it must not have the indentations of any particular key, otherwise it would not open all the doors it is meant to open. Comprehension therefore and extension are evidently in inverse ratio.

29. All that has just been said about the various degrees of logical extension or universality and of comprehension, together with their mutual relationship of superiority and inferiority, is usually illustrated by the Scholastics by what is called the *Porphyrian Tree*. This is a diagram designed in the shape of a genealogical tree by Porphyrius (234-304 B.C.), author of an Introduction to Aristotle's Logic, called the *Isagogue*. The Porphyrian tree consists in the logical grouping and classification of all the particular species contained under the general heading or supreme genus of substance. Substance is the first of the ten categories into which Aristotle divides all the things of this world. A similar tree could be likewise drawn up for any of the other categories.

Explanation of the Porphyrian Tree.

Substance is contained in the comprehension of, and contains in its extension, all and each species of spirits and bodies, physical elements and living beings, plants and animals, and all the individuals of the human race. But substance itself does not contain in its comprehension, and is not contained in the extension of, anything superior to it, because it is not a species of anything else, but the universal genus of all substances. It has therefore the greatest extension and no logical comprehension.

Bodies is contained in the comprehension of, and contains in its extension, all and each species of physical elements and living bodies, plants and animals, beasts and men. It contains in its comprehension, and is contained in the extension of, substance in general. Its extension is therefore greater than its comprehension.

Living beings is contained in the comprehension of, and contains in its extension, all and each species of plants, animals in general, beasts and men. It contains in its comprehension, and is contained in the extension of, bodies and substance in general. It has therefore a great extension, and a great comprehension.

Animals is contained in the comprehension of, and contains in its extension, all the species of beasts and the individuals of the human race. It contains in its comprehension, and is contained in the extension of, living beings, bodies and substance in general. Its comprehension is therefore greater than its extension.

Man is contained in the extension of, and contains in its compre-

THE PORPHYRIAN TREE

Substance in general
supreme genus of the two following supreme species

Immaterial substances (spirits)
an intermediate genus which contains many other species, namely the Angels

Material substances (bodies)
an intermediate genus which by the addition of the specific differences *inorganic* and *organic*, forms the following intermediate species

Inorganic substances (physical elements)
an intermediate genus which contains all the genera and species of inanimate matter

Organic substances (living bodies)
an intermediate genus which by the addition of the specific differences *vegetal* and *cognitive* forms the following intermed. species

Vegetal substances (plants)
an intermediate genus which contains all the genera and species of the botanical reign

Cognitive beings (animals in general)
which is an intermediate genus of the species

Irrational animals (beasts)
formed by the addition of the specific difference *irrational* and divided into many other genera and species

Rational beings (men)
formed by the addition of the specific difference *rational*, and constituting the lowest species in this line, because all men belong to one and the same human species

the lowest genus of the species

hension, animals, living beings, bodies and substance in general. But it is not contained in the comprehension of, nor does it contain in its extension any inferior species, but only the individuals of the human race. It has therefore the greatest comprehension, but has little logical extension.

DISTRIBUTION OF TERMS

30. From the foregoing chapter we gather that one and the same term can be used to represent all or several of the individuals which are contained in its extension. Thus the term *animal* can be used to mean all organic beings, or else some of them, for example, only lions. Now it is of the utmost importance in Logic to know whether the terms of a sentence are meant to designate all the individuals contained in their extension, or only a few. Hence we must lay down rules which will enable us to know exactly what is the logical extension of a given term in a sentence.

Distributive terms. We call distributive or universal a term which, in a sentence, is meant to represent each and every one of the individuals contained in its extension, as for example, *roses*, in *roses are flowers*.

Non-distributive terms. A non-distributive or particular term is one which is meant to designate some only of the individuals of a genus or a species. *Ex.* : *some roses*, in *some roses are white*, is a non-distributive or particular term.

Signs of distribution are particles which indicate whether a term is used in a distributive or a non-distributive meaning. These particles are: *all, every, no, many, some, a few.* They are also called *syncategorematic* signs. When these signs are present in a sentence it is relatively easy to recognize the distribution of its terms; the difficulty arises when there is no sign of distribution, and it then becomes imperative to have recourse to the following rules.

3:. *Rules of distribution for the subject.*

Rule 1. If the subject of a proposition is preceded by *all, every,* or *no,* it is a distributive term. *Ex.*: *All men are rational, no cats are dogs.*

Rule 2. If the subject of a proposition is preceded by *many, some,* or *a few,* it is a non-distributive term. *Ex.: Some men are tall.*

Rule 3. If the subject of a proposition is not preceded by any of these signs of distribution, it is a distributive term if the predicate is a necessary or an impossible attribute of the subject. *Ex.: Dogs* is distributive in *Dogs are animals. Cats* is distributive in *Cats are not birds.*

Rule 4. If the subject of a proposition is not preceded by any of these signs of distribution, it is a non-distributive term if the predicate is only a contingent attribute of the subject. *Ex.: Roses* is non-distributive in *roses are red,* and *men* in *men do not walk backwards,* because it is not meant that all roses are red, or that no men ever walk backwards.

32. *Rule for the predicate.*—There is only one rule for the predicate, which applies to all predicates whether the subject is distributive or not; it suffers no exception whatever, and must be remembered carefully, as it is all-important in the construction of syllogisms.

This rule is: A term used as predicate of a proposition, is distributive in all negative propositions, and non-distributive in all affirmative ones. *Ex.: Cats* in *no dogs are cats,* is distributive, because the whole class of cats is excluded from the subject; *cats* is still distributive for the same reason in *some dogs are not cats.* But *animals* is a non-distributive term in *all dogs are animals,* and in *some dogs are animals,* because dogs do not constitute the whole class of animals, but only part of it.

33. *Indivisible terms.*—Singular and indivisible terms are those which denote only one person or thing. They consequently have no extension, and strictly speaking, are neither distributive or non-distributive. Nevertheless they are treated as distributive or non-distributive terms, and follow the rules of distribution that have just been laid down. Thus, if the subject of a proposition is a singular or indivisible term, this term is treated as distributive or non-distributive according to rule 3 and 4, namely, according to whether the predicate is necessary or impossible, or else contingent. The

subjects of the following propositions are treated as distributive because their predicates are essential ones and apply to the whole subject: *Peter is a man, the sun is hot, prudence is a virtue.* But the subjects of the following are treated as non-distributive because the predicates are not essential: *Peter is tall, this dog is lame, the sun is veiled, prudence is easy to practice.*

As to the predicate, if it is singular or indivisible, it is easy to understand that in negative propositions it is considered as distributive because the whole of it is excluded from the subject. In affirmative propositions it is considered as non-distributive, because, although in a sentence like *my name is Dick Ronny,* there is probably no one else who has that name, yet it means that *I happen* to be called by that name, and does not exclude the possibility of someone else partaking of it. Thus also in *this is water,* we mean that *this* partakes of the nature of water, and not that *this* is the whole of water.

34. *Distributive propositions.*—The distribution of a proposition is entirely dependent on the distribution of its subject; the distribution of the predicate has nothing to do with that of the proposition. Therefore a distributive proposition is one that has a distributive subject, according to the rules given above. It is called an *A* or an *E* proposition according to whether it is affirmative or negative. *Ex.:* All men are rational (A), *dogs are animals* (A), *no cats are birds* (E).

A non-distributive proposition is one that has a non-distributive subject, according to the same rules. It is called an *I* or an *O* proposition according to whether it is affirmative or negative. *Ex.:* *Some men are tall (I), roses are red (I), men do not walk backwards* (O).

The *quantity* of a proposition is its distribution or non-distribution.

The *quality* of a proposition is its affirmation or negation.

35. To sum up all this, there are four different kinds of propositions:

1. Distributive (*quantity*) -affirmative (*quality*), called *A* propositions, which have a distributive subject and a non-distributive predicate. *Ex.:* All *dogs* (distributive) *are animals* (non-distributive).

2. Distributive (*quantity*) -negative (*quality*), called *E* propositions, which have a distributive subject and a distributive predicate. *Ex.:* No *dogs* (distributive) *are birds* (distributive).

3. Non-distributive (*quantity*) -affirmative (*quality*), called *I* pro-

positions, which have a non-distributive subject, and a non-distributive predicate. *Ex.*: *Some men* (non-distributive) *are tall* (non-distributive).

4. Non-distributive (*quantity*) -negative (*quality*), called *O* propositions, which have a non-distributive subject, and a distributive predicate. *Ex.*: *Some men* (non-distributive) *are not tall* (distributive).

CHAPTER 6

CLASSIFICATION OF TERMS OR CATEGORIES

36. Logical *Categories,* also called *Predicaments,* are the result of a logical classification of the terms we use. They are supreme classes to which all these terms belong, and into which we can divide the concepts represented by those terms. Now because our concepts are objective, that is to say, because they represent existing things, it is evident that any classification of terms or concepts must coincide exactly with that of existing things.

37. The general classes to which all created things belong or *the supreme modes of being,* are called metaphysical Categories or Predicaments, in opposition to the logical ones which are classifications of terms and of the concepts these represent. Aristotle has given us a complete and comprehensive classification of all created things, based on experimental observation. He found ten Categories or Predicaments, namely:

1. Substance. 2. Quality. 3. Quantity. 4. Relation. 5. Action. 6. Passion. 7. Time. 8. Place. 9. Position. 10. Habit.

This number however, is not constant even in Aristotle's works; he sometimes reduces it to nine, and sometimes to eight. In fact, the accident of position can be reduced to either that of quantity or dimension, or to that of relation, or even to that of place. Habit, which includes the exterior appearance of things, such as people's clothes, decorations or ornaments, animal's fur, and so forth, evidently does not concern philosophy, and Aristotle mentions it only to be complete in his enumeration.

In reality therefore eight Categories only deserve a separate mention, namely Substance, Quality, Quantity, Relation, Action, Passion, Time, Place. We shall deal with these Categories separately in Metaphysics and in Cosmology.

Here in Logic, it will suffice to remark that these Categories, in their turn, can be divided into two great classes, namely into *Substance*, and into *Accidents* of which there are nine. We must also remark that great care is to be taken not to confuse Predicaments with Predicables. Predicaments are different *classes* of terms and things; predicables are different *ways* of affirming one term or thing of another.

CHAPTER 7

PROPOSITIONS

38. A *proposition* is the verbal expression of a judgement. A judgement is a mental act by which we affirm or deny the identity of two ideas or concepts. Simple concepts do not give us complete and perfect knowledge. To know is not simply to have ideas; ideas must be connected, affirmed or denied of each other. The necessity of judgements arises from the discursive nature of our knowledge. We can only acquire knowledge by gradual steps, by proceeding from the knowledge of one thing to that of another. This can only be done by the mental comparison which we call judgement.

We first acquire a few primitive ideas, such as thing, matter, animal, man, and so forth. We then compare these ideas by saying *this man is an animal, this thing is matter,* etc. Judgement is so natural and essential to our knowledge, that we rarely have simple concepts, just as it rarely occurs that we have simple sense-stimuli, all our sense-knowledge being the outcome of several experiences joined together. Thus we rarely think about anything without making, at least implicitly, a judgement about it.

39. It is important to remark that the purpose of a judgement is not merely to compare the concepts of our mind. The judgement must reach to external facts, and refer to the relation existing between the objects represented by these concepts; otherwise our knowledge would be subjective. Therefore the relation affirmed or denied to exist between two concepts must hold in reality, must correspond to a relation existing or not existing in external fact. This correspondence to reality is the test of our knowledge; we call it truth. Truth has accordingly been defined: the correspondence of the intellect with reality.

40. Since perfect knowledge consists of judgements, it follows that complete and perfect truth is only to be found in judgements and in the propositions which express them. In simple concepts there is only an incipient and imperfect truth. A proposition consists of a subject and of a predicate joined together by the verb *to be*. All propositions can ultimately be resolved into a sentence containing the verb *to be,* and it is often necessary to reduce them to this simple form in order to analyse them logically. Our English language presents no difficulty in this respect, since we usually prefer the form *a dog is running* to *a dog runs*. If we say that a dog is not running, we are affirming the negative predicate *not running* of a dog. Therefore a proposition always contains an affirmation. Therefore, however long and complicated a proposition may be, it only contains two logical terms, namely a subject and predicate. The function of the predicate is to make us know in a more explicit manner the implicit meaning of the subject.

41. If the identity expressed by a proposition is of such a nature that the subject and predicate are convertible, the proposition is called a logical *definition*. This happens when the predicate expresses the essence of the subject, namely its proximate genus and its ultimate specific difference. There are however other kinds of definition which are not strict logical ones.

An Etymological definition is the mere explanation of a word-root. For example the etymological root of *legend* is the latin *lego,* which means *to read.*

A Nominal definition is a proposition which states the ordinary meaning in which a word is taken, independently of its etymological origin. Thus the word *species,* derived from the Latin *spectare, to look at,* would mean etymologically something that is visible or apparent; its nominal definition is however *the subdivision of a class or genus.*

A Descriptive definition is one which states the origin, purpose, or other circumstantial features of a thing, for example, an incunabulum is defined as a specimen of printing prior to 1500, or television as a process which permits one to see events which are taking place outside the range of normal vision.

A *Logical definition,* which is the one we are concerned with here, is that which states the next higher logical genus and the lowest specific difference of a thing. For example, to define an animal as a cognitive being. Logical definition expresses the logical elements contained in the comprehension of a thing, and is based on a strict logical analysis. It must be clear and short, it must not contain a negation, it must be proper to the defined thing and not applicable to any other thing, it must not contain the thing which is to be defined, but only contain the proximate genus and the specific difference, as already explained.

Logical definition is the only perfect definition, and must be used whenever possible. Some things however are not susceptible of such a strict logical definition; in this case we must have recourse to a descriptive or to a nominal definition. In fact, we cannot define in a strict logical manner: 1. Transcendentals, such as being in general, because of their logical simplicity, that is to say, because of their lack of logical comprehension. 2. Things of which we do not know the proximate genus or the specific difference, such as the soul or the angels. 3. A genus as such, since a genus as such has no specific difference.

CHAPTER 8

CONDITIONAL AND OPPOSED PROPOSITIONS

42. *A conditional proposition* is one which is composed of two propositions or members, one of which is the *antecedent* and expresses a condition upon which the other member, the *consequent,* depends. A conditional proposition is the opposite of what is called

a *categorical* proposition. There are two kinds of conditional propositions, namely the purely conditional, and the disjunctive.

A purely conditional proposition is one that does not affirm or deny either of its members, but simply asserts the dependence of the consequent upon the antecedent. *Ex.: If I become king, I shall not be poor. If law has no sanctions, it will not be observed.* It is evident from these examples that it does not matter whether the antecedent or the consequent be true or false; the sole object of these propositions is to stress the dependence of one upon the other. When I say *if I become king, I will not be poor,* I am neither affirming or denying that I shall be king or not be poor.

A *conjunctive* proposition is a conditional one constructed with incompatible members. *Ex.: I cannot sleep and study at the same time.* These propositions are entirely similar to purely conditional ones for all logical purposes and can always be converted into the form: *If I sleep, I cannot study.*

43. *Rules* of conditional inference.—Because in a conditional proposition, the consequent depends upon the antecedent, it is permissible to draw certain inferences from it, which however must conform strictly to the two following rules:

1. We may conclude from the *affirmation* of the antecedent to that of the consequent, but not from that of the consequent to that of the antecedent.

2. We may conclude from the *denial* of the consequent to the denial of the antecedent, but not from the denial of the antecedent to that of the consequent.

As example let us take the conditional proposition: *If the sun is shining, I will go out.*

From: / *We may conclude:*
The sun is shining (*aff. of ant.*)= Therefore I will go out (*aff. of cons.*)
I will not go out (*den. of cons.*)= Therefore the sun is not shining (*den. of ant.*)
From: / *We may not conclude:*
I will go out (*aff. of cons.*) = Therefore the sun is shining (*aff. of ant.*)
The sun is not shining (*den. of cons.*) = Therefore I will not go out (*den. of cons.*)

44. If either the antecedent or the consequent, or both, are negative propositions, they will, when denied, have two negations, and

be equivalent to an affirmative proposition. Thus in the example: *If it rains, I shall not go out,* in order to deny the consequent, we shall have to affirm that I shall go out. This gives rise to the following results:—

From:	We may conclude:
It rains (*aff. of ant.*)	= Therefore I shall not go out (*aff. of cons.*)
I shall go out (*den. of cons.*)	= Therefore it is not raining (*den. of ant.*)

From:	We may not conclude:
I shall not go out (*aff. of cons.*)=	It is raining (*aff. of ant.*)
It is not raining (*den. of ant.*)=	I shall go out (*den. of cons.*)

45. A *disjunctive* proposition consists of two contradictory members, connected together in a consequential manner by the words *if, either, and,* etc. *Ex.*: *Quantity is either continuous or discreet. A thing cannot be and not be at the same time.*

Since a disjunctive proposition really consists of two contradictory propositions joined together, the only condition required in order to construct a disjunctive proposition is that its members conform strictly to the conditions laid down for the validity of contradictories.

Disjunctive inference has none of the intricacies of conditional inference, because one of the contradictories must necessarily be true and the other false, and therefore we may infer from the affirmation or from the denial of either of them, to the affirmation or the denial of the other.

46. *A contradictory* proposition is one which denies what another affirms, or affirms what another denies. In two contradictory propositions, the affirmation of the one and the negation of the other must bear exactly on the same subject and the same predicate; great care must be taken that no variation whatsoever takes place; one of the propositions must affirm exactly what the other denies. *Ex.*: *The soul is immortal, and the soul is not immortal,* are two contradictory propositions.

In order to be really contradictory, the four following conditions must be realised: 1. One of the propositions must be affirmative, the other negative. 2. The propositions must exclude each other. 3. One of them must be true, and the other false. 4. There must be no other possible alternative.

47. *Two rules* govern the formation of contradictory propositions:

The first rule is that if a proposition has a subject which is not preceded by a sign of distribution, its contradictory is formed by adding or taking away the negative particle, thus changing the quality but not the quantity of the proposition. *Ex.: Man is not mortal* is the contradictory of *man is mortal*; *my coat is black* is the contradictory of *my coat is not black*.

48. The second rule is that if a proposition has a subject which is preceded by a sign of distribution, its contradictory is formed by changing both the quality and the quantity of the proposition. This is done by adding or taking away the negative particle, *and* by changing *all* or *none* into *some*, and vice-versa. *Ex.: Some men are not liars* is the contradictory of *all men are liars*.

By changing the quantity of these propositions, as we are told to do, that is to say, by changing *all* or *none* into *some*, the subject is not really changed, as it would seem to be. The words only are changed, not their meaning. In fact to affirm that all men are liars is to affirm that every single man is a liar, and to deny or contradict this statement we have to say that every single man is not a liar; but this means that there are some who do not lie, i.e., some men are not liars. Similarly to affirm that no men are liars is to say that there is not one single man who tells lies, and to contradict this statement we must say that there are one or two who tell lies, which is equivalent to saying that some are liars.

The form *all men are not liars*, or *all roses are not red* for a distributive negative proposition, instead of the form *no men are liars*, or *no roses are red*, must be avoided as ambiguous. In fact, *all are not*, could mean either *none are*, or *some are not*. By using the form *no men are*, we avoid this equivocation, and definitely signify that none are.

49. *Contrary* propositions are those which are incompatible with one another, but do not exclude the possibility of other alternatives. Only one of several contrary propositions can be true; but they could all be false since the number of alternatives is not restricted. *Ex.: My coat is white* and *my coat is black*, are two contrary propositions. They cannot both be true, since if the coat is white, it cannot be black; but they could both be false, as the coat could be of another colour.

There are *two rules* to be observed in order to construct contrary propositions. The first rule is that if a proposition has a subject not preceded by a sign of distribution, its contrary is formed by changing its predicate into one that is incompatible with it. *Ex.*: *My coat is black* or *my coat is red,* are contraries of *My coat is white.* *My* is not a sign of distribution.

The second rule is that if a proposition has a subject preceded by a sign of distribution, its contrary is formed either by applying the preceding rule of changing the predicate into an incompatible one, for example, by saying that *all* roses are red instead of *all* roses are white, or else by adding or taking away the negative particle without changing anything else, i.e. by changing the quality but not the quantity. *Ex.*: *No men are liars* is the contrary of *all men are liars.*

50. *Square of Opposition.* The manner in which two contradictory or contrary propositions are opposed to each other is generally illustrated by what is called the Square of Opposition:

ALL MEN ARE LIARS = is *contradictory* of = SOME MEN ARE NOT LIARS

↓   ↑   ↓   ↑

is *contrary* of: is *contrary* of:

↓   ↑   ↓   ↑

NO MEN ARE LIARS = is *contradictory* of = SOME MEN ARE LIARS

51. *Dilemma.* Sometimes disjunctive propositions are joined together in the form of an argument, which is then called a dilemma. A dilemma is an argument that concludes against an opponent from both members of a disjunctive proposition, called the horns of the dilemma. Examples:— When Omar Caipha in 640 burnt the Alexandrian library, he argued in this way: These books either contain the doctrine of the Coran, or they do not contain it. If they contain it, they are useless, the Coran being sufficient; if they do not, they are harmful; therefore they must be burnt.—Our Lord argues thus: No man can serve two masters. Either he will hate the one, and love the other; or he will sustain the one, and despise the other; you cannot serve God and mammon (Math. 6. 24).—He also said: If I have spoken evil, give testimony to the evil; but if well, why strikest thou me? (Jo. 18. 23).

A dilemma can be answered by pointing to an incorrect disjunctive which does not exhaust all the possible alternatives, or by retorting, that is by rebutting, the dilemma; this is done by drawing contrary conclusions from the disjunctive.

CHAPTER 9

MODAL PROPOSITIONS

52. *A modal* proposition is one that contains a word altering the way in which the predicate refers to the subject, namely a word directly affecting the verb *to be,* which verb is implicitly contained in all propositions. In propositions like *he runs quickly, he works well,* the words *quickly, well,* do not affect the verb *to be,* but the predicate *running* and *working.* Therefore these are not modal propositions. There are only four words that affect the aforesaid verb, and consequently only four kinds of modal propositions. These are: *possible, impossible, necessary* and *contingent.* But since *possible* can not only mean *not impossible,* but can also be taken to mean *not necessary,* which is equivalent to *contingent,* we are left with three kinds of modal propositions: necessary, impossible and possible.

The following scheme will show in what precise relation these modal propositions stand to each other, and which is a contradictory statement of the other, and which is only a contrary one.

1	2
Necessary to be	Necessary not to be
Impossible not to be	Impossible to be
Not possible not to be	Not possible to be

3	4
Not necessary not to be	Not necessary to be
Not impossible to be	Not impossible not to be
Possible to be	Possible not to be

Remarks

I. The three propositions contained under No. 1 are equivalent and interchangeable; so also are those contained under each of the other numbers, namely 2, 3 & 4.

II. All the propositions of No. 1 are contradictories of each and all those of No. 4, and vice-versa. All the propositions of No. 2 are contradictories of each and all those of No. 3, and vice-versa.

III. All the propositions of No. 1 are contraries of each and all those of No. 2, and vice-versa. All the propositions of No. 3 are contraries of each and all those of No. 4, and vice-versa.

CHAPTER 10

SYLLOGISMS

53. We now come to the main point of the study of Logic, namely the construction of a valid and correct argument. The following explanations and rules will enable us to draw correct conclusions and avoid the pitfalls and fallacies to which reasoning and discussions so often lead. The Scholastics call *Syllogism* the verbal expression of an argument. The rules they give for the correct construction of a syllogism automatically ensure the soundness of an argument, provided it is based on true premisses. But even when both the premisses and the conclusion happen to be true statements, if the rules for the correct framing of syllogisms are not faithfully observed, the conclusion will have no logical value since it would not follow from the premisses; in other words it will not prove or demonstrate anything at all. As the Scholastics say, the *consequence* will be false, or rather will not exist at all, as there can be no logical connection between the premisses and the conclusion, although the *consequent*, namely, the statement contained in the conclusion, taken by itself, may happen to be true.

54. A *Syllogism* is an argument composed of three terms and of three propositions related in such a manner that the last proposition follows necessarily from the first two.

The first two propositions of a syllogism are called its *premisses;* the first one the *major*, the second one the *minor*. The last proposition is called the conclusion.

One term of the major is repeated in the minor, and is called the *middle term*. This term must not be used in the conclusion. The remaining terms of the major and of the minor serve as subject and as predicate of the conclusion. Therefore, although there are three distinct propositions in a syllogism, and each one of them has two terms, there are only three terms in the syllogism, because each term of the premisses is repeated twice. Example:

Major premiss : All dogs (middle term) are animals (major term)
minor premiss : All terriers (minor term) are dogs (middle term)
conclusion : All terriers are animals

It is of the utmost importance to remember that there must be only three terms in a syllogism. The argumentative value of the syllogism is based on the principle that if two things are similar to a third, they are similar to each other: a syllogism compares two terms to a third, and thus infers their equality in the conclusion. It is evident that there is no place for a fourth term in this comparison. Ambiguous terms, namely those having more than one meaning, must therefore be avoided, since the double meaning of an ambiguous term would be an implicit multiplication of terms.

The construction of syllogisms is governed by what are known as the figures and modes of syllogisms.

55. The *figure* of a syllogism is the form it assumes according to the various positions of its middle term. The middle term is that which is common to both the major and the minor premiss. Now there are four ways in which this middle term can be arranged in these premisses, and these four different arrangements give to the syllogism four different configurations, which we call its figures.

In the first figure, the middle term is the subject of the major premiss and the predicate of the minor. *Ex.:* All *dogs* are animals; but all terriers are *dogs*; therefore all terriers are animals.

In the second figure, the middle term is the predicate of both the major and the minor. *Ex:* No cats are *dogs*; but all terriers are *dogs*; therefore no cats are terriers.

In the third figure, the middle term is the subject of both the major and the minor. *Ex.:* All *dogs* are animals; but some *dogs* are terriers; therefore some animals are terriers.

In the fourth figure, the middle term is the predicate of the major, and the subject of the minor. *Ex.:* All terriers are *dogs*; but no *dogs* are cats; therefore no terriers are cats.

56. *Quantity* and *Quality* of propositions. In order to understand what we are going to say about the modes of syllogisms, we must recall what has already been said about the quantity and the quality of the propositions which make up a syllogism. (See No. 34.)

The *Quantity* refers to the distribution or extension of a proposition, namely to the fact of whether it is a distributive or a nondistributive proposition.

The *Quality* of a proposition refers to the fact of its being an affirmative or a negative proposition. By taking into consideration these two factors of Quantity and Quality, we are faced with four different kinds of propositions:

1. Distributive Affirmative propositions, with a distributive sub-

ject and a non-distributive predicate. We call them for brevity's sake " A " propositions.

2. Distributive Negative propositions, with a distributive subject and a distributive predicate. We call them " E " propositions.

3. Non-distributive Affirmative propositions, with a non-distributive subject and a non-distributive predicate. We call them " I " propositions.

4. Non-distributive Negative propositions, with a non-distributive subject, and a distributive predicate. We call them "O" propositions.

57. *Modes*. The Mode of a syllogism is the configuration given to it by the quantity and the quality of the A, E, I, O propositions of which it is composed. Now there are 64 mathematical permutations of these four letters A, E, I, O, that is to say, there are 64 possible ways of arranging these propositions together, according to whether they are affirmative or negative, and distributive or non-distributive. We call these arrangements Modes. Furthermore, each one of these modes can be constructed in any one of the four figures, thus giving us a total of 64 times 4, namely 256 possible ways or modes of constructing a syllogism.

But of these 256 modes, there are only 19 that have a logically valid conclusion. The others are of no reasoning value, and are useless. These 19 modes are the traditional forms of syllogisms given in text-books of Logic.

58. A careful study of all these modes is a most useful drill for the logician, but it is most bewildering for the beginner. Experience shows that only five of these modes are ever used, and that a thorough mastery of these five modes enables the student to construct with ease and correctly all the syllogisms he needs for practical purposes. He will therefore be well-advised to concentrate exclusively on the study of these five modes only. This little departure from the usual method of studying the structure of syllogisms, acts as a stimulant towards an exhaustive enquiry into the whole syllogistic process.

The reason for which five modes only are of practical use, is that five modes only have distributive conclusions. There is no point in proving a non-distributive conclusion when it is possible to prove the corresponding distributive one. Thus it is useless to prove that *some* souls are spiritual when it is much easier to prove that *all* souls are spiritual. In fact, the object of study is generalisation.

Science of any kind endeavours to establish general laws and principles, applicable to whole classes of things.

It might be objected that we sometimes have to prove the truth of singular propositions, namely those which have as subject a proper name, or *this, that.* We might have to prove for example that St. Peter is the head of the Church, or that Jesus Christ is truly God, that *this* argument is erroneous, or *that* Sacrament was established by Christ. Such propositions however are not considered as non-distributive, but as real distributive ones, since the predicate of a singular proposition extends to all that is, or can be, included in the subject. Therefore they are included in the five distributive modes of syllogisms.

CHAPTER II

CONSTRUCTION OF SYLLOGISMS

59. To each of the five modes, a mnemonic name has been given. These names are entirely meaningless agglomerations of letters, and have been coined for the sole purpose of assisting memory. These names are: *Barbara, Celarent, Cesare, Camestres, Camenes.* These names are like index-words that show at a glance which A.E.I.O. proposition is to be used, and where to place the middle term in a syllogism. Each of them contains three syllables. The first syllable represents the major of the syllogism; the second, the minor; the third, the conclusion.

Each syllable of these names contains either an A, or an E. The letter A stands for a distributive affirmative proposition, and the letter E stands for a distributive negative one. No syllable contains an I or an O, precisely because I and O stand respectively for non-distributive affirmative and negative propositions. Since we are dealing, as has been said, with syllogisms having distributive conclusions only, their premisses also, according to the rules of syllogism, must be distributive.

60. *Barbara* and *Celarent* belong to the first figure, which means that the middle term must be the subject of the major premiss and

the predicate of the minor one. *Cesare* and *Camestres* belong to the
second figure, which means that the middle term must be the
predicate of both premisses. *Camenes* belongs to the fourth figure,
which means that the middle term must be the predicate of the
major premiss and the subject of the minor one. No syllogism must
be constructed in the third figure, as this figure cannot have a
distributive conclusion, and we are not dealing here with non-
distributive conclusions.

The conclusion of a syllogism can be either a direct or an indirect
one. The first mode, that is to say syllogisms in Barbara, must always
have a direct conclusion, in which the subject must be taken from
the minor premiss and the predicate from the major. But in the other
modes, that is to say in syllogisms in Celarent, Cesare, Camestres and
Camenes, the conclusion can also be an indirect one, in which the
terms are inverted, the subject being taken from the major instead
of from the minor premiss.

We will give an example of each mode:

BARBARA: (first figure)

All *flowers* are plants	(A)
all roses are *flowers*	(A)
all roses are plants	(A)

CELARENT: (first figure)

Direct conclusion		*Indirect* conclusion	
No *flowers* are trees	(E)	No flowers are *trees*	
all roses are *flowers*	(A)	all roses are flowers	
no roses are trees	(E)	no *trees* are roses	

CESARE: (second figure)

Direct conclusion		*Indirect* conclusion	
No trees are *flowers*	(E)	No *trees* are flowers	
all roses are *flowers*	(A)	all roses are flowers	
no roses are trees	(E)	no *trees* are roses	

CAMESTRES: (second figure)

Direct conclusion		*Indirect* conclusion	
All roses are *flowers*	(A)	All *roses* are flowers	
no trees are *flowers*	(E)	no trees are flowers	
no trees are roses	(E)	no *roses* are trees	

CAMENES: (fourth figure)

Direct conclusion		Indirect conclusion
All roses are *flowers*	(A)	All *roses* are flowers
no *flowers* are trees	(E)	no flowers are trees
no trees are roses	(E)	no *roses* are trees

61. *Rules* for the construction of syllogisms in the five aforesaid modes.

If a syllogism conforms to one of these five modes, it is necessarily correct, because these modes have been purposely designed to ensure the fulfilment of all the conditions which a correct argument could possibly require. These conditions are summed up in the following rules:

I. *Three terms.*—The very first and essential rule is the one already given, namely that there must be only three terms in a syllogism, and that these terms must not be ambiguous, since ambiguity would multiply them.

II. *Middle term.*—The second rule is that the middle term must be distributive in at least one of the premisses, otherwise it would not necessarily refer to the same individuals, and consequently there would be more than three terms, as for example if we said that gold is a *precious metal*, but silver is also a *precious metal*, therefore silver is gold.

III. *Distributive terms.*—The third rule is that a distributive term in the conclusion must also be distributive in the corresponding premiss, otherwise we should be proving more than is contained in the premiss.

IV. *Affirmative premiss.*—The fourth rule is that at least one premiss must be affirmative, otherwise no comparison would be established.

V. *Affirmative conclusion.*—The fifth rule is that the conclusion cannot be affirmative if one of the premisses is negative, because there would be no inference at all.

62. *Reduction* of syllogisms.—A syllogism can be constructed in any of these five modes, at choice. But of course if the conclusion is an affirmative one, we must use the form Barbara, because all the others have negative conclusions. Syllogisms in the fourth figure, namely in Camenes, are better avoided, as this figure inverts the position of the middle term and makes the argument more difficult to follow; it has no advantage over the straightforward form in

Camestres. The most perfect forms are those of the first figure, namely those in Barbara and Celarent. It is therefore useful to know how to reduce to this first figure syllogisms which have been constructed in the other figures, namely in Cesare, Camestres or Camenes.

To facilitate this reduction, certain letters have been purposely inserted in these mnemonic words, Cesare, Camestres and Camenes, namely the letters C, S, and M. C indicates that the syllogisms must be reduced to the mode of the first figure which begins with a C, namely to Celarent. No. syllogism can be reduced to Barbara. S indicates that the proposition represented by the syllable which this letter follows, must have its terms transposed by simple conversion. M indicates that the premisses themselves must be transposed, the major and minor exchanging places. We will give a few examples:

CeSare (2nd figure)	=*reduced to*	=*Celarent* (1st figure)
No cats are dogs	— S =*invert terms*	= No dogs are cats
all terriers are dogs		all terriers are dogs
no terriers are cats.		no terriers are cats

CaMeStreS (2nd figure)	=*reduced to*	=*Celarent* (1st figure)
All terriers are dogs	—M =*transpose premiss*	= No dogs are cats
no cats are dogs	— S =*invert terms*	= all terriers are dogs
no cats are terriers.	— S =*invert terms*	= no terriers are cats

CaMenes (2nd figure)	=*reduced to*	=*Celarent* (1st figure)
All terriers are dogs	—M =*transpose premiss*	= No dogs are cats
no dogs are cats		all terriers are dogs
no cats are terriers.	— S =*invert terms*	= No terriers are cats.

63. *Conversion.* The student will have noticed that in order to reduce a syllogism of one of the other figures to the first one, it is sometimes necessary to invert the terms of a proposition. We call this conversion. Now this can only be done in compliance with certain definite rules, as would be apparent from the fact that we could not infer from *all lions are animals,* that *all animals are lions.* Conversion is the transposition of the terms of a proposition, so that the subject becomes predicate and the predicate subject. There are several kinds of conversion, but the only two required for practical purposes are what can be called *simple,* and limited or *accidental* conversion.

64. *Simple conversion* is performed by making the subject and predicate change places without any other alteration. All *E* and *I* propositions can be converted in this way. Thus we can convert *no immortals are men* (E), into *no men are immortals* (E); and *some substances are minerals* (I), into *some minerals are substances* (I).

Accidental conversion is performed by making the subject and predicate of *A* propositions change places, and furthermore by changing the quantity of the subject. This means that after having transposed the terms, we must either change the distributive sign *all* which precedes the subject into *some,* or add the sign *some* if there is no other sign. *Ex.: All roses are flowers,* or *roses are flowers,* must be converted into *some flowers are roses;* it would be wrong to convert these *A* propositions into *all flowers are roses.* But *no immortals are men* (E), can be converted into *some men are not immortals,* or into *no men are immortals.* Conversion is impossible in *O* propositions, except by what is called *per contrapositionem,* which is a useless contortion of words.

65. *Sorites.* Several syllogisms can sometimes, for brevity's sake, be joined together by omitting their conclusions and drawing only one final one. We then have what is called a Sorites. A Sorites is a polysyllogism with more than two premisses disposed in such a manner that the predicate of the first is used as the subject of the second, the predicate of this premiss as the subject of the following one, and so on. To be valid, the term repeated as subject must be absolutely identical with that used as predicate in the preceding premiss. Furthermore, only the first premiss can be non-distributive; all the others must be distributive. And finally, only the last premiss and the conclusion can be negative; the other premisses must be affirmative.

66. *Fallacy.* By Fallacy we mean an erroneous argument which has the appearance of truth. Few errors in reasoning can occur if the rules of syllogisms are faithfully observed. On the other hand, a syllogism badly constructed is bound to be a fallacy, its conclusion having no argumentative value, although it might, for other reasons, happen to be true.

The following are a few of the most frequent causes of fallacy :

1. *Ambiguity,* which can occur either by using equivocal terms, or by constructing a sentence in an equivocal manner.

2. Fallacy of *composition* and *division* consists in applying to each thing separately what is only true of all together, or vice-versa.

3. Fallacy of *accident* is turning an exception into a rule and vice-versa, or arguing from the mere accidental qualities of a thing to its very nature, and vice-versa.

4. *Evading the point,* which includes the famous argument *ad*

hominem, which means to retort by saying *tu quoque,* you also.

5. *Begging the question,* which includes arguing in a vicious circle.

6. *Bad induction,* which means to assume something to be the cause of an event because that event happens to follow it.

7. *No argument,* which means that there is a flaw in the process of reasoning. This happens especially when we contravene the rules given in the treatise on syllogisms.

8. *Fallacy of many questions,* which consists in putting into one sentence several questions which would require separate answers.

CHAPTER 12

INDUCTION

67. There is another form of argument which is called Induction, in opposition to the mental process of Deduction involved in syllogisms.

Induction consists in a logical inference from particular instances to general conclusions. Inductive methods are also called scientific, experimental or empirical. These methods are of the greatest value to the philosopher; but what is still of more importance to him is to investigate the fundamental principle on which the value of Induction is based. Indeed Induction faces us with a serious problem, namely with the fact that scientific experiment, of however an accurate nature, is not able to cope with the entire multitude of natural phenomena; even if this were possible, we should never have the assurance that it had in fact exhausted all the possible variations of those phenomena. What is the motive for which we assent to scientific laws based on a comparatively small number of experiences? In virtue of what principle do we conclude, from one or several instances of a phenomenon which we have sense-experienced, to many other instances which have not been, and cannot be verified?

68. This principle is that of the *Uniformity of Nature.* This means that the universe is governed by general and uniform laws, that the

course of nature is uniform in its manifestations, and not erratic, that unexpected and different effects are not produced by constant natural causes. This principle is one of those primordial truths, the evidence of which is immediately and naturally apparent to our minds. We instinctively adhere to it. Its truth results from the fact that physical causes have no choice as to the effects they produce; as soon as circumstances are favourable, they are compelled to act and to produce the natural effect for which they were intended.

Because the Author of nature is an intelligent being, he created the world and all the things it contains for a definite purpose. Each physical substance tends to the fulfilment of that purpose by displaying its own special activity. The resulting effect specifies and characterises the substance from which it results, and becomes what we call its specific and distinguishing property, whereby we recognise and label that substance as distinct from all others. That each thing must have a definite purpose and produce a definite and constant effect, is not a knowledge obtained by observation and experiment. It results from the very definition of a physical cause. The free actions of men are not uniform, precisely because man is the free cause of his actions, and at liberty to do as he likes. But physical causes have only one pre-established course of action, because they are physical and not free causes, and have no power to interfere with the recurring sequence of their effects.

69. The purpose of induction is to discover by observation and experiment which are these uniform actions of nature, in accordance with known and approved scientific methods. When we have accurately verified by sense-experience that a phenomenon is due to a certain cause, which we have disentangled and isolated from the multiplicity of other apparent causes, we are justified in affirming that this cause will always produce a similar effect under similar circumstances. Our general conclusion will then be, not a simple generalisation of several separate instances, but a logical and rational inference, namely, the inference that if a cause is truly proved to produce a certain effect even in one single instance, it will always do so in similar circumstances. It is in this manner that we know that all solids are heavier than air, although we may not have experimented with many of them. Archimedes lost no time in concluding that all bodies lose weight when immersed in a fluid, as soon as he had noticed it had happened to himself.

Without this inferential principle of nature's uniformity, we should not be justified in drawing general conclusions even if we had experimented with all known individual instances. There would always remain the possibility of having overlooked some of them.

70. Uncertainty in inductive conclusions is the result of insufficient observation and experiment concerning the circumstances under which the phenomena occur. These circumstances are due to the influence of other substances which change the nature of the phenomenon under observation. The whole task of scientific observation and experiment is to isolate a phenomenon from all others, by preventing these from interfering, or by overcoming their interference. But man's power of induction is limited. In spite of the greatest accuracy, some circumstances are, and always will be, overlooked. Thus accidents happen, due to the unforeseen influence of exterior causes. Nevertheless the laws of nature and of science can be known and applied with sufficient accuracy to give us moral certainty that nothing abnormal will happen. We can confidently travel by train, climb a ladder, or undergo an operation, with sufficient assurance that there will be no accident. Accidents are the exception, not the rule, and they do not destroy our belief in Nature's Uniformity of action.

PART II

MAJOR LOGIC

SUBJECTIVISM

71. We now come to Major or Material Logic, which is called by moderns *Epistemology* or *Criteriology*. These names can be assumed as being synonyms for practical purposes. The ultimate scope of Major Logic is to find out whether we can be certain that what we know is in accordance with fact or reality.

Some philosophers deny the objectivity of our knowledge, and maintain that we cannot be certain of really knowing what we imagine we know. Views of this kind are entertained by those to whom we can give the general name of Subjectivists and Idealists, all tainted with a certain degree of Scepticism. They say that there is nothing outside our mind to justify the formation of the universal and abstract ideas which form the basis of our intellectual knowledge, since everything that exists is concrete, and to conceive it as abstract is to falsify it. Consequently our ideas and our knowledge would be merely subjective impressions, and all we really know are the modified states of our own minds. They say that we know our own ideas and not the outside world, since we are not justified in claiming that ideas are faithful reproductions of what exists outside our mind. From this to doubting the very existence of the outer world there is only a step.

They corroborate their views by reminding us of the many evident illusions to which we all admit to be subject, and which make us perceive things differently from what they are in reality, the proportions of a landscape for example, the shape of an object according to our angle of view, and generally all optical illusions, sensations of heat, cold or pain according to our different bodily dispositions, and so forth.

72. Others attack the reliability of our cognitive powers; they say that conclusions logically deducted from straightforward principles have no probative value, experimental observation being the only sure means of acquiring knowledge. But even this experimental study cannot give birth to absolute certainty, since, they say, we can never be sure of not being under the influence of a sense-illusion. They also consider common sense as a kind of blind intuition, as an

unfounded belief that the man in the street accepts without the slightest idea of why he is doing so, a belief which is utterly unreliable in scientific problems, and which leads man astray in his research for truth, especially in the difficult problem of the objectivity of cognition. In fact, solidly established common-sense beliefs have time after time been shown to be wrong and in total contradiction with the discoveries of science.

73. We are therefore faced with a most important and exhaustive problem to which we cannot pretend to do full justice in the few pages of a simple Philosophy for beginners. A thorough treatment of this subject would require a careful and lengthy inquiry into the views and opinions of all those who have doubted or denied the objectivity of our knowledge and the trustworthiness of our cognitive powers. This would be beyond the scope of the present work.

74. We therefore simply intend to lay down a few principles which will enable the student to follow the intricate discussions to which the problem has been subjected by philosophers. We will do this by examining first of all the much debated problem of the Universals. We will then deal with the final motive and basis of our assent to truth, namely with the question of evidence and its various aspects.

CHAPTER 2

THE PROBLEM OF THE UNIVERSALS

75. It is surprising that so many philosophers scorn the study of the universal as of little or of no importance, that they consider it far more conducive to the solution of philosophical problems to study the brain process in the formation of mental images which represent things as they really are, rather than the genesis of universal and abstract concepts which would seem to falsify our knowledge, and that they find it hard to understand why philosophers quarrel with each other as to whether the mind can frame those vague and confused ideas we call *universals*.

76. Yet, unless the existence and objectivity of universal ideas is firmly and satisfactorily established, there would be no possibility of ever drawing a general conclusion concerning the nature of a thing. We could not define coal for example, or a dog, since in the hypothesis, our knowledge would consist solely of particular images of bits of coal and individual dogs. We could never get beyond the tedious and unprofitable act of thinking of a lot of individual things and facts one after the other.

77. Indeed, the very nature of knowledge demands that we be able to transcend the particular dimensional limitations of individual objects, and to form universal ideas of things abstracted from these hampering quantitative characteristics. Statements of the most simple kind postulate universal ideas, since any statement consists in affirming that a subject is included in a general idea expressed by the predicate of a proposition and consequently abstracted from its particular individuality. Thus to affirm that lions are animals, we have to conceive universal ideas, namely those of *lion* and of *animal* in general, in the abstract. It is not enough to sense-perceive, or to form a mental picture of a particular lion and of a particular animal. In other words, there can be no knowledge without generalisation, and in order to generalise, we have to abstract from that which restricts a thing to a particular individual. Even a child conceives abstract and universal ideas when it grasps what its mother means by explaining to it that an aeroplane is a *thing* or a machine that flies, or that a negro is a black man. In fact, *aeroplane, thing, machine, negro, man* are universal ideas, because they do not refer to any single individual.

78. The scholastic doctrine of the Universals is based upon an important and undeniable fact, namely on the difference between the *mental image* of an individual object and the *abstract concept* or idea of the hidden nature of a thing. There is a fundamental difference between a mental image and an abstract concept, because the concept abstracts from, that is to say, does not represent, the quantitative characteristics which define the mental image. Therefore whilst a mental image represents a tree, for example, which is either big or small, a sound which is either loud or faint, a piece of white paper or a piece of brown paper, the concepts of *tree, sound, paper* are invariably the same however many times and by whomsoever they are formed, precisely because they abstract from all the individual dif-

ferences these things have in their concrete reality, and contain only the essential components included in their nature.

It is a matter of common sense that beneath external appearances, there is in all things something which the intellect alone can perceive, a hidden nature which remains invariable when its exterior appearances change. There must be in all things something which makes those of the same species similar to each other in spite of variations in size, volume, shape, colour, and so forth, and which also makes them differ from those of another species, something which makes a perfect substitute or a counterfeit different from the real thing.

79. This constituent nature of a thing is exactly the same in all the specimens to which it is common. A spoonful of water is of the same nature as a bucketful; ten yards of material is not of a different nature than a sample of a few inches, stone is always stone, whether it be white, brown or grey, whether it be that of a rock or that of a pebble. It is evident that the abstract concept which represents this immutable nature of things, must itself be immutable and always the same. The doctor, the psychologist, the biologist, may be able to form many more judgements about the causes, the properties, the powers, of *man,* for example, than I can; but their concept of the nature of man is not different from mine; they are all thinking of exactly the same thing as I am when they form an abstract concept of *man.*

In fact, if ten people were asked to form a concept of *tree* in general, they would have to abstract from all individual differences, and would consequently have the very same idea, namely, that corresponding to the definition of a good dictionary. But if those ten people were asked to form a mental picture of a tree, it would be highly improbable that two of those pictures would be alike, as would be evident if they were asked to draw on paper a picture of a tree.

80. Now this nature which makes a thing just what it is, is hidden to the senses and comes under the grasp of the intellect which is endowed with the power to abstract it from the individual characteristics which hide it, such as its size, shape, the degree and intensity of its qualities, and to consider it without them. And since each and every man, for example, really has exactly the same human nature as all other men, the intellect does not err when it considers that human nature as being common or universal to all men. And precisely because the abstract concept does not represent things as

individuals but as being common to many individuals, we call it a
universal concept. It is *formally* and *actually* universal in the mind
which conceives it as such. The nature however itself, as it exists
outside the mind, is not formally and actually universal, but individual; but since it can be considered as universal by the mind, we
say that it is *fundamentally* and *potentially* universal.

81. Therefore the Conceptualist and Nominalist point of view is
to be rejected. Conceptualists admit that we are able to form general
and universal ideas, but say that such concepts do not correspond
to any kind of extra-mental reality, that they are mere subjective
creations of our mind, whilst the Nominalists consider the universal
concept as a mere name given for the sake of convenience to a lot
of things which happen to resemble each other by their concrete
qualities. According to the Nominalists a universal concept would
represent a class of things, a lot of individual objects considered
together in a bunch; this kind of collective idea would, they say,
have the advantage of avoiding a useless repetition of words.

CHAPTER 3

TRUSTWORTHINESS OF KNOWLEDGE

82. We must now deal briefly with those who pretend that,
although endowed with the power of reasoning, we are unable to
arrive at trustworthy conclusions, and are habitually and normally
subject to error. This is inconceivable; it would be a blot on creation.
Even those philosophers who would make us believe it, use logical
arguments to prove their own conclusions which, they maintain, cannot be doubted. They thus show that they at least trust their own
reasoning faculty. They believe in their own inferential powers, but
not in that of others. Thus they implicitly adjudge to themselves
powers which we have not.

83. We have as much right to accept the dictates of common sense
as they have to reject them. The rare cases in which common sense
has been subject to correction, such as that of the popular conviction

that the sun turned round the earth, do not justify the denial of its reliability. Common sense has always graciously given way as soon as it has realized its error. But there are certain theories which it obstinately refuses to accept, such as that of the incompetency of our reasoning powers to arrive at trustworthy conclusions. People as a whole are always ready to accept new philosophical and scientific conclusions; that they persist in rejecting sceptical and subjectivist conclusions is a sure sign that these are unsound.

84. The main reason for which these philosophers deny the validity of our inferential powers is, they say, that the very principle of Inference, which is at the base of all reasoning, cannot be proved unless we make use of, and presume as true, the very principle we are trying to prove. This is evidently a vicious circle. Furthermore, they extend this objection to all conclusions, which would thus also be based on a vicious circle, because they are all necessarily contained in the principles expressed in the premisses, and must consequently be presumed to be true by the very fact of laying down those principles.

85. Thus, for example, the premiss *all men are mortal*, by which we try to prove that Socrates is mortal, assumes that the conclusion is true before having proved it, since if we did not already know that Socrates was mortal, we would have no right to affirm in the premiss that all men are mortal. Therefore they say that we cannot acquire knowledge by reasoning, because a reasoned conclusion is either contained in the premisses and consequently already known before it is actually drawn from them, in which case it teaches us nothing new and is useless; or else it is not contained in the premisses, and then it is false.

86. The answer to this apparently formidable objection is, first of all, that the principle of inference needs no proof and can be unhesitatingly presumed to be true. We know that this principle is true by common sense and intuition. No one of sound mind can deny that if A equals B, and B equals C, A is necessarily equal to C; in other words that two things equal to a third are equal to each other. Therefore a reasoned argument does not contain a vicious circle, since it would be absurd to deny the common-sense principle of Inference under the pretext that it cannot be presumed to be true because it cannot be proved.

87. Neither is it true to say that a conclusion does not prove anything because it is either useless or false. Of course a conclusion must be contained in the premisses, otherwise it could not be drawn from them. But it is not contained in them explicitly, only implicitly. The object of an argument is precisely to show in an explicit manner that the conclusion is implicitly contained in the premisses. All the conclusions of Euclid for example are contained implicitly in a few fundamental axioms; but it takes a very long time and a great deal of study to find them out.

There is however another remark to be made, namely, that the form of syllogism which these philosophers criticize is not a typical form of syllogism. The proof that *Socrates is mortal* from the premiss *all men are mortal*, is not a strict logical inference, because it only concerns a *fact* that needs no real proof, and that cannot be strictly proved by a logical argument, since there would be no contradiction in terms to say that all men were not mortal; indeed in the beginning, man was not doomed to death. Therefore, that all men are mortal is not a logical principle contained in a more general one, but a simple fact known by experimental observation. Neither is the conclusion *Socrates is mortal* a strict logical inference, but a simple statement of a particular instance or example of a fact known by experience.

88. The same answer can be given to those who not only deny the validity of logical conclusions, but also maintain that even plain definitions are totally useless for the purpose of furthering knowledge and of serving as premisses to our reasoning process. They argue from the identity between a subject and its predicate expressed by the verb *is*, that the predicate is a useless repetition of the subject, the definition being a mere tautological proposition. Thus to say that an animal is a cognitive being, is a mere repetition of words, and amounts to saying that an animal is an animal. A thing cannot be defined unless its meaning is already known, and thus a definition does not give us any new knowledge.

89. Now there is certainly no doubt that the predicate of a definition must indeed be contained in the comprehension or analysis of the subject, otherwise we should not be justified in affirming the identity of the two terms. It is not however contained in it explicitly, but only implicitly. Words are abbreviated signs which we use to express compound and sometimes intricate ideas. They are handed

down to us as the result of much reflection on the part of those
who have preceded us, and their meaning has to be explained. A
stenographic sign may represent a whole sentence to the expert; but
it means nothing to the profane until its meaning has been explicitly
stated. A definition is therefore not useless; it explains in other more
intelligible words the meaning implicitly contained in a word. A
definition is the breaking up of a complex idea into parts which are
more simple and easy to understand. The breaking up or analysing
must go on until we arrive at ideas which we can grasp.

90. *Sense Illusions.*—We must finally add a word about the sense
illusions which, according to some philosophers, would prove that
our knowledge of the outside world is unreliable. The general proof
of sense-trustworthiness is that our sense-faculties were made by the
Creator for the precise purpose of cognizing the objects they were
made to perceive, the eye to see, the ear to hear, and so forth. To
say that they are unable to cognize these objects is equivalent to saying that they are perfectly useless, that there is no sense in using
them at all, and that we ought to be able to learn without using them,
to acquire knowledge without observation and sense-experience.
This however is against all known facts.

91. Of course our senses must operate in normal conditions; functional disorder and lack of objective proportion impair their normal
activity. We cannot expect to see properly if our eyes are not healthy,
the light too strong or too weak, the object too small.

92. In proper working conditions our senses are not subject to
illusion. Illusion occurs in the interpretation of sense-stimuli, not in
the sense-stimulation itself, and these erroneous interpretations of
sense-stimuli are mostly only temporary. Some are quasi-deliberate,
such as illusions of perspective or the optical illusion of movement
in the cinema. Anyhow, there is no illusion which cannot eventually
be detected by research and reasoning. Although it took some time,
Galileo did detect the illusion of the sun turning round the earth.
Permanent illusions are the exception, not the rule.

93. That our senses have no useful function to perform or that
they are utterly incapable of performing it, is such a fantastic assertion that it cannot be seriously entertained. Furthermore, to say that,
in sense-perception, all that we perceive and are aware of, are the
modified states of our senses, bears no corroborative evidence. We

are seldom aware of our sense-impressions or of our ideas; we become aware of them only when we deliberately stop to think about them. We frequently read a book, or enjoy the sight of an artistic painting, or hear fine music, without reflecting upon the fact that we are reading, looking or listening. What we perceive directly is the object of perception, not the perception itself. To say otherwise contradicts our personal experience.

CHAPTER 4

EVIDENCE AND TRUTH

94. We have seen that no uncertainty concerning the objectivity of our knowledge can be seriously entertained. We must now endeavour to discover what makes us sure that what we know is true, what makes us certain of knowing the truth.

95. To be certain is to give a firm assent of our mind. *Certitude* is a state of intellectual acquiescence by which the mind accepts, and agrees upon, something as being true, and in this sense it is subjective. But it is not subjective in the sense that it is produced by the mind without any regard to reality. Certitude is caused by objective motives; it is objective because its object forces the assent of the mind, irrespective of personal opinion.

96. The characteristic of certitude is that it must exclude all reasonable or founded fear of error, otherwise the assent would not be firm. Certitude is thus distinct from ignorance, doubt, or opinion. It is generally divided into metaphysical, physical and moral certitude. Metaphysical certitude is that which is based on the intrinsic nature of things; physical certitude is based on physical laws, and moral certitude on the normal course of natural phenomena or on the general conduct of mankind.

97. Certitude is also divided into common and scientific. Common certitude, or common sense, is the unwavering assent given spontaneously to truth in virtue of an instinctive logic of the mind; it is

not a blind credulity, but is based on motives upon which the mind
has not sufficiently reflected, but which upon consideration would
be found valid and convincing. Thus anyone would agree without
hesitation that two material objects cannot be present at the same
time in exactly the same place; yet it would take a lot of thinking to
explain why this is not possible. Scientific certitude is the assent
given to truth on account of motives which have been thoroughly
analysed and found to be worthy of that assent.

98. The ultimate and formal motive of our assent is what we call
objective evidence. This means that the reason for which we give our
assent to a proposition is that we are forced to agree that there exists
a necessary connection between its subject and its predicate because
the subject is contained in the logical extension of the predicate.
Objective evidence therefore depends upon a fact, not upon the considering mind; whether we realize it or not a cat, for example, is and
always will be a member of the animal species.

99. Whilst objective evidence arises from the fact of the agreement between subject and predicate, subjective evidence on the contrary results from the fact of our perceiving and realizing this agreement. Subjective evidence is therefore defined as a clear vision of the
agreement between a subject and its predicate. And because the mind
was made for the very purpose of perceiving this agreement between
two things apprehended as subject and predicate, it is compelled to
assent whenever it is faced with two such things which agree. It can
no more withhold its assent, than the eye can help seeing when
faced with a luminous object.

100. Thus objective evidence is the final motive of subjective
evidence, the causal factor of our certitude. Some even call it the
criterion of truth; we will explain however how this is to be understood. What is important to remember is that although subjective
evidence is a necessary condition of assent, it is not and cannot be
its final motive, unless we approve of the subjective and sceptical
theories mentioned before.

101. *Truth.*—Logical truth is defined as the correspondence of the
intellect with reality, or the agreement between mind and fact. It is
a state of mind which arises from knowing a thing as it really is,
namely from formulating, at least implicitly, a judgement. This
judgement is true or false according to whether it corresponds or not

to fact. This does not mean that to form a true judgement the mind must know absolutely all that there is to be known about a thing; partial knowledge is sufficient as long as it corresponds to fact.

102. Logical truth, also called *formal truth*, is the kind of truth implied by the usual and popular acceptance of the term. Truth considered from another point of view, has quite a different meaning and is called metaphysical or *material truth*. It is defined as the correspondence of a thing to its archetype. It is an inherent property of all things which makes them correspond exactly to the plan which existed in God's mind when he made them. In this meaning all things are necessarily true, since God made all things just as he wanted them to be. Gold for example is either true gold, or not gold at all. Nothing can be metaphysically false. When we speak of false money, for example, there is nothing wrong with the coin itself; it is called false simply because it appears to be what it really is not. The lack of truth is not in the object, but in our mind which forms a judgement not corresponding to facts.

103. *Error.*—Error is the absence of logical truth. It is not the same thing as ignorance. Ignorance is complete or partial absence of knowledge of a certain subject, whilst error presupposes knowledge, a knowledge however which does not correspond to fact.

104. Error, like truth, is a state of mind; therefore, strictly speaking, the senses are not subject to error, although sense-illusions can lead the mind astray and thus occasion intellectual error. Neither does error strictly occur in the simple act of intellectual apprehension, namely in mere concepts, because error necessarily implies a judgement by which we affirm a predicate of a subject to which it does not belong, or vice-versa deny a predicate of a subject to which in reality it does belong. As a matter of fact, practically all our concepts implicitly contain some kind of judgement; in adult life especially, there are few, if any, pure intellectual concepts; and even if we did happen to conceive a pure concept without forming any judgement whatsoever about it, the state of our mind would be that of ignorance and not that of error if the concept did not happen to correspond to reality. Ignorance, in fact, is lack of knowledge, whilst error is a positive judgement of the mind.

105. Error cannot occur with regard to first principles which form the basic elements of all knowledge; it is not possible either to doubt

them, or to err in forming them. It is when we come to conclusions drawn from these principles that error occurs. But even in framing conclusions the mind is infallible *per se*; this means that the mind instinctively adheres to truth and rejects error, because it is naturally attracted by the objective evidence of truth and cannot be so by anything else, namely by error, just as the ear cannot perceive anything but sound.

106. But *per accidens*, that is to say accidentally, on account of exterior influence, it can be pressed to accept as evident that which possesses no real objective evidence. This happens by command of the will, which can prevent the full development of the process of the mind's deliberation and put a premature end to its enquiry for truth. In other words, the will can consent to the rash judgements which the intellect forms through habit, through hasty inference or wrong interpretation of sense-stimuli, or from insufficiently controlled associations of ideas. Except in the case of first principles, it is always the will which decides when it is that there is sufficient evidence, and declares that a judgement shall be the one to which the mind should give its final assent. The will ought to allow the mind to deliberate sufficiently, until the evidence is so strong that assent can no longer be withheld; if such evidence is not forthcoming, then the will ought not to allow the mind to give its full assent, but make it remain in a state of doubt.

107. Error therefore, although essentially an act of the mind, is nevertheless finally attributable to the will. Circumstances generally excuse us from responsibility in the matter, because there are what are called the first movements of the will, a kind of impetuous act for which we are not responsible, but theoretically error is always deliberate, in the sense that it is always due to the hasty and premature act by which the will determines the final judgement of the mind.

108. *Doubt* is a state of mind in which assent is suspended through fear of error. It is called positive doubt if the fear of error arises because the evidence for and against is so equally balanced that it is impossible to arrive at a decision. It is called negative if the fear arises from the absence of sufficient motives on either side. It differs from certitude and opinion, because in doubt there is no assent at all, since it is suspended; whilst certitude is a firm assent, and opinion is a wavering or hesitating assent.

Methodical doubt is not a suspension of assent; it is really not a doubt at all. It is a state in which we deliberately place ourselves with regard to judgements to which we have given our full assent, but with regard to which we only act as if we doubted them. We do this by considering what would happen if we doubted them, that is to say, we try to find reasons which could be alleged against them, not in order to confirm our doubt, but in order to strengthen our assent. This is the method St. Thomas adopted in the articles of his *Summa*, and it is a necessary preliminary to metaphysical certainty. This kind of doubt is sometimes called fictitious doubt.

CHAPTER 5

EVIDENCE OF JUDGEMENTS

109. We have seen that logical truth is a property of judgements and propositions, which are true or false according to whether the predicate belongs or does not belong to the subject. In other words we know a judgement to be true and accept it as such in virtue of its objective evidence. All judgements however have not the same degree of evidence. Some are immediate or *self-evident,* because their objective evidence is forced immediately upon the mind, of its own self, by its own natural clarity. These propositions become evident to us as soon as we gather the meaning of the terms, as for example: *the whole is greater than the part.* These are called principles. Other propositions on the contrary need to be demonstrated by means of intermediary propositions until it becomes evident that they are but applications of self-evident principles. These are called conclusions or mediate propositions, because their truth becomes evident only through the medium of other explanatory propositions, namely by demonstration or reasoned inference of which the syllogism is the verbal expression.

110. *First Principles.*—There must be some principles, namely some propositions, immediately evident, without any demonstration. It would be impossible to prove all propositions. We could not go

on for ever proving each one by another; there must be a starting point.

We are not talking here of those principles which every science takes for granted as axioms and postulates, and which are assumed to have been proved in previous studies. Such axioms are in reality conclusions, and are only considered as principles when referred to by particular sciences. We mean by principles, those of the most elementary kind, common-sense ones, which we generally call first principles, such as *two and two are four, the whole is greater than the part.* The truth of these principles is known by intuition. Man's intellectual faculty is essentially a reasoning one; he is meant to discover truth by deduction. Angels have an intuitive intellect; they do not reason, but grasp all truth directly, with more ease than we grasp that of the most elementary principles. Yet man has necessarily been endowed with enough intuitive power to understand without reasoning these first principles, without which he could not reason at all.

III. *Principle of contradiction.*—Amongst these elementary principles there must be one that is the very first of them all, and upon which the whole edifice of our knowledge is subsequently built. There is much debate as to which principle can vindicate the honour of being the very first and essential one. Some contend that it is the principle of contradiction, namely: *Nothing can at the same time exist and not exist,* which can also be expressed in this way: *Contradictories are impossible.* When we have a thought, we must necessarily think of something; the difference between something and nothing is that the one exists and the other does not. The first thing we realize therefore, when we have a thought, is that the thing we are thinking and forming a judgement about, exists, and that it is something distinct from those things that do not exist. Thus the very first act of our mind would be to imply this fundamental truth, namely that things that exist cannot at the same time be non-existent. We then proceed to ask ourselves how, why and when they exist. Therefore all propositions would seem to imply this principle of contradiction, because whenever we affirm something, we imply the negation of the contradictory of that statement.

112. *Other principles.*—Others however prefer as the first principle that of causality, namely that every event must have a cause; or the principle of inference, namely that two things that are similar

to a third are similar to each other. This last principle is sometimes called that of the excluded middle. And others contend that the first principle is that of identity, or the principle of the uniformity of nature. We do not intend to enter into this discussion in this reference manual.

CHAPTER 6

ANALYTIC AND SYNTHETIC PROPOSITIONS

113. An *Analytic* proposition or judgement is one whose predicate necessarily belongs to the subject and could not be conceived as not belonging to it. The connexion between subject and predicate results from their very nature and is apparent from their logical analysis without any confirmation from outside experience. An analytic proposition corresponds to what the scholastics call a proposition necessarily true or *in materia necessaria*. Thus from the meaning of the terms *triangle*, *angle* and *side*, I can deduce the truth of the proposition: *a triangle has three angles and three sides*. Sense-perception is of course a necessary preliminary to the formation of the concepts expressed by the terms, but no further sense-experience is required in order to gather the truth of the proposition. It becomes at once evident, since the predicate is but an explicit expression of the very thing implicitly designated by the subject. The truth of these analytic propositions depends upon whether the analysis of their terms proves that the subject is contained in the comprehension of the predicate, that is to say, upon whether the predicate is either the genus, the difference or the species of the subject. If it is, its denial would involve a contradiction; in fact, if a subject belongs to a certain genus, it cannot possibly belong to any other. Hence analytic propositions are always and necessarily true.

114. These analytic propositions are also called *universal* precisely because they are necessarily and universally true. But all universal propositions are not analytic. *Dogs bark*, for example, is a universal proposition because it is a distributive one, the predicate being affirmed of all the individuals to which the subject is common. But

we know that all dogs bark through experimental observation and not
by analysing the nature of dogs; there would, in fact, be no contradiction in terms to think of a dog unable to bark. Therefore it is not
an analytic proposition.

115. A *Synthetic* proposition is one the predicate of which
expresses something which is not included in the analysis of the
subject, and which is known to belong to the subject, not by theoretical reasoning, but by experimental observation. It is something
which as a matter of fact happens to belong to that subject, but could
be conceived as not being connected with it. Thus, no reasoning on
the nature of the earth could ever give us the knowledge of its
spherical form, which in fact it has not always been thought to
possess. Neither would any amount of logical analysis of the
terms of *arsenic is poisonous* ever show us the truth of this proposition; it is only after having experimented with arsenic that we
know it to be poisonous. These propositions are therefore based on
experimental observation, not on logical analysis. Their denial would
often contradict facts, but would involve no contradition in terms.
Therefore we say that they are not necessary but *contingent* propositions, and that they correspond to what the scholastics call propositions not necessarily true, *in materia contingenti.*

116. Modern philosophers use these terms in a different sense.
They call analytic or *a posteriori* those propositions which we call
synthetic, because, they say, they result from the scrutinizing and
analysis of facts; whilst for them, synthetic propositions which they
also call *a priori*, would be those which we call analytic, because they
maintain that they are syntheses of the several particular instances in
which they have been found to be verified.

We cannot enter here into a deeper examination of this terminology
which, to say the least, is misleading. It is not exact to use the analysis
or synthesis of mere facts as a criterion of the classification of propositions. Neither is it exact to call a proposition or a judgement *a
priori*, meaning anterior to any kind of sense experience, since the
objectivity of our knowledge demands that it be derived from the
outside world. Thus we cannot know that the whole is greater than
the part, until we have gathered through sense experience the meaning of *whole* and of *part*. Neither is there any judgement or proposition which can rightly be called *a posteriori*, resulting only from
sense experience, since inductive methods and scientific laws would

have no sure basis if they were formulated independently of some theoretical principle such as that of the Uniformity of Nature.

117. Scholastics do use the terms *a priori* and *a posteriori*, but in quite a different meaning. They use them exclusively to denote two distinct kinds of arguments. An *a priori argument*, also called an argument *propter quid*, is a strict logical demonstration expressed or expressible in strict syllogistic form. It is called *a priori* because the proof is taken from the definition or from the essential properties of a thing, and from these as from a cause, which by its nature is prior to an effect, the truth of the conclusion is shown to result as a natural effect. An *a posteriori argument*, also called an argument *quia*, is a special kind of deductive argument used when the nature or properties of a thing are unknown, and consists in ascertaining the exact cause of certain effects from a careful scrutiny of the latter. It is called *a posteriori* because an effect is always posterior to its cause. Thus the existence of God is proved by the knowledge we have of created things, and modern science is continually using arguments *a posteriori* to determine the causes of natural phenomena.

CHAPTER 7

THE EVIDENCE OF FAITH

118. First principles are self-evident, that is to say, so clear and obvious that they command our assent; the mind cannot help acknowledging and accepting them as true. In other words, their objective evidence automatically generates subjective evidence and the full assent of our mind. But propositions which are not first principles are neither obvious nor self-evident, and the mind is brought to assent to them by two different processes. The first process is that of rational argument, which consists in resolving these propositions into the first principles upon which they are based, and in which they are implicitly contained. The mind then gives its assent because it recognizes them as logical and necessary conclusions of self-evident principles.

119. The second process is that by which the will commands the

assent of the mind. It can happen that, through lack of time or opportunity, or for some other cause, the mind cannot find any convincing reasons or arguments, and consequently fails to understand why a proposition is true. In such a case a further motive is required to induce the mind to give its assent. This motive is to be found in the authority of someone who knows that these propositions are true. Thus we can acquire much knowledge by simply accepting the conclusions at which other people have already arrived, without questioning the reasons on which their conclusions are based. In fact, no one could possibly investigate the ultimate reasons of all he knows; it would take too much time and too much intellectual effort.

120. But in order to accept these conclusions on authority, the mind requires to be prompted or moved. In the case of the first principles it is prompted by the objective evidence of truth, and in the case of reasoned conclusions it is prompted by its trust in its inferential powers. But in the case of non-obvious conclusions there is no evidence, and in order to put an end to its hesitancy, the will has to command the mind to give its assent. Assent in this case is an act of the mind commanded by the will, and it is called *belief* or *faith*. Belief is the more general term and is used to signify the assent of the mind to any kind of truth which is neither self-evident nor satisfactorily verified by logical argument or sense-experience. It can produce sufficient evidence for intellectual acquiescence and assent, although it does not always exclude a remote possibility of error. Thus we believe we are the children of those whom we call our parents, we are convinced that New Zealand exists although perhaps we have not been there, we accept unhesitatingly the fundamental principles of, let us say, trigonometry, although we may not have taken the trouble to verify them ourselves.

121. The terms *faith* and belief are sometimes taken as synonyms, but as a rule faith implies a firmer assent than simple belief. It excludes all possibility of error, and signifies an assent based on the authority of someone whom we know cannot deceive us, and as a rule, is used exclusively to signify our belief in divine revelation. Faith is not a blind assent; its object must be evident because without evidence our mind cannot give its assent to truth. But the evidence of faith is not based either on sense-experience or on rational argument; it is entirely rooted in the authority of the person who tells us the truth.

122. The measure of our faith depends on how much value we set on the testimony on which it is based, as for example, on how serious is the newspaper which gave us the information, or how learned is the professor who is teaching us something unusual. Now there is no greater authority than that of God, who is infinite truth. We can therefore accept without any fear of error whatsoever he teaches us, and can have entire faith in the truths he reveals; as a matter of fact, it is really only with regard to these truths that we can have absolute and complete faith.

123. It is important to remark that the act of faith does not entail an abdication of our reasoning power, since it does not contradict reason, and is based on reasonable evidence, namely on that guaranteed by God himself. Neither is it a derogation to the exercise of our free-will, as if we were forced to accept something of which we were not convinced. The act of faith is really no exception to the general rule by which the will always has to intervene to put an end to the deliberations of our mind, except in the case of the very first principles of knowledge which are known by intuition. If we gave free vent to our mind, we should never arrive at a final conclusion, but should for ever remain involved in doubt and in fear of error. The will always has to intervene to close the deliberations of the mind, and decide that the mind should stop in its enquiry for truth and evidence.

Therefore in the act of faith, as in any other case, the will fulfils its normal function by deciding that there is enough evidence, although it be only exterior evidence, to justify a complete assent of the mind. Moreover, in matters of supernatural faith, the will is strengthened and the mind is enlightened by the virtue of Faith.

CHAPTER 8

THE CRITERION OF TRUTH

124. We must now briefly outline the much discussed question of what is called the *Criterion* of truth. There is no general agreement as to the exact meaning of the term criterion. Some call it the reason

of our adherence to truth, namely the ultimate motive of our assent, and maintain that this criterion is to be found in objective evidence. Others mean by criterion of truth a standard, a supreme test, or the means whereby we can be sure of the truth of the judgements we form, and they find in the principle of contradiction such a test. It would seem possible to proceed in an intermediate manner in this question, by distinguishing between different kinds of truths.

1. First of all there is the fact of our own existence and of our own mental states or acts. The criterion of the truth of this fact, namely the motive of our assent or belief in this fact, is evidently its objective evidence which is supplied by the testimony of consciousness. No proof or test is necessary or possible; we accept the fact as evident.

2. There are those truths which we call first principles. Here again there can be no doubt that their objective evidence is their criterion. The obvious clarity of these principles is such that we cannot deny them without denying our own capacity to think and to reason. In this case, criterion must again be defined as the motive of assent, and not as the test of truth, since there exists no test or proof of these principles, which are known by intuition.

3. Thirdly, we have all those truths which are implicitly contained in these principles, and which are called conclusions. Here again it is because they are evident conclusions that we assent to them; it is their objective evidence which is their criterion, if we mean by criterion the motive of our assent. But these conclusions, unlike other truths, admit of a test, of a kind of verification. They not only admit of it, but they need it, because their truth is not known to us intuitively like that of first principles. We arrive at their knowledge only through the process of reasoning, and it is quite within the limits of possibility that our reasoning is not correct. It therefore becomes imperative to retrace our arguments, step by step, until we arrive at those first principles of which they are presumed to be conclusions: a process somewhat similar to that of proving the exactitude of an arithmetical multiplication by dividing the product by the multiplying factor, thus arriving once more at the initial number which served as multiplicand. We call this process the resolution of propositions into its first principles, and use it as a criterion of the truth of our conclusions, criterion in this case being taken as a test of truth and not as a motive of assent.

PART III

METAPHYSICS

INTRODUCTION TO METAPHYSICS

Metaphysics are treated by many to-day as old fashioned and fallen into desuetude, like the scientific convictions of past ages such as sidereal astronomy or the belief in the four simple elements. In fact, Metaphysics are taught in practically the same way as they were written by Aristotle 2,000 years ago at the very beginning of civilisation! How can we expect such old theoretical speculations to be acceptable in the present age of unlimited horizons in the field of scientific progress? How can we expect them to be viewed with favour by philosophers who reject not only the evidence of their senses, but that also of rational arguments? It is therefore not astonishing to hear Metaphysics called the finding of bad reasons for what we believe on instinct, a will-o'-the-wisp, a tissue of sophisticated and irrational utterances, an unsatisfactory science doomed to failure.

But although it might seem that the progress of modern science outshines Metaphysics and throws upon them an unfavourable light, yet it is a fact that never before has mankind been so superficial in its quest for truth. Although experimental methods have led to many marvellous discoveries, the modern mind is so hampered and absorbed by the great multitude of the natural phenomena it explores, that it either neglects entirely the pursuit of abstract truth, or errs grossly in its endeavour to discover it. The old philosophers were not encumbered by the difficulties and illusions of experimental observation; they used their minds more than their senses and went straight to the point. They grappled directly with that very nature of things which science is still endeavouring to explain experimentally.

Aristotle is the author of Metaphysics, which he divided into twelve books. This magistral work reveals Aristotle as a man of exceptional intellectual capacity and power of concentration. Why should we be reluctant to accept the unrivalled work of this great man just because he happened to live such a long time ago? Until someone can explain more clearly the hidden mysteries of abstract being, Aristotle's Metaphysics remain the most constructive system yet put forward.

Metaphysics deal with being in general or in the abstract, that is to say with the plain fact of being or existing, without regard to any concrete or individual existing thing. Its object is to discover what we mean by saying that something is *a being*, that something exists, whether that something be a material or an immaterial and spiritual object. Therefore Metaphysics first enquire into the nature of being. They then deal with the different categories of being, always in the abstract, and with the general abstract properties of being. And since Philosophy is mainly the study of the supreme causes, Metaphysics finally deal with the important problem of causes and causality.

THE ANALOGY OF BEING

125. *Being.*—The term being is the present participle of the verb *to be*, and denotes the state of existing, just as *burning* points to that of something that burns. Here *being* is taken as a participial noun and signifies that which *is* or *exists*. The concept of being is a transcendental notion, that is to say, it is not confined to any single category of things, because it is above, and common to, anything that can in any way be said to be or to exist. The contradictory of being is *nothing*. Nothing is the negation of being, and cannot even be conceived by the mind, since concepts must represent something.

Although the beings that exist in this world form the matter of the very first concepts of a child when it calls them all *things*, yet the metaphysical study of the notion of being is one of the most difficult, not because of its complexity, but because of its extreme simplicity. Being has no logical comprehension and therefore cannot be defined. This is precisely why it is called a trancendental notion.

126. Being is taken in two different meanings, namely to signify logical and real being. *Logical* or rational being is that which exists only in the thinking mind. When concepts are generated in the mind, they acquire a conceptual or logical existence which justifies the use of the verb *to be* in judgements, as when we say that a genus *is* a universal. Concepts are therefore a kind of being, since they are real modifications of the thinking mind. They are called beings of the second intention, *entia rationis*; they are not however real beings, but only conceptual ones, and form the object of the study of Logic.

127. *Real being* is that which is not produced by, and which exists outside of, our minds. It includes not only that which we can sense-perceive, or which exists independently as an individual object; it has a much broader meaning than that to which it is restricted by those who maintain that the only real beings are those which form the object of positive science. Indeed, the hidden and inner nature of things is also a real being. Furthermore, the metaphysical components of things, as, for example, potency and act, essence and existence, are objective realities and not mere subjective fictions. The

accidents of things, namely their properties and actions, irrespective of any scientific interpretation, are also real beings. Science discusses the nature of colour, energy and so forth; the philosopher considers them as parts of objects, the real existence of which they partake. They co-exist in the thing to which they belong, and unless we deny the reality of the external world and of the objects it contains, we have no reason to deny that of the accidents.

128. All these imperfect and incomplete metaphysical realities nd even conceptual entities can truly and really be called beings. We are thus faced with the difficult problem of determining how one and the same term *being* can apply to things so widely different from one another, and how even God, who is Infinite and Eternal, can be called a being. The answer is that the term being is analogous, or in other words, that it can be affirmed of all these things by analogy. This is what we have to explain in the present chapter.

129. There are three different ways in which one and the same term can be affirmed of several others: as an equivocal, a univocal, or an analogous term.

An equivocal term is one which has a completely different meaning when used to designate several things, although it is written or pronounced in the same way, for example *seal* used to designate an animal and a wax impression. Clearly, being is not an equivocal term, because all things that are called beings have in common the fact that they are or exist, in however an incomplete and imperfect manner, which fact justifies their appellation of beings, whilst there is nothing in common between the meanings of equivocal terms.

130. *A univocal term* is one which has always exactly the same meaning when it is used to designate several things, for example the term *animal* as applied to a dog and a horse. Things designated by a univocal term have therefore not only a community of name, but a real community of meaning. Thus the term *animal* is not simply a common name given to a lot of individuals, but it expresses something real that all those individual animals have in common, namely an animal nature or essence. A univocal term is therefore a real logical universal, because it is truly common to all the things which it designates; since there are only five classes of logical universals or predicables, a univocal must belong to one of them.

131. Now it is evident that the term *being in general* is neither a

particular species, or a specific difference, or a logical property, or an accident of being. It remains to be shown that it is not a genus. A *genus* is common to several species into which it can be divided by the addition of specific differences. These differences cannot be already contained in the genus, but must be added to it from the outside, because, if they were already contained in the definition of the genus, the species would not be different from the genus. Thus a dog must have something that is not contained in the meaning of the term *animal*, otherwise all animals would be dogs. But it is impossible to add anything to being that is not already contained in it, because outside of being there is nothing, and all that is added to it must be something. Therefore being cannot be a genus, since it is not possible to add to it specific differences not already contained in it. For this reason being cannot be strictly divided into species.

132. *An analogous* term is one which has not quite the same meaning, though not an entirely different one, when it is used to designate several things. Since being is not an equivocal or a univocal term, it follows that it must be an analogous one. In fact, it is only by analogy that all things, whatever they be, can be called and are beings.

Analogy is a partial resemblance of things which differ in certain aspects. In general, analogy implies some kind of proportion or similarity between two or more things, or between relations. It is expressed by a term which is neither completely univocal or completely equivocal in its meaning. There are however three different kinds of analogy which we must now proceed to explain. These are, analogy of attribution, that of proportion, and that of proportionality.

133. *Analogy of attribution* is a similarity of meaning between two things called by the same name, on account of some mere extrinsic resemblance, or of some relation they bear to one another. The definition of the one does not apply to the other; strictly speaking it belongs only to one of them, and is merely *attributed* to the other on account of the relation this one bears to the first one. Thus there is an analogy of attribution between a healthy man and healthy food; *healthy* properly is a quality of man, and is only attributed to food inasmuch as this helps to give health. Likewise a healthy colour is merely a sign of health. Neither food nor colour really possesses health.

134. *Analogy of proportion* consists in a real identity of meaning

between two things designated by the same name, although this identity is not complete, and only applies when those things are considered under certain particular aspects. It differs therefore from analogy of attribution in that the same definition can be applied to both under certain aspects, whilst in analogy of attribution the definition of the terms is entirely different. As an example, there is an analogy of proportion between the *head* of a family and the *head* of the human body; in both cases we could define *head* as that which is primary and essential, and which directs the rest of the body. So also *light*, as applied to that of the sun and to the light of reason; in both cases we could define *light* as that which makes things clear and visible, although in different ways.

Analogy of proportion is therefore not a complete resemblance, otherwise the terms would be univocal and not analogous; yet these terms are not equivocal since there is a real resemblance. The analogy of attribution can hardly be called a resemblance at all, but is really an equivocation.

135. It is by this kind of analogy, namely that of proportion, that being is common to all created things. Because being is not univocal it is not called a *universal*, but a *transcendental*, and the various kinds or classes of being into which it is divided and which it transcends, are not called species, but *modes* or *manners of being*.

Therefore *being*, although not a logical genus or a univocal universal, is really common to all things; all things can be called *beings* by analogy. In fact whatever we can think of has some kind of reality even if it be an incomplete being and only partakes of the reality of the whole, such as primary matter or accidents. Act and potency, substance and accident, exist, although in a different way: potency exists as a perfectible reality, act as a perfecting one; substance exists by itself, accidents in and by the substance.

CHAPTER 2

ANALOGY OF PROPORTIONALITY

136. *Analogy of proportionality* is an analogy based on a one-sided or mixed relation between two things. This third kind of analogy is

introduced in order to explain how the term *being*, which designates created things, can be used with regard to God himself who is uncreated and infinite.

We have seen that in order to establish an analogy of proportion, we have to be able to define both terms of the analogy and thus discover a definite bi-lateral relation between them; this relation forms the basis of the analogy and is the cause of the resemblance between the two terms. But an analogy of proportionality exists between two things one of which we are unable to define and which consequently we cannot really relate to the other. Such an analogy is vague and imperfect, and would at first sight seem rather useless, since the sole purpose of any analogy is to help us to understand the meaning of one of its terms by comparing it to the other. If it cannot be compared or related, there would seem to be no object in making the analogy. Nevertheless the analogy of proportionality is helpful in that it is the only manner in which we are able to acquire some kind of knowledge of a Being which transcends all efforts of understanding. It is for the purpose of explaining how we can know God, that we distinguish between the two analogies of proportion and proportionality. By this distinction it is possible to refute those agnostic theories which call God the *Unknowable*.

137. A real relation adds something to both its terms and establishes a mutual dependence between them. For example, in the relation between an author and the books he writes, it is evident that the books depend entirely upon the author, and also that the author depends upon the books as an author, because without them he would not be an author; the writing of them adds something real to the author, makes him different to what he was. But although the fact of creation makes creatures dependent upon the Creator, it leaves the Creator himself unchanged, since nothing can be added to his perfection. Therefore the relation between God and his creatures is a one-sided relation, and only exists in the creature; God is not related to, or dependent upon, the creature. We have an example of this in the relation based on knowledge; this relation is something real in the knower, but it does not affect in the least the thing that is known.

138. Yet this one-sided or, as it is called, mixed relation, is sufficient to establish a kind of analogy between God and his creatures; we call this analogy an analogy of proportionality. We make the analogy by conceiving God as being one of the terms of a real rela-

tion, and by thinking of him as if he were related to us by creation, just as material things are related to one another. Thus by analogy, or by comparison to the manner in which natural causes are related to their effects, we are able to think of God as the cause of all things.

This concept is not false, since it is only an analogy, but it is very imperfect. We can however improve upon it by eliminating all that is material and by endeavouring to add all possible perfections. Thus we conceive God as not having the limitations of our finite nature, and call him the Infinite being, the infinitely good, just, perfect, and so forth. Or we conceive him as exceeding all the perfection of this world and call him Omnipotent, the First Cause, Eternal.

But we do not know the meaning of these words, and cannot define them. They simply sum up the result of the analogy we have made between a term which is known to us, and one of which we have no positive knowledge. Our analogy runs like this: Since created things are actual beings on account of their created existence, so also God is an actual being on account of his Uncreated and Infinite existence, whatever that may be; as man is kind through his kindness, so God is kind on account of a goodness that we can only conceive as being greater than any human goodness. In one word, we conceive creatures as imitating in a very distant manner the perfections of God, and thus compare them to him by an analogy of proportionality.

CHAPTER 3

POTENCY AND ACT

139. In order to grapple with Metaphysics, it is of the utmost importance to have as clear an idea as possible of what we mean by Potency and Act. These terms, which we shall see recurring quite frequently, had to be purposely coined on account of the extreme difficulty of explaining the meaning of certain metaphysical notions. Although they are rather puzzling at first, they are really very descriptive and helpful when properly understood.

As to the term *Act*, it is taken in three distinct meanings, to designate: 1. The act of being, namely existence as distinct from essence.

2. The act of the essence, namely form as distinct from matter. 3. The accidental acts or the accidents.

140. *Act of Being.*—In its popular meaning the word *act* or action conveys to the mind the idea of something that is being done or accomplished, of something which makes a thing exist in a different manner to that in which it existed previously. In fact, an action always produces an alteration of some kind, by transferring a thing from one state to another, as for example the act of running, burning, or that of radiating. By extending the meaning of the word *act* from that which makes a thing exist in some particular altered manner, to that which makes a thing *simply and purely exist*, we have a fairly accurate description of the act of being.

A thing comes into being, or begins to exist, when its essence acquires existence; before receiving existence, that essence evidently does not, although it could, exist; when it receives existence, it passes from the state of purely possible things to that of physical objects. Now this new state is said to be acquired by an act, but *act* in this case simply means that which causes a thing to pass from the realm of possibility to the domain of concrete existence, and is not to be confused with an act or action which merely modifies an existing thing, such as painting for example. Instead, therefore, of conveying to the mind the idea of something which makes a thing exist in a particular accidental manner, the term *act* is used here to mean *that which makes an essence purely and simply exist*, and is therefore a synonym of existence.

Existence is a real manner or mode of being; not an accidental, but a substantial one. It is called the act of being or an entitative act, *entitative* being derived from a Latin word meaning *being*, because it makes the essence become a real concrete being. And since this act makes the essence exist, the essence is said to be *actuated* by existence.

141. *Act of essence.*—This is the substantial form of things, also called a quidditative act, *quidditative* being derived from a Latin word meaning *essence*.

We have called existence an act because it places the essence in the realm of concrete things; likewise we call form an act because it causes each particular essence to have a special place amongst the great variety of other essences. The special function of the form is to specify the essence and make it belong to one particular species

of things rather than to another; the act of essence gives to a thing
its *specific actuality*, whilst the act of being gives a thing its
existential actuality. It is important to bear in mind this distinction
between the act of being and the act of essence.

142. *Accidental acts.*—These are the accidents. They are
secondary forms which are added to an essence already actuated by
its primary or substantial form. They complete the essence by
actuating it in a secondary manner, and are therefore called secondary
acts of the essence, or secondary quidditative acts.

143. *Pure act* is the name given to those acts which are not dependent upon a corresponding potency. There are three kinds of pure
acts :

1. The human soul which is a complete substance by itself;
although it is united to the potency of matter as the form of a complete species, it can exist without that potency.

2. The Angels are called not only pure, but separate acts, because
they are not united to any potency of essence, namely matter; they
have however a potency of being because their existence is distinct
from their essence.

3. God is a pure and infinitely perfect act, because in him there
is no potency whatever. His essence is absolutely identical with his
existence. His essence is to exist; there is nothing in him but pure
act.

144. *Potency* has three entirely distinct meanings :

1. *Active* potency is the power to perform an action. It includes
not only the physical forces of things, but also the vital powers of
living beings, the latter having the special name of faculties.

2. *Objective* potency means possibility. It has a purely logical
entity, and exists only in the mind. The possible result of an election
is an example of objective potency or possibility, whilst a square
circle is not an objective potency because it involves a contradiction
in terms and cannot even be conceived.

There are three kinds of possibility. The first is called *intrinsic*
possibility; this is the mere fact that the concept does not involve a
contradiction; thus it is intrinsically possible for snow to be black,
but it is impossible for a circle to be square. The second kind is the
extrinsic one, namely that which depends on a thing's cause. It is
called *natural* potency with regard to natural causes, and *obediential*
potency with regard to the First Cause to whom certain effects are

possible which are not so to other agents. The third kind of possibility is the *moral* one, which refers to the normal and usual way in which efficient causes produce their effects.

3. *Subjective* potency is something real, a real part of an existing thing, something that exists outside the thinking mind. Because it is a potency, it is only an incomplete and imperfect reality which cannot exist by itself. But when united to the act which perfects it, it really exists as one of the component elements of a concrete and individual subject.

There are three kinds of subjective potency. Potency of *being* or the essence; united to existence which is its act, it becomes a complete being. Potency of *essence* or primary matter; united to a substantial form which is its act, it forms a complete essence. *Accidental* potency, namely that of substance considered as subject to the accidents which complete and perfect it.

A certain amount of confusion and uncertainty might arise regarding the use of the terms *subjective* and *objective*, unless we carefully observe the different meanings of these terms in connexion with potency and knowledge. By *subjective potency* we mean a potency which, instead of being a mere object or concept of the mind, forms part of something that is *subject* to real concrete existence. *Subjective knowledge* is a knowledge of things, not as they exist outside the mind, but only as the thinking mind, namely the thinking *subject*, represents them.

Objective potency on the contrary is a pure concept of an *object* considered as not containing a contradiction in terms, whilst *objective knowledge* is the knowledge of *objects* or things as they really exist.

145. *In Act*, or *actu*, is an expression used to signify that a thing is no longer in a potential state with regard to the act it is meant to have; it is thus opposed to the expression *in potentia*, *in potency*. There are four principal cases in which this expression is used, namely:

1. Primary matter is in act when it is united to its quidditative act, namely to its substantial form, and is thus no longer in potency.

2. The essence of existing things is in act with regard to its entitative act of existence, whilst an essence considered in the abstract is only in potency towards that act.

3. The nature of a thing is a universal in act when conceived by the mind as such, and is called an actual universal, but it is only a universal in potency or a potential universal in the concrete things

to which it belongs. In this sense the term *formally* is also used as a synonym of actual, and has as correlative the term *fundamentally* or *materially*.

4. An efficient cause is in act when it is actually using its operative powers and performing an action, with respect to which it is otherwise said to be only in potency. Sometimes however, instead of saying that an agent is in potency or in act towards its functions, we say that it is in the *first* or in the *second act*; in the first act means that it has the power to act, in the second act that it is actually performing an action.

CHAPTER 4

ESSENCE AND EXISTENCE

146. Having grasped the meaning of potency and act, we are now prepared to deal with the two intrinsic metaphysical components of all created beings, essence and existence.

Essence is the sum of all that is expressed by the comprehension of a term, or by the concept of species. The word *quiddity* has been coined to denote the essence, from *quid*, Latin for what a thing is. We can describe essence by calling it that which makes a thing what it is, and different from things of other species. A definition expresses the essence of a thing. Essence is often used as a synonym of nature, although there is a slight difference between the two.

147. It is practically impossible to give an example of an essence, as all our words, such as *man*, *flower*, and so forth, represent the whole individual with all its particular features; there are no words to designate the essence by itself, abstracted from its existence and its individuality. We should have to coin words as the Scholastics did in Latin; but it is far more difficult to do so in English. The equivalent of the Latin word for the abstract nature or essence of man, for example, would be *humanity*, but this word has quite a different meaning to-day. So all we can do is to speak of the *essence* of a thing, of *that by which* a thing is ultimately constituted, and by which it differs from other things, whatsoever *that* may be.

148. In view of this difficulty, we have recourse to the next best thing, namely to that of defining essence in respect of its function towards existence. Considered apart from existence, but with relation to it, essence is something that has the capacity of existing. To express this capacity, we call essence a potency, correlative of the term act which is used with respect to existence.

We call essence a subjective potency, according to the meaning of this term as explained in the preceding chapter. It is a potency because it is an incomplete reality and cannot exist by itself. It is subjective because it is not a mere concept of the mind, but one of the real and substantial components of an existing subject. Until it is united to existence, it is a pure objective potency still in the realm of possibility. But once united to existence, it becomes something real and substantial, namely a subjective potency.

It still remains a potential reality even when it is united to its act, because although its capacity has been fulfilled by existence, it still retains that capacity. As an example, a jug still retains its capacity of containing water even though it is filled. It is precisely in virtue of its continued potency or capacity of being united to existence, that essence is kept in existence. In fact, an existing essence does not exist by its own power, but by that of the actuality of existence which continues to fulfil its capacity or potency. In other words, the potency of essence does not disappear by the fact of its existence, because at every moment of its existence, it is still in need of, that is to say, in potency to, an existence which it has not of itself. But this potentiality does not detract from its reality; essence has a reality of its own, distinct from that of existence, although of a different kind. The reality of existence is an actual subjective reality, that of essence is a potential subjective reality.

149. Therefore essence is *something*, a being of some kind; but because it has no existence of its own, it is an incomplete being. Neither the essence or the existence can exist by itself, separated from the other; neither of them is therefore complete without the other; they are both incomplete beings, made for each other in such a way, that when united, they blend admirably together, to form one single and complete individual being. They each partake of the other's reality. The essence partakes of existence, more or less, according to its potential capacity, and existence partakes of the multiplicity and specific diversity of the essence.

150. *Essence and existence are really distinct.*—From what has been said so far, it ought to be clear that essence is a reality of its own, distinct from that of its existence. It is however extremely important to stress this point of the real distinction between essence and existence, because it forms the basis of several theological arguments. The point in question consists in showing that the nature or essence of a thing, does not constitute the whole of that thing's reality. In other words there are in each thing two distinct realities, one the reality of its essence or the potential reality of being, the other, the reality of existence or the actual reality of being.

151. When we say that essence and existence are distinct, we are speaking of a real distinction. In fact, distinction, which is the non-identity of two things, is two-fold:

1. *Logical* or mental distinction, or the distinction between two aspects of one and the same thing. Such is the distinction we make between the attributes of God. This distinction is also called *rationis ratiocinatae,* or virtual, in opposition to actual or real.

Text-books introduce another kind of logical distinction which they call *rationis ratiocinantis;* there is, they say, no foundation for such a distinction. Consequently it is of no practical use. An example would be the pure mental distinction we could make between a concept and the definition of this concept, such as between *man* and a *rational animal.*

2. *Real* distinction is between two existing things. There are two kinds of real distinction, absolute and modal. A *modal* distinction is that of two things one of which has only a modal reality; this means to say that one of them can only exist as a modality of the other and could not even be conceived as existing by itself. Thus there is a modal distinction between a suppositum and the individual nature, between a point and the line it terminates, between an object and its shape or position.

An *absolute* distinction is that of two things which have an independent reality of their own. It is however very important to remark that there can be a real absolute distinction between things which are not separable. Failure to admit this is at the basis of those systems which deny the reality of anything which cannot be sense-perceived, and which consequently reject the science of metaphysics. In fact, metaphysics, by analysing the nature of things, discover that this nature is not a simple one, but composed of many real and distinct elements, such as essence and existence, matter and form. These metaphysical elements are real components of a thing. Essence and existence, matter and form are not mere subjective concepts; every material object has a real essence, a real existence, real matter and real form. Each of these elements has a completely different definition, and is consequently quite distinct from the others, although they have not an independent existence or an independent reality. They are therefore absolutely and really distinct. We could say that an absolute distinction is twofold, namely physical or numerical, when things have a separate concrete existence, and metaphysical, when things are metaphysical components of being and exist only by partaking of the existence of the whole.

152. The difficulty of conceiving two distinct realities in one and the same existing thing, arises from the fact that when we think of something real, we immediately try to imagine it in terms of sense-experience. But there is another sphere of reality beyond the range of our imagination and senses, known only to the intellectual mind. In fact, whilst the senses can only perceive as a whole the physical reality of things, the intellect is able to consider separately any of their several components. It can dwell on the shape of a flower, for example, to the exclusion of its colour, or on the sharpness of a knife to the exclusion of its appearance. It is by this abstractive process of the mind, and not by any experimental observation, that we come to the real distinction between essence and existence. But because this distinction can only be perceived by an act of the mind, it is not a mere mental distinction. The mind discovers it, but does not create it. It is based upon sane logical argument, upon which we can rely better than upon the testimony of our senses, and upon which we must rely for all those things which surpass the range of the senses.

CHAPTER 5

REALITY OF ESSENCE AND EXISTENCE

153. *Reality of existence.*—We gather the general idea of existence from the fact that we can see and feel a thing. Thus, after gazing

at a thing which appears to be a shadow or a phantom, we put out
our hand to feel whether it really exists or not. But when we
endeavour to analyse the abstract meaning of existence, we are confronted with a very difficult problem; so difficult indeed that we
have to content ourselves with a mere nominal definition, by saying
that existence is *that by which* a thing is or exists, by which it has
a place in the domain of concrete objectivity.

154. Now we can assume that the things which surround us,
really do exist; it is a well-known fact, a common-sense truth which
constitutes the primordial stage of every child's knowledge. But if
things really do exist, existence must be something real. Existence
however has nothing whereby, of itself, any kind of difference can
result in the things which it actuates. It is the bare fact of being,
and there is only one way of being: a thing must either exist properly, entirely, or not at all. This is evident especially in organic
natures whose existence is known as life; there is no intermediary
stage between life and death. Therefore the mere fact of existence is
not different in a man, a tree or a stone.

As an example, water, of itself, has no measure or shape; water
as such is the whole indefinite amount of liquid of that name which
exists or could exist. There is no limit to it. It only assumes a definite
shape or measure on account of the nature of the thing which contains it. So also, existence, of itself, is unlimited, it has no boundaries,
and has nothing that can in any way be the cause of the specific and
individual variety of things. If there were nothing but existence in
the things that surround us, these would all be one and the same
thing; they would form one big, indefinite mass, identical and uniform. Incidentally, this is precisely why God is one and infinite,
namely, because there is nothing in Him but existence: His essence
is to exist.

155. *Reality of essence.*—Essence is something real apart from
the reality of its existence. At first sight essence would not appear
to have any reality apart from that of its existence, since we naturally
relegate that which does not exist, into the wishful and creative
efforts of our mind, void of all concrete reality. But we do not maintain that essence is something real *when* it does not exist, as this
would involve a contradiction, but that when it actually *does* exist
it has a reality of its own besides the reality it acquires from the
fact of its existence. It differs from existence in that it is necessarily,

in virtue of its component elements, the principle of the multiplicity and differentiation of things. It cannot be conceived otherwise, since matter, which is one of its elements, is the principle of the numerical individuation of things, and form, which is its other element, is the principle of their specific differences. But essence could not contain these differential principles if it were identical with existence, since there is no such differentiating principle in existence which excludes all idea of plurality and distinction.

To make a rather banal comparison, if we had several balloons of different material, shape and size, and blew them out, they would all assume different appearances, not because of any difference in the air that filled them, but because of the differences in the material of the balloons. Or if an electric current was connected with many bulbs of different shapes, sizes and colours, the different effects produced would be due to the bulbs which receive the current, and not to the current which itself is uniform.

156. Therefore, because essence and existence have completely different functions, essence being the cause of the multiplicity and variety of things, which cannot be attributed to existence, we are in a position to conclude that the one cannot be identical with the other, and that there is a real distinction between the essence and the existence of all created things.

157. We can arrive at the same conclusion in another way. To maintain that existence is the essence of a thing would be to say that it is of the very nature of a thing to exist. This, however, is obviously not true, because many new things come into existence, and many cease to exist. And furthermore, if essence and existence were identical, the knowledge of the one would lead to that of the other. Thus if I say that a trapezium is a four-sided figure of which no two sides are parallel, by the very fact of knowing all about this kind of four-sided figure, I know all about trapeziums, and vice-versa. But no amount of study and investigation of the essence of a thing can ever make us know whether it really exists or not; all we can be sure of is that such a thing is capable of existing, that there is no intrinsic contradiction to its actual existence. On the other hand, the deepest understanding of the metaphysical nature of existence cannot reveal to us the nature or essence of one single thing. If essence and existence were identical, one would necessarily lead to at least a partial knowledge of the other.

158. In the course of philosophy, the term *nature* is often used as a synonym of essence. The two terms are practically synonyms, but whilst the term essence can also be considered under a logical aspect as something consisting of a genus and of a logical difference, nature generally refers to a metaphysical essence. Nature is used to denote essences composed of matter and form, pure essences not composed of matter, and even the infinite essence of God. It is also sometimes used to designate the constituent character of accidents, and thus we speak of the nature of an accident. But its primary meaning is that of a substantial essence to emphasize the distinction between the essence or substance of a thing and its exterior appearances or accidents; in this sense we speak of the hidden nature of a thing.

Nature is the root and the remote principle of all activity. It is in virtue of its nature that an individual performs special functions. But the proximate and immediate principle of action is the operative power itself, whilst the individual is the subject which performs the actions its nature makes it capable of performing. The student need not worry about this distinction between nature and essence; he can always use the two terms indiscriminately.

159. The nature of a thing is *fundamentally* universal, that is to say it is, or could be, common to many individuals. The nature of man, for example, is to be found in all human beings. We say fundamentally, because it is the foundation and the reason of the identity of the species in many individuals. But *formally*, that is to say, actually, it exists only in one individual at a time. If it were not fundamentally universal, there would be no ground for our general and abstract concept, let us say, of man; concepts would be void of meaning, mere concepts or words.

CHAPTER 6

SUBSTANCE

160. We have seen in Logic that there are ten Categories which, however, can be reduced to eight, namely, substance, quality,

quantity, relation, place, time, action and passion. We saw that by Categories we meant the supreme modes into which being can be divided. We call them modes of being and not species, because we have also said that being is not a genus and cannot be divided into species properly called. Now although Metaphysics would be the right place to deal with all these metaphysical categories, some of them, namely quantity, place and time are exclusive categories of material things, and therefore are dealt with in Cosmology and not in Metaphysics. We are thus left with five categories, those of Substance, Quality, Relation, Action and Passion.

161. As there is little of importance to say about Quality, we will deal with it briefly before the other categories. There are four kinds of quality. The first kind are the habits of the soul and of the mind. Moral philosophy and psychology deal with habits and dispositions. The second kind is active power or potency; this is dealt with under causality. The third kind denotes all those physical attributes that produce material modifications or alterations in a thing, such as colour, sweetness, hardness and so forth; this is the domain of experimental science. And finally the fourth kind is external form or figure; this is the domain of geometry, natural science and aesthetics.

162. *Substance.* Substance is the first of the Categories. There are three kinds of substance, namely material substances, immaterial or spiritual ones such as the human soul and the Angels, and finally the infinite and eternal substance of God.

The term *substance* can be taken in three different meanings, to signify:

1. A logical universal or predicable, namely the supreme genus of the first logical category. To consider substance as a predicable requires a reflex act of the mind, or as we say, a second consideration or intention, and therefore substance in this sense is called *second substance.*

2. A formal suppositum or person. In this sense substance designates an existing individual thing or person. It is then called *first substance.* We shall see in the next chapter what we mean by suppositum.

3. A radical suppositum, namely an individual considered without, and as distinct from, its subsistence. We call it a radical suppositum precisely because in this case we consider substance as something apt to exist but not actually and formally having that which makes it exist

by itself and independently. This also will be made clear in the next chapter.

163. It is in this last sense that we define substance as *that which can exist by itself without a supporting subject.* This is the characteristic of substance, namely to be able to exist by itself. By this we mean that it does not have to partake of the existence of something else which supports it, as the accidents do, such as colour, shape, and so forth, which depend entirely for their existence on the subject to which they belong. If substance could not support itself in existence, it would have to be supported by something else; this in its turn would have to be supported, and so we should have an infinite process, which is impossible. We do not, of course, mean that it is independent to such an extent that it does not depend on an efficient cause, namely on the First Cause who gives existence to all things and maintains them in existence.

Since it is self-supporting, it is able to support in its turn the accidents, which have no proper existence of their own, but depend entirely on that of the substance to which they belong.

CHAPTER 7

THE SUPPOSITUM OR PERSON

164. Suppositum and person are synonyms, the only difference being that the term person is reserved for a suppositum endowed with intellectual faculties. Person is therefore an intellectual or a rational suppositum. The student will find no difficulty in applying all that we shall say of the person to any other suppositum.

Person is defined as a complete, subsisting and incommunicable nature or substance. The suppositum is defined in exactly the same way. We call it a complete and subsisting nature, because it is endowed with all that is necessary to make it exist independently and by itself. Thus the soul alone is not a person, because it is not a complete individual without the body; neither is the body alone a person, because it cannot exist independently of the soul. For the same reason we shall see that the individual nature by itself is not a person, because it depends on existence in order to be.

165. We add that the person must be incommunicable. This follows from the fact that it exists by itself and as an independent individual; an individual is necessarily distinct from all other individuals and is not communicable to them.

But there is a very special reason for adding this term *incommunicable* in the definition, because when dealing with the mystery of the most Holy Trinity, theology teaches us that the individual nature of God is a subsisting nature, although communicable to Three Persons, and thus provides us with an example of a complete and subsisting nature, which however is not incommunicable.

166. In fact, a deep enquiry into the metaphysical notion of person, leads us to the conclusion that a complete individual nature is something really distinct from the person itself. When we say that there is a real distinction between person and nature, we are speaking of a real modal distinction, not of a real absolute one. An absolute distinction is between things which have nothing in common, one of which does not include anything included in the other, that between two apple-trees, for example. These things have an independent reality of their own.

167. A *modal distinction* on the contrary is between two things, one of which does contain something belonging to the other. This happens when one of them has only a modal reality. This means that one of them can exist only as a modality of the other, and could not possibly even be conceived as existing by itself. Thus the difference between a shaped finger and its shape; the shape belongs to the finger, yet it is not the finger.

Another example is that of a line terminated by its indivisible extremity or point. The point, which is indivisible, is necessarily distinct from the divisible line. Therefore although the line cannot exist without its terminating point and cannot be separated from it, the line as such, considered without the point, is not the same thing as the line with its point. Without the point it is something indefinite, non determined, non-existent. With it, it is a real and complete line. Therefore there is a real distinction between them, but it is modal, because they belong to each other.

168. Now an individual essence or nature has all the constituent

elements of its individuality, but it has not in itself any principle of existence; it does not actually exist of itself; existence must come to it, as it were, from the outside. Without existence, although it is an individual substance, it is not a complete and self-supporting one, and is incapable of performing the functions of which it is the remote principle. Therefore it is logical to conclude that an individual nature as such, is not the same thing as a complete and subsisting one, that is to say, it is something really different from a person.

This distinction however is only modal, because the person includes the individual nature, without which it would not be a substance at all. Our conclusion therefore means that an individual nature considered without existence is distinct from that same nature considered with its existence. But because this distinction can only be grasped by considering separately two things which are inseparable, we must not think that it is only a mental distinction; it is real, because existence is something really distinct from essence or nature. We even have an example of a nature actually separated from the person, since the human individual nature of Christ actually existed without a human person.

169. Thus it will be seen that the term *individual*, which means that which cannot be shared by anything else, as opposed to universal, can designate two distinct things: the individual substance and the individual nature.

170. An individual *substance* is a concrete existing suppositum or person. It is often called simply an individual. It is clear that it can belong to one thing only and that it is something distinct from all other individuals. An individual *nature* is the essence or substance considered by itself, apart from that which makes it exist, not however in the abstract, but in the very suppositum to which it belongs. This is more difficult to grasp, but we must remember that an essence is distinct from its existence not only in the considering mind, but in reality.

This means that my essence or my individual nature is not my existence. Therefore my individual nature considered without my existence, is something distinct from my individual nature considered with my existence. Considered with existence, my nature is a self-supporting individual person. Considered without existence my nature is still an individual one, because, although a nature or essence as such is universal and can be shared by many individuals, my own nature belongs to me only and is necessarily an individual one. Thus it is clear that I have an individual person and an individual nature which are manifestly two distinct things.

To avoid confusion, the complete existing nature or person is called a *formal* suppositum; the individual nature as such is called on the contrary a *radical* suppositum, meaning that it is the root of the formal suppositum or person, a kind of embryonic suppositum which can become a formal one.

171. Common sense itself admits this distinction between nature and person. We do not say that it is the nature of a thing or of someone that exists and does things, but that it is the whole complete existing individual or person that exists and acts. The dog runs and barks, not his nature. There is a philosophical axiom to express this: *Actions belong to the suppositum or person.* The suppositum or person is the subject of existence and the efficient cause of all activity; it is called *that which* exists, lives, and acts; it is the *principium quod*. The individual nature on the contrary is the principle in virtue of which the suppositum is able to exist, live and act; it is called *that by which* the suppositum had these properties; it is the *principium quo*.

CHAPTER 8

SUBSISTENCE

172. We still have to explain what we mean by subsistence, before putting an end to our abstruse discussions on the suppositum, because the question arises as to why substance can become a suppositum, independent and self-supporting, while accidents cannot, and are doomed to exist only in and by the substance. This entirely different way of existing cannot originate from the existence itself, because existence of itself is one and the same in all things and has nothing whereby it can make substance exist in a different manner than accidents do. Existence is the mere fact of being, and

makes a thing exist; the different way of existing must come from
something other than existence. We say that substance exists by
itself and thus becomes an individual suppositum or person on
account of what we call *subsistence*.

173. Subsistence is the *ultimate terminus of an individual nature*.
We can compare subsistence to the terminating point of a line to
which it belongs and which it terminates. It is a mode, a way of being
of a nature which it makes ultimately ready to exist by iself. But
instead of being just an accidental mode, as the curvature of the
finger for example, it is a real and substantial mode, which terminates
the nature and makes it an individual nature, capable of existing by
itself. It makes a substance partake of existence in a different manner
than the accidents do. Existence makes a thing exist, subsistence
makes it exist by itself, makes its existence self-supporting and
independent. Therefore, although all scholastics do not share this
opinion, it would seem that subsistence is really something different
from mere existence.

Individual and self-supporting existence immediately follows subsistence as a natural result, just as the carpenter's finishing touch to a
piece of furniture immediately and naturally results in a completed
and finished object. Before the sculptor gives the statue he is making
its finishing touch, the statue does not yet really exist as an individual and completed object. It is the last stroke of his labour which
completes it, makes it exactly what it is meant to be, and at the same
time, without any further action of the artist, makes it exist independently by itself.

Thus subsistence, by terminating the individual nature, releases
the tide of existence, which sweeps over that nature and places it
among the things that are. It is the last finishing stroke or touch
which ultimately disposes the nature to receive an existence of its
own, independent of, and incommunicable to, any other, and thus
distinguishes it from those things that have no proper existence of
their own.

174. It is therefore subsistence that makes substance a real formal
suppositum or person. It precedes existence; but there is no question
of any precedence in time, just as there is no lapse of time between
the very last moment in which a match is actually ready to ignite
and the moment when it actually ignites. It reaches its climax of heat
gradually, but the last moment of transition is the same as the first

moment of ignition, one same indivisible instant joining the past to the future. Thus, when a thing is produced, it receives a nature which has at one and the same time subsistence and existence, together with all the accidents which accompany its existence.

CHAPTER 9

ACCIDENTS

175. An *accident* is a manner of being which does not exist by itself as substance does, but only in and by a substance which supports it and keeps it in existence, and which the accident modifies. The First Cause, however, can maintain in existence an absolute accident without the aid of the substance by which it is normally supported. We shall explain this in the chapter on quantity.

Nothing can be added to the infinitely perfect actuality of God's essence but much can be added to material essences, because the vast potentiality or capacity of primary matter is far from being exhausted by its substantial form; it is therefore still in potency to many ulterior secondary determinations or forms. It is precisely the function of the accidents to actuate some of this remaining potentiality, although no accidents are capable of totally perfecting all the capabilities of material essences, which are, and always will be, to some extent imperfect.

176. Strictly speaking, accidents have no existence of their own, but share the one and only existence of an individual substance. Their existence is really a co-existence; they exist in and by the substance to which they belong. Since accidents only exist in and by the substance to which they are united, it would seem more logical to maintain that they do not add any new kind of existence to a thing, besides that which it has as a substance, although the contrary opinion is consistent with scholastic philosophy. There is in fact only one kind of existence; existence is in itself one and uniform. Things are said to have various kinds of existence only because existence is communicated to them in different degrees and manners according to the different potential capacities of their essence.

177. The potential capacity of a thing to exist in a certain definite individual manner, is due to its accidents, because although accidents are *acts* of the essence which they complete and modify, yet they are *potencies* with regard to existence, namely accidental *potencies of being*. In fact they do not make a thing exist, but make it capable of existing in a certain way. Therefore they are not entitative acts or acts of being, since there is only one act of being, namely existence, which actuates the whole being, namely its nature and its accidents. This is expressed by saying that with regard to existence, *in linea existentiae*, accidents are potencies, not acts, viz., potencies of being or entitative potencies.

178. But with regard to the essence, *in linea essentiae*, they are acts, acts of the essence or quidditative acts, which complete and modify the essence or quiddity. As water for example, takes the shape of the vessel into which it is poured, so the essence is shaped by its accidents and receives from them its individual features. It is in this sense that accidents are called *secondary, complementary, acts, or accidental forms,* the primary act of the essence being the substantial form. Therefore accidents must not be conceived as a sort of rind, which, when stripped away, would reveal the essence or substance as a core or kernel. There is no super-position or joining together. Accidents are acts, and their union to the essence must be thought of only as that of an act to its potency.

179. We know very little about the hidden substance of things, our knowledge being arrested at their surface, at their effects and properties, that is to say at their accidents. It would therefore seem at first sight that the knowledge of these accidents, sound for example, shape or colour, ought to present no difficulty. Yet it is surprising to find how little we know about the nature of many of them. Our knowledge of accidents is often limited to that of the impressions they create on our senses. We are conscious of seeing colour, of hearing sound, of feeling soft things, and so forth; but it is extremely difficult to analyse and define colour, sound or softness, although science provides us with plausible hypotheses as to their nature.

Yet, just as the difficulty of arriving at the knowledge of the underlying nature of things is not a proof of its non-existence, so also, we are not entitled to conclude that accidents are mere sub-jective illusions because they are difficult to define. The objective reality of accidents is a common-sense truth based on the reliability of our sense-perceptions.

180. There are several kinds of accidents:

Proper or specific accidents, also called specific properties, are those that are always found in every individual of one species only; they are essential and invariable characteristics of one particular substance, such as the particular shape of a crystal, the size and colour of each species of flowers, the specific reactions of the elements.

Common or contingent accidents, also called common properties, are those that do not necessarily belong to any particular substance.

Predicable or Logical accident is the name of one of the five predicables, and is that which may be used as predicate of a proposition, but is neither part of the definition or a specific property of the subject. It is opposed to logical property. All common or contingent accidents are logical accidents.

Predicamental or metaphysical accident is the name of the nine categories of physical accidents, namely of those things which cannot naturally exist by themselves, but only in and by a substance which they modify. It is therefore opposed to substance, and thus, not only contingent, but also specific properties of things are metaphysical accidents. All metaphysical accidents are not always logical ones, such as specific properties.

181. *Absolute* accident is an accident which has some kind of reality besides that of being a mere modification of substance. Quantity is the only accident which everyone agrees to call absolute; it can in fact be conceived, and even, by supernatural power, exist, independently of a measurable subject, viz., without a substance which it actually modifies. Since the whole reason for considering the distinction between absolute and modal accidents is the permanence of the accidents in the Sacrament of the Eucharist, it is not necessary to postulate the existence of any other absolute accident, and it will lead to less confusion if the name of absolute accident is reserved for quantity alone, in spite of the contrary opinion of some authors. The discussion is one of pure terminology. In fact all accidents, including quantity, but excluding relation, could be called absolute, since they modify substance independently of anything else; although they are dependent on, and related to, the substance which supports them, they are nevertheless absolute and independent in their own sphere of reality. Relation of course is not an absolute but a relative accident, because the modification

it causes in a thing is entirely dependent upon some other object to which that thing is related.

182. *Modal* accident is that which has no other reality than to be a mode or modification. It cannot even by divine power exist or be thought of without that which it modifies. Thus it is impossible to think of a position or an action, and so forth, without thinking of an object affected by these modalities. Here again we are up against a question of terminology, since all accidents, including quantity and even relation, are really modifications or modes which affect substance, and could therefore strictly speaking be called modal accidents. There is however a general understanding that quantity should not be called modal. It is with regard to quality that there is a certain amount of disagreement. It is however best to classify quality as a modal accident, since even in the Holy Eucharist it does not really exist without a subject, quantity being the quasi-subject of quality and of all other accidents.

In conclusion, quantity is generally called an absolute accident, relation is a relative accident, and all the other accidents are called modal.

We must finally add that spiritual substances also have accidents, such as quality, relation and action.

CHAPTER 10

RELATION

183. We now come to the most difficult of all the Categories, that of Relation. Relation is extremely difficult to explain and to understand, because, besides being an accident with no independent existence of its own, it cannot even be conceived without thinking about two things at the same time, namely the two things that are related to each other.

Relation is a state of dependence which exists, or is conceived as existing, between two things. Relation conveys the idea of dependence, just as absolute conveys that of independence and self-sufficiency. A relative thing necessarily depends upon something else for its relationship; relation, being a ratio or proportion, can only be conceived as existing between several things. The thing to which another is related is called its correlative. If the correlative disappears, so does also the relation.

184. There are three kinds of relation. The first kind is *predicamental* relation. This is an accidental relation, and is proper to created substances. It is, as we shall see, subdivided into real, logical and mixed relation.

The second kind is *transcendental* relation. This is an essential relation; it is not a mere contingent accident as is predicamental relation, but something belonging to the very nature of a thing, without which that thing could not be imagined and could not exist. Such a relation is that of matter to form, of the effect to its cause, and so forth; the whole reason of being of the one is found in its relation to the other.

The third kind is *subsisting* relation. This is a self-existing or substantial relation, found in God alone. A subsisting relation is the whole actual essence or substance of God, whilst a transcendental relation is only an essential property, and a predicamental relation only a contingent accident. A subsisting relation exists by itself; transcendental or predicamental relations do not exist by themselves. There are three subsisting relations in God, which are the Three divine Persons of the Holy Trinity.

185. Here we are concerned only with predicamental relation which is one of the nine accidents or modes of being; it is called a relative mode in opposition to the other accidents which are absolute modes.

A modal accident can be an absolute or a relative *mode*. There is no contradiction in saying that a modal accident can be an absolute mode; all accidents, except quantity are modal accidents or manners of being of the absolute accident, namely quantity, upon which they directly depend. But most of these modal accidents are nevertheless absolute modes, because the nature of their modality is quite independent of anything else. One of them however, namely relation, is not an absolute mode but a relative one, because everything in it, its very modality, is dependent on something else, namely on its correlative.

186. Therefore relation is dependent for its existence on some other thing than the subject in which it exists. It consists in a mere

respect, a *towardness* of one object to another. Thus the relation of paternity is a real attribute of a father, but it is dependent for its reality upon that of his son.

Now the fact of being a father gives to a man something real that he did not possess before. He becomes related to a son, and thus acquires a real, although relative, mode of being which he had not before. When we think of a mode, we must not imagine it as a coat of paint on a door. A mode can be real though not tangible or visible. If I become sad for example, I undergo a real change, I acquire a real mode of being that I did not have before, although the change may not be noticeable to anyone. Relation is an awkward thing to grasp and to define, yet it is a real predicamental accident, that is to say, something real and not a fiction; otherwise it would have no right to figure among the ten categories of real things.

187. A few examples will make this abstract notion of relation clearer. If we draw two parallel lines, A and B, on a piece of paper, they will have a real relation to each other. One would be tempted to say that such a relation is not real, that the fact of having a parallel B does not make A any different from what it was. So let us draw the same lines again, A as it was, but B at right angles to A through its centre; we shall now have a cross instead of parallel lines. It is quite certain that A has now acquired a new mode of being on account of the new position of B, and consequently on account of the new relation of A to B: before, A was one of the two parallel lines, now it is a section of a cross.

Again, let us take a number, 26943 for example, and then change the order of its figures thus 63492. Through a mere change of order or relationship, these ciphers have definitely acquired a completely new and real status, or mode, since they have a different function and value. If we draw a picture of a house and place the house right in the centre of the paper, the picture would be ugly for want of perspective and proportion. Let us draw it again with the house to one side and lower down, below the line of the horizon; the picture will then assume a totally different reality, by a mere change of proportion or relation of one part to another.

188. Proportion, or relation of one thing to another, is one of the essential characteristics of this world. The world is full of relations, everything and every event being related in some way or another to something else. The arrangement of the flowers in a vase, of the

furniture in a room, of the objects in a landscape, the social relations of mankind, the proportions of a scientific apparatus, and so forth, are all true and real relations. They do not modify things in the same way as would an alteration in shape or colour; but they do bring about real modifications, real manners of being which those things did not possess previously.

189. There are therefore such things as real relations. But there are also two other kinds of predicamental relation, namely logical and mixed relation.

Logical relation, unlike a real one, does not give to the related things any real mode of being they did not possess; it exists purely in our minds which create it. Such relations can exist only between two things of which one at least is a concept, for example between being and non-being, or between genus and species.

Mixed relation gives a real mode of being to one of the related things but not to the other. For example the relation of the creature to the Creator arises from the fact of creation which gives existence to the creature. But it leaves God entirely unchanged, as he is in no way richer or more powerful because he has a world to govern, and is completely independent of his creatures for his happiness. Therefore creatures are really related to, and dependent on, God; but God is only related to creatures by an act of our minds, by a logical relation. Likewise the relation between the object of our knowledge as compared with our cognitive powers is a mixed relation; knowledge is something real in us, but leaves the things we know indifferent and unchanged.

CHAPTER II

ACTION AND PASSION

190. The last two categories which we have to explain in Metaphysics are action and passion. Action is the execution of a movement. Its correlative is passion, which is the fact of a thing being subjected to an action or movement. It would hardly seem necessary

to warn the reader that the term passion is not used here in its popular meaning of strong emotion.

A second remark is that the term movement is not taken in the exclusive sense of local motion, but in its most general acceptance, to signify any kind of change wrought in a subject, thus including any alteration occurring either in matter, in the mind, or in the will. By alteration or change we do not mean that which results in a thing on account of this change, but the very change itself, the actual fact of being changed. The change itself produced by an action is called *Passion*.

191. Now this passion or effect wrought in a subject, is not really different from the action of the agent which produces it. The motion of the agent is not different from the motion of the thing moved. There are not two movements, but only one, the difference between them being purely logical, and arising simp'y from a different point of view. An action is a movement considered as proceeding from an agent; that same action becomes a passion or passive change, if considered as received in a moved subject.

As an example, if I move a chair from one place to another, the movement I perform in order to move it is my very own; it belongs to and is performed by me; yet it is the chair that is displaced and moved. Therefore the movement I perform pertains to the chair that is moved as well as to me who am moving it; in reality the displacement of the chair is not distinct from the movement I make to move it. If I were to move my pen to write, my action or movement would be the same movement as that by which the pen would be moved.

192. There are two kinds of agents, namely the principal agent and the instrumental one. A *principal* agent is one which acts in virtue of its own power alone. An *instrumental* agent is one which acts by the power of the principal agent. Thus if I paint, I am the principal agent of the picture; my brush is the instrumental agent. An instrumental agent receives from the principal agent the power to perform an action it could not perform of itself; but at the same time it uses its own native power, since it is the knife that cuts, although it could not cut by itself. But neither could I cut without the knife.

Now second causes, that is to say created agents, are instruments with regard to the First Cause; the concept of second cause is incomprehensible without that of instrumentality. It is only in virtue of their instrumentality that created things can be called real causes of the total effect produced by them and by God. An instrumental cause acts on the one side in virtue of the motion of the primary cause, but on the other it uses its native power, which makes it a real, although instrumental, cause.

193. As principal cause, God moves secondary causes to produce their effects; therefore God himself is the cause of, and produces the effects, of which created things are secondary causes. Thus an acid burns in virtue of its natural corrosive power, but it is God who makes it able to burn at that moment, thus using it as an instrument.

To understand this action of the primary cause, we must reflect that it does not destroy the action of the secondary cause, because the principal and the instrumental agents are not two partial agents both of which perform part of the total effect, as would be the case of two horses pulling the same cart. On the contrary the effect produced by the principal and the instrumental agent is due in its *totality* to both of them; each one of them does not perform part of the effect, but the *whole* effect. This is readily understood, since it has been said that the movement of the patient, in this case the instrument, does not differ from the movement of the agent who performs it. There is one action only, not two; one effect, not two. The effects produced by secondary causes are to be ascribed totally to them and totally to the first Cause, without any prejudice to the efficacy of either of them.

194. God therefore is the principal agent, created things are instrumental causes. These instrumental causes are real efficient causes, but cannot make use of their natural activity without an actual motion of the primary cause, as a knife cannot cut unless it is made to cut by some exterior agent. God moves every secondary cause according to its special nature, that is to say that he moves natural elements towards the attainment of their effects by means of fixed and unalterable laws to which they are compelled to conform. He moves human free-will according to its free nature, that is to say freely. How he does it will always remain a mystery; but being the author and creator of free-will, surely he knows enough about it to be able to move and direct it without destroying its free nature.

Finally let it be added that when God produces some effect or other in this world directly by himself, without making use of created instrumentality, he is said to work a miracle.

CHAPTER 12

CAUSE AND EFFECT

195. We have defined philosophy as the knowledge of causes. In fact we have so far investigated the supreme causes of all things and shall continue to do so. We must now try to determine exactly what we mean by *cause* and by its correlative *effect*.

A *cause* is that which contributes to the production of something that follows it. Man has always been inclined to wonder how the phenomena he observed in nature were produced. The mystery which surrounded these phenomena led him in early times to personify and even deify the power responsible for the most simple phenomena such as rain, fire and the like, a personification which was sometimes called by the vague names of chance and fate. Later on, he began to make methodical enquiries into the nature of this power. This was the beginning of philosophy, which is, and always was, an enquiry into the causes of things, and is in fact defined as the knowledge of causes.

196. Aristotle was the first to give an adequate and logical answer to the problem. What he set out to find were not the particular causes of particular things, but the very nature of causality. He first of all established the difference between a principle and a cause. These terms were not unknown before him, but their meaning was vague and inconsistent. He therefore analysed them thoroughly, and called *principle* that which simply precedes something else, and restricted the meaning of *cause* to that which influences, or contributes to, the production of that which it precedes. Thus all causes are principles, but not all principles are causes.

He then proceeded to demonstrate that the meaning of cause must not be restricted to the producing agent or to the efficient cause. Active power is in itself mysterious and obscure, and can give no real insight as to the nature of causality in general. In fact, the mystery which surrounds it has led modern philosophy to the incredible assertion that there is no such thing as causality, and that there is no other relation between natural phenomena than a mere succession of events. Aristotle's investigations led him to the conclusion that there are several kinds of causes, four in number, namely the material, formal, efficient and final cause. He based his conclusion on a methodical observation of the changes which take place in the production of natural phenomena.

197. There are in fact, two different kinds of change, namely substantial and accidental changes. A *substantial change* is that which occurs when the very substance of a thing is changed into something else, the test of such changes being the disappearance of the specific properties of the preceding substance. In fact, since these properties are always present in all the individuals of one kind of substance only, their disappearance necessarily entails that of the substance which they characterize. An *accidental change* on the contrary is a mere modification of some of the common properties and qualities of a thing.

The phenomena of which Aristotle was bent on discovering the causes, were not merely the accidental changes of things, but their more deeply rooted substantial changes. It was to substantial change that he especially directed his attention; and modern science has shown how right he was, by discovering that chemical or substantial changes are at the root of many phenomena the accidental nature of which were taken for granted at his time, such as combustion for example.

198. Now when a thing is changed substantially, something must remain throughout the change in order to justify the reality of the change. If, for example, when a piece of coal is changed into ashes, nothing whatsoever remained in the ashes that was in the piece of coal, there would be no connection between the two; ashes could not then be said to have been formed out of coal; the coal would have simply disappeared and ashes appeared from nowhere. The *material* cause is precisely that which remains, and is called the primary matter of things. It is considered as something indetermined and potential which can exist in different ways according to the different determining elements which make it exist in one way rather than in another.

The *formal* cause is that which makes the material cause exist in one particular manner, that which makes one thing a piece of coal and another ashes. It is a determining and actual element.

The *efficient* cause is the active power which makes it possible for the formal cause to be united to the material one.

199. The *final* cause is the purpose for which the change is effected. The study of the final cause is called Teleology or Entelechia which holds that there is purpose and design in every event and in every action. This purpose drives the agent to act and

is for this reason called a cause. The drive to reach a goal is due to an interior and immanent impulse in all living beings. This impulse is more or less immanent according to the degree of perfection of their life. Other beings are driven towards their goal by exterior agents, for example an arrow, which is driven towards the target by the bow. Only intelligent beings are conscious of the purpose of their actions and can act for a deliberate motive. The purpose and design of all other agents is chosen and determined by the First Cause and Author of their nature. Teleology is opposed to those systems which hold that events are due to a blind and casual force.

200. We have said that a cause influences in some way that which it precedes. We must therefore explain how these four causes contribute towards the final result of the change which is effected. As to the material cause, its influence must not be conceived in the same manner as that of the efficient cause; its contribution is not that of any action or activity; it provides the support, the basis upon which the change is effected; it contributes in a passive, or more precisely, in a potential way. Since it is indetermined towards the manner in which it is to exist, it is said to be *potentially* any kind of material being, to contain in potency any of the substantial forms which can determine and actuate it. Its causal contribution is therefore that of its potentiality or capacity of being any particular thing.

The formal cause contributes by determining matter, in order to exist in one particular manner. Here again there is no action in the common acceptance of the word. It influences the existing thing by actuating its matter; it is therefore the substantial act of the essence, not an accidental act like action.

201. The efficient cause contributes to the change which is wrought in a subject, not by adding or transferring something to the effect, but by reducing the potentiality of matter into actuality, namely by bringing forth from matter the forms contained in its potency. Its action is therefore not productive of the effect in its totality; it does not produce the effect in the full meaning of the word, as if it made something exist which did not exist at all before; this would be to create, to make something out of nothing. Its causality is merely a transforming power. To make a comparison, it starts the machinery which of itself results in the desired effect. All

we do, for example, is to put a match to a piece of paper, which then of itself burns and is reduced to ashes. The action of the agent consists in producing favourable circumstances under which the phenomenon will take place; it brings into proximity two elements, which then of their own accord react in a manner which we cannot control. In other words, we cause the latent forms contained in the potency of matter to become actual, but we produce neither the matter nor the form.

The contribution of the final cause consists in prompting the agent to act. The efficient cause is determined to act in one way rather than in another only because of the influence of something that is being sought for as an end. All agents act for an end, although for some of them this end is pre-established by a superior agent. The end is the reason for which a particular form is drawn out of the potency of matter by the agent.

Thus in all effects, of whatever nature they may be, we find a quadruple cause. All four concur to the final result which cannot be rationally explained without them. They apply not only to those things which are the result of substantial changes, but also to those which are produced by accidental changes. In these latter, however, the material cause is the individual substance, namely secondary matter, and the formal cause is an accidental form.

202. An *effect* is the change or alteration produced by an agent. There are two kinds of effect, remote and proximate. The proximate or primary effect, is that which follows immediately and necessarily from a cause. The remote effect is a secondary one which follows, but not necessarily, the primary effect. The primary effect consists in the actual change wrought in a thing by the agent. By change we do not mean that which results in a thing on account of this change, since this would be a remote effect, but the very change itself, the actual fact of being changed, the actual production of the change. Considered with regard to the object which is thus being changed, this change or effect is called *passion*.

The proper and immediate effect of an agent consists therefore in the completion of the action or movement of that agent. An effect is a completed action. The intended effect is produced, for example, when I have finished writing, even if the ink had disappeared from the paper whilst I was writing. The effect is the actual movement of writing, not the visible letter which results from the writing; the letter is only a remote effect.

203. This remark enables us to understand how it is that an effect always resembles its cause. A painting can reproduce a man with features totally different from those of the artist who made it; yet the painting itself bears a likeness to the artist: people will recognize his style in all his works. It is therefore the manner in which a change is wrought, the actual production of the change, the immediate, not the remote effect, which is like the agent, and which is a faithful expression of its power to accomplish it, an outward expression of the pent-up energy of the agent.

204. When, besides the production of the action, the remote effect, that is to say the thing in which the change is wrought, also resembles the agent, this agent is called a univocal cause. In this case the total effect is of the same species as the agent, as in the reproduction of living beings. Whereas when the production only and not the thing produced is like the producing agent, the agent is called an equivocal cause.

CHAPTER 13

THE EFFICIENT CAUSE

205. We must call the student's attention in a special manner to the efficient cause, which has the power to make matter possess in reality, *in act*, a form which it previously possessed only *potentially*. We express this by saying that the efficient cause draws the form from the potentiality of matter. No created cause can produce the form itself. Efficient power consists in moving or displacing matter and its parts, and thus bringing about quantitative and qualitative modifications which gradually render matter unable to exist under its previous form and thus dispose it to the reception of a new one.

There are different kinds of efficient causes, the principal of which are the following :

1. The *univocal* cause which produces an effect of the same species as the agent; thus a child belongs to the same human species

as its father. The equivocal cause has an effect of a different species; thus a statue is not of the same species as the artist.

2. The cause *per se* is that which produces the natural and specific effect it is meant to produce; thus fire is the cause *per se* of heat, an artist is the cause *per se* of his artistic work. The cause *per accidens* on the contrary is one that produces an effect not directly and necessarily intended to be produced by that cause; thus food can accidentally produce death, or a hunter can accidentally kill a man.

3. The cause *in act* or actual cause, is that which is actually producing an effect, for example a painter who is actually painting. The cause *in potency* or potential cause, is that which can produce an effect which however it is not actually producing, as for example a painter who is not painting at the moment.

4. The *necessary* cause, also called natural or physical cause, is that which always and necessarily produces the effect for which it is intended when it is placed in favourable conditions; all physical elements, plants and animals are necessary causes. A *free* cause, also called voluntary or moral cause, is one that is free to choose the effects it wishes to produce. Only intellectual beings are free causes.

5. The *proximate* or immediate cause is that whicn produces an effect directly without any other intermediary cause. The *remote* or mediate cause on the contrary only reaches its effect with the help of one or several intermediary causes. The immediate cause of all activity is the operative power or faculty of the agent; but in the last resource the effect is due to the whole individual agent or to the suppositum, which is therefore its remote and mediate cause, because it produces this effect by means of the operative power it possesses. Thus my whole person is the remote and mediate cause of vision, but the proximate and immediate cause of vision is my visual power.

6. The *principal* cause is that which acts in virtue of its own power. The *instrumental* cause uses the power of the principal cause to produce an effect. This distinction is equivalent to primary and secondary cause.

206. *Existence of efficient causality.* The existence of efficient causality has been strongly denied by some philosophers. They maintain that nothing has a real influence on anything else. What we call cause and effect, would be mere successions of separate events which we are in the habit of associating; these associations are

arbitrary, there being no ground in reality for any casual connection between two events or phenomena. In fact, they say, we cannot point with certainty to the cause of any particular effect, because what is commonly believed to be the cause of an event is subsequently often shown not to have any connection with it at all.

207. The obvious answer is that although we may err in attributing a certain effect to one particular cause, our mistake is only brought home to us because we discover a new cause which we believe to be the right one. And even if it were not possible to ascertain the exact cause of a particular phenomenon, we would not be entitled to conclude to the universal denial of causality.

Indeed the principle of causality is obvious to the mind; it is an elementary and self-evident principle of common sense. No intellectual effort is required to realize that an event must have a cause, and that it cannot just happen by itself without the interference of any agent whatsoever. To have recourse to chance and fate is not a scientific answer, but an open admission of ignorance.

208. In fact, there is no such thing as chance if this term is taken to signify a causeless event. The law of causation is a universal one, and all men act upon the assumption of its truth. To assume that an event has no efficient cause, contradicts the common-sense principle that there can be no effect without a cause. Furthermore if there is no causal agent, there can be no motive to justify the event, since a motive can only be conceived by an agent, and thus there would be no purpose or object for such an event to happen; this would contradict facts, since the purpose and harmony of the universe cannot be denied.

Neither is there such a thing as chance, if the word is taken to mean a blind force or fate which directs events irrespective of any motive or purpose. The assumption of this blind force is unwarrantable since the first and universal cause of things must necessarily be intelligent and therefore must act for a purpose.

209. If however by chance we mean the unknown cause of an inexplicable or unpredictable event, the use of the term is justifiable. Thus we can attribute to chance events which really have a cause, which cause however we are unable to discover, especially if those events happen to be contrary to our expectations, as when we say that dice-throwing, surprises, the unexpected meeting of a friend and so forth, depend on chance.

210. Unless we adopt a sceptical view of all natural phenomena, we are forced to admit this principle of causality. It is the basis of scientific induction; the whole course of our daily life depends upon it. It is in virtue of this principle that natural sciences, such as mechanics, astronomy, biology and so forth, foretell the nature of the event we are to expect to follow from another one. Thus we rely upon the traction power of the engine which is to set our train in motion, we know that the earth will revolve upon its axis to-morrow in the same manner as it did to-day, we are confident that a strong ladder will not break down under our weight, we know in advance that the turning of a switch will put on our electric light, that the striking of the A on the piano will yield a different sound from that of the F, that the absorption of a poison will cause sickness and death. If causality were denied, no reliance whatever could be placed upon the occurrence of these phenomena.

211. We must however admit our incapacity to probe into the intimate nature of causality. The great physicist Laplace declared that the nature of force is, and ever will be, a mystery. He did not for this reason deny its existence. The unsophisticated mind will easily trace this mysterious causal power to the First and Almighty Cause. Although we do not understand how God makes things partake of his own active power, we are certain that it is He who has given to radium, to steam, and to all other things their marvellous properties, and to man his sensitive and intellectual faculties.

As to how energy is transmitted from cause to effect, there is no ready answer. But the fact remains. There is no possible doubt that if an electrified wire contacts an earthed piece of steel, the current will immediately flow into the steel, whatever may be the scientific interpretation of the fact.

CHAPTER 14

TRANSCENDENTAL PROPERTIES

212. The term *transcendental* is used in opposition to that of predicamental or categorical to signify something that soars above the range of the categories. A transcendental is therefore not confined to

one category only. Thus being, act and potency, essence and existence, essential relations, are transcendentals.

A transcendental is not a strict logical universal, since a universal must be predicable univocally of its inferiors. It could be called universal since it is common to many things, but it is not called so in order to distinguish it from univocal universals, and in order to show that it only applies analogically to things. We arrive at the knowledge of transcendentals, not by simple abstraction as in the case of ordinary universal concepts, but by establishing an analogy between concepts which have been abstracted in the usual manner from phantasms. Therefore ultimately, the concept of a transcendental is gathered from, and owes its origin to, the impressions made upon our senses.

Here we are concerned with the transcendental properties of being in general, which are found in every single being, namely the three properties of Unity, Truth and Goodness. We have already dealt with metaphysical truth in Major Logic. We will therefore now consider Unity and Goodness.

213. *Transcendental unity* is the oneness of a thing, and consists in the fact that a thing is whole and undivided. It is another name for the individuality of a thing. In fact an individual is that which is whole and complete in itself and distinct from other individuals. It is called transcendental because it applies not only to material things, but to every existing being, and to God himself. God is essentially one.

Everything is necessarily one, because if it were not, it would be divided into parts and thus cease to exist as an individual. Unity is therefore a transcendental property of being as such. Since it is a property, it is distinct from the nature of things, and is a real addition to the nature. This is why we have said that the nature of a thing is really distinct from the individual substance or person, namely from the individuality or unity of a thing. But there is no real distinction between the existing individual or person and its unity, since it is precisely its unity that makes it individual. The scholastics express this by saying that *unum et ens convertuntur*, which means that to be one and to exist is the same thing.

There is also a *predicamental unity*, also called quantitative, namely that of material things only, which consists in the continuity of the quantitative parts of matter. This will be dealt with in Cosmology.

214. *Goodness.* Transcendental goodness is a property of being which results from its perfection. Perfection is a synonym of actuality, since an act perfects the potentiality of a thing. The goodness of being therefore consists ultimately either in the quidditative actuality which results from its substantial form, or in the entitative actuality due to its existence, or in the accidental actuality it receives from the accidents, foremost amongst which are its specific properties.

Now everything naturally tends towards the perfection or actuality of its nature, and clings to that perfection when it has it. Therefore goodness can be described as something which answers the natural tendency of being, or, as we say, *that to which all things tend*. No individual being can possibly be without some kind of actuality which perfects it and consequently makes it good. All things necessarily have a certain amount of actuality and perfection, and it is for this reason that it is said that *all things are good*. This means that all things are good because they are actual, since all actuality is a perfection of the thing it actuates. But it does not mean that nothing is evil.

215. *Evil* consists in the absence of some actuality of being. Being cannot be deprived of all actuality, because it would then be nothing and not a being. Therefore a being cannot be totally evil; all bad things are in some way or another good.

216. There are three kinds of evil, which we will call the evil of nature, the evil of pain, and the evil of sin or moral evil. *Evil of nature* is a kind of inherent evil of all created things. It results from the necessary limitations of these things. God made them all good, but not absolutely and infinitely good like himself; this would have been impossible, since in such a case he would not have been the only God. Therefore the perfection of created being is relative; things are perfect and good only because they are not wanting in that which is due to their nature. Manifestly they are wanting in many other perfections. In this sense we have the apparent paradox that all good things are evil, and all evil things are good. In fact, each thing is only good and desirable in certain circumstances and for certain particular purposes.

Thus, what is good for one is not good for another. A perfect specimen of the animal or vegetal kingdom can be good in itself, such as a poisonous plant or insect, yet harmful and evil for man. So also a cancer is something evil with respect to the organism, but a surgeon will perhaps find that it is a perfect specimen of fungoid growth. No created thing is absolutely good, but neither is anything absolutely evil. There is nothing that cannot serve some useful purpose and thus be good, because desirable by something or other. The order of the universe is dependent on this evil of nature; the decay and destruction of one substance is a necessary condition for the growth and production of new ones, or as we say, the corruption of one thing is the generation of another. Decayed animal and vegetal organisms fertilize the earth, the preservation of life requires the destruction of certain animals and plants for consumption, natural elements are continually being thwarted from attaining their ends in order to contribute to those of other elements. Thus fire depends on the destruction of wood or coal, chemical reactions on that of the elements they react upon, natural phenomena are the result of the conflict of the forces of nature. Therefore what we call the evil of nature is evil or good according to the point of view from which we consider it

217. *Evil of pain* includes all that causes suffering to man in body and mind. The problem of pain and suffering belongs to ethics. We will merely observe that physical pain in itself is a natural effect of nerve reactions, and consequently from a purely theoretical point of view is good, and serves the good purpose of warning us of what might be harmful to the organism, by informing us for example of just how far we can exert our strength. The evil of pain lies in the irritating effect it has on the sufferer. We must remember that the evil of pain was not intended by the Creator, and that it is a consequence of sin, inflicted as a punishment after the fall of man. As to animal suffering, some think that it is also due to the fall of man with whose welfare that of inferior beings was bound up; in any case, it is generally agreed that animals do not suffer to anything like the same extent as man, since they lack the power of reflection which greatly increases all the sufferings of man.

218. *Evil of sin* consists in the deviation of the human will from the moral order and again belongs to the subject matter of ethics. We must remember that the whole of this evil consists only in the deformity of the act of the will; the act itself by which man wills that which is evil is something good, since it is the act of one of the greatest faculties of man.

PART IV

COSMOLOGY

INTRODUCTION TO COSMOLOGY

Cosmology is a word generally adopted to-day to signify a branch of Natural Philosophy which studies the nature of the inorganic world in general. Natural Philosophy is the study of being as subject to variation and change in the concrete individuals in which it exists. Natural Philosophy thus differs from Metaphysics which is also the study of being, but in the abstract and without regard to the changes to which it is subject in material things.

Now there are two great classes of material things, inanimate and living ones. So Natural Philosophy is divided into two parts, namely Cosmology or the study of inanimate or inorganic nature, and Psychology which is that of living beings.

Cosmology would at first seem to coincide with modern Physics; they both investigate the natural phenomena to which inorganic substance is subject. But whilst Physics study each particular phenomenon by means of experimental research, Cosmology investigates the general nature of these phenomena by means of rational arguments. The main enquiry of Cosmology centres on the nature of change itself and all that is connected with it, such as place and time. It is precisely by investigating the nature of substantial change that it arrives at the fundamental theory of Hylomorphism.

HYLOMORPHISM

219. Hylomorphism is the name of the scholastic theory of matter and form. It constitutes a philosophical analysis of the essence of material things. Although the real nature of things has not yet been discovered in the experimental laboratories of science, the metaphysician has no hesitation in maintaining that it is composed of two constituent and distinct elements, one constant and unchanged throughout all the substantial changes to which a thing is subjected, and called *Primary Matter,* the other variable which comes and goes with each successive change, and called *Substantial Form.*

220. *Change* is the fact of becoming other or different, the passage from one state to another. There are two distinct kinds of changes, namely accidental and substantial changes. An accidental change is a variation in the exterior appearances or accidents of things, and can occur by alteration of colour, size, shape or any other exterior quality, or by change of position or place; this last kind of change is properly called motion or movement.

221. A *substantial change* occurs when the very substance of a thing is altered, when wood for example is burnt to ashes. It implies the destruction of a substance and the production of a new one in its place. We generally use the terms corruption and generation instead of destruction and production.

222. *Generation* strictly speaking is the production of a living being from another living being of the same species. This term, however, is also used in a broader sense to mean the production of anything which results from a substantial change, and thus implies the disappearance of a substantial form and the advent of a new one. The subject of generation is primary matter, which cannot possess two substantial forms at the same time; the previous form disappears at the advent of the new one and thus entails the destruction, or, as we say, the *corruption* of the substance to which the previous form belonged. This explains why the terms generation and corruption, or production and destruction, as also the terms transformation and

substantial change, really mean one and the same thing, although they point to different aspects of it.

223. Since the theory of Hylomorphism is based on the substantial changes which occur in material things it is of the utmost importance to establish the existence of such substantial changes in opposition to mere accidental ones. Now the basic proof of the occurrence of a substantial change is derived from the fact of the disappearance of certain characteristic properties of a thing and the appearance of new ones. Indeed, our knowledge of substance is entirely dependent on that of its properties. Thus the organicity of living beings stands for their specific difference, but organicity is only a property of living beings, not their intrinsic constituent or their specifying principle. It is merely a mark or sign of this principle, something which always accompanies it and tells us that it is there.

Now a substance of one kind cannot at the same time be a substance of another kind. Therefore if a substance ceases to exhibit certain specific properties of its own and begins to exhibit different ones, we are entitled to conclude that it has undergone a substantial change, or a change of kind.

224. A serious *difficulty* is encountered in the fact that compounds still possess some characteristics of their elements, such as their typical spectra and their global weight. The same difficulty applies to the reverse process, namely to the resolution of a compound into its elements. This is a fact recognized by the scholastics who say that the elements remain *virtually* in the compound. Different explanations have been put forward as to the meaning of the term *virtually* in this case, in order to explain how the elements remain. We will not enter here into this rather complicated question. It will suffice to remark that not all the specific properties of the elements remain in the compound, and on the other hand that the compound possesses several specific properties not to be found in its elements. To give one example only, many of the properties of water are entirely different from those of hydrogen and oxygen. Therefore our principle of discrimination between two substances still holds; different characteristic properties necessarily point to different kinds of substance, even if some characteristics remain the same.

225. Now scientists agree that nothing is wasted in the Universe. Therefore a substantial change cannot involve the total destruction of a thing, but can only *transform* it into something else. To be

transformed means to assume a different internal structure, different properties and different features.

We are thus led to the conclusion that there must be in all things a permanent basis or subject that undergoes the change, since there must be something which can lose its structure and assume another one, something that can pass from one state to another, as for example from the state of wood to that of ashes. Science acknowledges the existence of this common substratum, and endeavours to-day more than ever, to discover the nature of this ultimate and invariable constituent of all things. But even if this ultimate component were discovered, it would still be an object of experimental perception, and would not satisfy the metaphysician, who, abstracting from all that is sense-perceived, is in quest of the constituents of the essence hidden to the senses. From the obvious fact that this hidden essence does change, and that when it does so, it does not totally disappear by a kind of conjuring trick to give place to something entirely new, he argues that it must contain an element that does not change or disappear, which he calls primary matter.

226. Care must be taken to distinguish between *primary* and *secondary* matter. Secondary matter is the actual mass of matter perceptible to the senses, and is the substance we can actually touch and see. Primary matter cannot be touched or seen or sense-perceived in any way; it is not the residue of any chemical or physical analysis, and can only be known by an act of intellectual abstraction, by the same process as the hidden essence to which it belongs.

227. *Substantial form* is not the figure or shape of things, but the hidden specifying principle of the essence, also known as the specific form. It stands for that part of the nature which changes when a thing is transformed. The very etymology of the word transformation testifies to the belief in a substantial form. When wood is burnt, its primary matter remains throughout; its substantial form disappears to make place for the substantial form of ashes.

Things have also accidental forms. *Accidental forms* are only found in things which already have a substantial form, and are therefore also called secondary forms. They consist in accidental or contingent manners of being, such as the shape, colour, position, activity and any other external quality of a thing. They can be either natural or artificial.

CHAPTER 2

MATTER AND FORM

228. In order to understand a little better the nature of matter and form, we have recourse to the terms potency and act. These terms are not used as a makeshift expedient whenever there is nothing better to say. On the contrary they are used here very deliberately. We are trying to explain things that are nearly beyond the grasp of man, and extremely difficult to express in words. Words have to be coined to express metaphysical notions, and among these words are those of potency and act; there might be better ones, but so far no one has found them. We therefore make free use of them because they do help us to understand these abstruse questions.

229. Matter is a *subjective potency*, because, as it is the common element of all things, it is capable of becoming any one of them. Its potency is its power to be something definite; of itself, primary matter is nothing definite. This capacity of primary matter corresponds to the notion of potency as described with reference to essence. But there is a difference between the way matter is in potency to form, and that in which essence is in potency to existence. Essence is a potency because it has no existence of its own; but it has a certain actuality of its own, given to it by its substantial form. Primary matter on the contrary has no actuality whatsoever; it is an absolutely pure potency, nothing but potency. It constitutes the elementary, *qualityless-stuff* of all individual things, without any definite structure of its own. It could be said that primary matter is the raw material, not of one particular thing such as pulp which has not yet been made into paper, but of all the things in the world. The senses cannot detect it, since sense-experience is only able to perceive definite objects with the whole array of their specific and accidental properties. Even the mind, which argues peremptorily to its reality, cannot form a clear concept of it, precisely because, in order to know it, the mind must abstract from every kind of actuality whereby it might be known. In fact, primary matter is that which remains when our mind has abstracted from a thing, not only its external qualities and its existence, but also the inner specifying principle which we call its substantial form. What remains has no feature or form whereby it can be known.

230. In an attempt to give an example of something that cannot

be properly illustrated, let us take a marble statue. A statue has many features which make it different from other marble structures, and which give to it what we call an accidental, artificial or secondary form. Now if it were to be stripped of these special features, it would not be that statue any more; it would not even be a statue at all, but just a block of marble. This block of marble would differ from a block of wood, because it would have the substantial form of marble. We could continue this abstractive process, and mentally strip this block even of its substantial form of marble. It would then simply be a piece of stone. And so on, by successive abstractions, we would finally arrive at matter in general, stripped of its last substantial form, of everything that could in any way define and characterize it; this would be primary matter, all alone without a rag of form on it. But primary matter does not exist in this nude state. It is only found in some kind of structural state, united to a substantial form of some kind. Between this, however, and concluding that it does not exist at all, there is an abyss. It does really exist as a potential reality when it is dressed up in, and united to, a substantial form.

Primary matter must be something real, because it is the physical substratum of substantial transformations. If it did not really exist in each individual thing, it would be impossible to explain how a thing could be changed into something else. Furthermore, primary matter is the root of quantity and of many other real qualities, which make material things really different from spiritual ones. It must therefore be real itself.

231. It is more easy to understand that substantial form is something real, since, although it does not exist by itself, it has an actuality of its own, which causes the actual distinction of one species from another. But neither matter or form is real unless the one is united to the other. We must not think of matter as of something already existing, awaiting the arrival of its form, since then it would not be a pure potency, void of all actuality. Neither has form any kind of reality outside our mind until it is united to matter. There is no real matter and no real form except in the complete essence. They are strictly correlative, transcendentally related to each other; this means that their very nature is to be thus related, that they cannot exist or even be distinctly conceived by the mind without each other. Form is necessarily the form of a definite quantity of matter, and matter necessarily belongs to a particular specific form.

232. When united they acquire a reality which they retain throughout the whole time of the existence of the individual to which they belong. Their union does not resemble that of two elements which are united to compose a third substance, as hydrogen and oxygen to make up water. Their union is called a *substantial union*, and in a more general way, the union of an act to its potency. Form actuates the transcendental capacity of matter, namely the transcendental need of matter to be of a particular kind and to arise from its state of pure potentiality.

233. There can only be one substantial form in a thing at any one time, otherwise a thing would belong to more than one kind of being. Created causality is a transforming power, the effect of which is merely the disappearance of the substantial form possessed by an object and the appearance of a new one, or the superseding of a new form to the form previously possessed by an object, and not the production of a thing out of nothing. To allow for the arrival of the new form, the previous one must disappear, or, as we say, *the destruction of one thing is the production of another*. This succession of forms in matter, is what we call a transformation. But transformations do not happen in a haphazard way; they are subject to a definite order and to definite working conditions. No agent can turn butter into coal, or change cabbage into silver. Matter which has the form of wood, is in immediate potency to the form of ashes or dust, but not to that of gold. It can be transformed into coal, but only after a long succession of intermediate changes. The philosopher expresses this by saying that when an agent transforms matter, it draws from matter the form to which it was in potency. Form is therefore *drawn out of the potency* of matter, because, by filling or satisfying some of the capacity of matter, it draws some of its potentiality into the actuality of essence.

234. The actual change of one substance to another is instantaneous. There is no interval of time between the disappearance of the preceding substantial form and the appearance of the new one, between, for example, the corruption of coal and the production, let us say of ashes. In other words, at no moment is primary matter without a definite substantial form of some kind. However, the process leading up to the substantial change is gradual, and consists in a gradual change of the qualities of a substance These changing qualities are called the *remote dispositions* of substantial change.

At a certain moment these qualities become modified to such an extent that they require a new kind of substance to support them. They become *proximate* dispositions at the moment of the arrival of the new substantial form, which is brought out of the potency of matter; they proximately dispose matter for this form, which appears without any further interval of time. Thus when milk is churned, the qualities of milk gradually change until at a given moment the substance that is being changed can no longer be called milk but butter.

235. The superseded form is said to return to the potency of matter. Form does not exist by itself, and so, strictly speaking cannot lose an existence which it did not have. It is the whole individual being which loses existence, when, on account of the disappearance of its form, it ceases to be what it was. By the appearance of the new form, the individual acquires a new existence. The previous form is not destroyed, but just disappears, as light does when it becomes dark, as cold does when a thing is warmed, or as the shape of a thing does when that thing is moulded into a different figure. Because, under appropriate conditions, it would be possible to make that thing exist again with its previous form, we say that matter is still in potency to that form, and that consequently the form has returned to the potency of matter.

236. The *human soul*, which is the substantial form of man, differs from all other substantial forms, in that it has an existence of its own and is self-subsistent. It is immaterial and spiritual, not dependent on matter for its existence; it is not drawn out of the potency of matter, but created directly by God, and it does not disappear or return to the potency of matter, but continues to exist after death.

237. Theology teaches us that there are also what we call separate spirits, namely the good and the bad angels. Angels have no matter. Their essence is not compound but simple, and consists only of form. The essence of an angel does not therefore result from the union of matter and form, body and soul, but is a pure and simple substantial form, joined directly to existence to constitute a complete being.

CHAPTER 3

QUANTITY

238. Quantity is that which gives to a material substance a plurality of distinct parts. A part is that into which a whole can be divided. There are three kinds of parts, and consequently three kinds of corresponding wholes.

Logical or specific parts are concepts representing either the species or the individuals contained in the extension of more universal concepts, as for example, men and beasts are contained in the general concept of animal.

Essential parts are the constituent elements of the nature of a thing. These can either be physical or chemical parts such as the atoms which constitute matter, or hydrogen and oxygen united to form water. Or they can be metaphysical parts, namely the abstract elements of being, such as matter and form, or essence and existence.

Integral, quantitative or aliquot parts are those of discrete or continuous quantity. *Discrete* quantity has actual parts which are separated from each other, such as those of a broken cup; *continuous* quantity has only potential parts, which are not separated from each other, as those of a bar of iron. Integral parts really exist in a whole continuous quantity, but, and this must be carefully noted, they do not exist as parts. This means that they form one integral whole, the extremity of each part being identical with that of the next.

239. It is of integral parts of a whole continuous quantity that we are speaking here. It is precisely the continuity of these parts in the whole which constitute what we call a continuum or magnitude, in opposition to a discrete quantity or a multitude, the parts of which are actually separated and disconnected. But although the parts of a continuum are not separate, they are not mixed and mingled together, but distinct. There is a fixed order or invariable sequence amongst them which gives to each one its own special ordinal position; this order is a natural and serial one that cannot be changed or inverted, there must be a first, a last, and intermediate parts in each continuum. This internal arrangement of its parts, or the *order of its parts in the whole,* is the primary and essential characteristic of continuous quantity and is sometimes called internal quantity. For this same reason a continuum or a continuous quantity is also defined as a quantity with ordered parts.

240. *Internal quantity* is the order of the parts in the whole, an internal arrangement of the parts which makes one precede or follow the other in a fixed manner. This order cannot be inverted without destroying the quantity; the part that is at the beginning, for example, cannot be put at the end, a continuous quantity being essentially an *ordinal* one. As has been said, quantity consists primarily in this internal order of its parts, and only secondarily in their relation to the surrounding place they occupy. As long as the order and the distinction of parts is preserved, a thing may vary in shape or even in volume, without losing its essential quantity and its individuality. On the contrary the order of parts in a *cardinal* quantity, namely a discrete one, can be changed without changing the quantity; the number ten, for example, is the sum of ten units irrespective of the serial order in which we count them.

The continuum is therefore necessarily an ordinal quantity. Discrete quantity on the contrary is objectively cardinal, and is only made ordinal by the mind which cannot count a multitude of objects all at once, but has to take them successively, first one, and then another, thus arranging them in a certain order.

241. *Dimensions* of quantity.—Quantity has three dimensions, namely length, breadth and depth. In fact, dimension is defined as the linear measurement of a continuous quantity in length, breadth and depth. The genesis of these notions is to be found in the sense-perception of the things that surround us, especially by tactual exploration. By moving its hand over its own body and then over other objects, the child gradually discovers extension, first in length, then in breadth and finally in depth.

These three dimensions form the basis of the three fundamental geometrical figures known as volume, surface and the line. Volume is a quantity with all three dimensions. Surface is breath and length without depth. The line is length without breadth or depth. By means of the point it is possible to define in still another way the three dimensions. The point is the indivisible and unextended extremity of a line. A line is the track of an imaginary point moving through space. A surface is the track of an imaginary line moving through space, and a volume is the track of an imaginary surface moving through space.

242. *Indivisibles.*—Indivisible is that which cannot be divided into parts. There are no such things as mathematical indivisibles

since numbers and magnitudes can be indefinitely divided by the
mind into ever smaller numbers or magnitudes. But there are logical
and physical indivisibles.

243. Logical indivisibles are those simple and transcendental
concepts which are common to all things, such as being, and which
cannot properly speaking be divided into logical parts, namely into
species. The subject of a proposition is also called indivisible when
it denotes things which are unique of their kind or when it represents the whole of a class or species, for example, sun, fire, man,
scissors; but this last kind of indivisible is rather a grammatical
than a logical indivisible.

Physical indivisibles are the *form*, the *point* and the *instant*. We
shall see what has to be said about the point and the instant in the
chapter on time and motion. As to forms, they are indivisible since
they are physically simple, that is to say that they have no physical
parts into which they can be divided. Nevertheless, the substantial
forms of inorganic matter, those of inferior living beings such as
worms and certain plants, and all accidental forms, are *indirectly*
divisible, or as we say *per accidens*, that is to say that they are subject to physical division, not on their own account, but on that of
the divisible quantitative mass of matter to which they are united.
The form or soul of other living beings is absolutely indivisible; it
disappears when the material mass is divided. As regards the human
soul we shall see in Psychology that it preserves its individuality
even after the corruption of the body.

244. We have said that the divisibility of matter is a necessary
consequence of its quantitative extension. From this it follows that
matter cannot be composed of indivisible parts, since no amount of
indivisibles can constitute a divisible whole, just as the sum of many
negative numbers cannot make a positive one. As a conclusion it
would seem that matter were divisible indefinitely, namely that there
could be no part of it, however small, that is not divisible into still
smaller parts. This is theoretically true, just as it is true that another
digit can always be added to the decimal part of any figure and thus
produce a fraction smaller than the preceding one. There would
seem however to be an end to the physical possibility of dividing
matter since the divided parts would at last become too small to be
subjected to further mechanical division.

245. Quantity is an accident, that is to say, it is something dif-

ferent from the substance of a thing. This is easily shown by the fact that if substance and quantity were one and the same thing, a change of quantity would entail a change of substance; yet it is obvious that a bucketful and a thimbleful of water contain exactly the same substance, and that a needle is made of the same substance as a steel girder, although those things differ very considerably in quantity. But although an accident, it is an essential and necessary one. Material substance cannot exist without quantity, to which its primary matter is essentially related. This need for quantity is a specific and certain sign of the materiality of a substance, whilst its absence is a sign of immateriality and spirituality.

246. Quantity is also, of its own native power, an individuating principle, because, of its own self, it causes the parts of a material substance to be distinct from one another and consequently from those of other material substances. This means that quantity, of its very nature, causes a thing to be of a definite amount and consequently to be distinct from other things, or in other words, to be an individual. For the same reason it is possible to conceive a quantity such as a line or a square as being individual by itself, without reference to anything else, whilst other accidents, and even substance itself, can only be conceived as numerically distinct with reference to a definite quantity upon which they depend for their individuation.

CHAPTER 4

QUANTITY AND THE SUPERNATURAL

247. From what has been said it follows that, since nothing can exist unless it be individual, all other accidents depend directly upon quantity for their concrete existence, and only indirectly, namely via quantity, on the substance in which they are rooted. Quantity thus becomes the *quasi-subject* of the other accidents because it makes them capable of concrete existence by making them individual, although of course it does not give them existence. Matter without

quantity would not only be wanting in the plurality of its parts, but it would have none of the other accidents, since these are directly dependent on quantity.

The conclusion at which we are aiming is that the other accidents of a thing could not, even by divine intervention, exist without quantity, because to exist at all they must exist individually, and to exist individually is to have a certain quantity. But there would be no contradiction involved if the First Cause were, in an exceptional case, to support these accidents in existence without their natural subject which is substance. On the one hand, they would not cease to be accidents, since they would not exist by themselves as substance does, but would be supported in existence by the First Cause; on the other hand, the individuality of their concrete existence would be maintained by the quasi-subject quantity.

As regards quantity itself, since it requires nothing else to individuate it and has of its very self definite and distinct parts, it could be conceived to exist without substance if its existence were supported by divine power. But neither substance nor the accidents could possibly be conceived to exist without quantity, because they cannot exist otherwise than individually, and they cannot exist individually without quantity.

248. In the light of these principles, we are able to understand the possibility of the permanence of the sacred species in the Blessed Sacrament. The quantitative dimensions of bread are kept miraculously in existence by divine power without the substance of bread; the other accidents are rooted in, and supported in existence by their quasi-subject, namely quantity.

249. These same principles explain how the body of Christ in the Holy Eucharist has no *local extension*. This is possible because local extension or location in place, which results from the contact of the quantitative parts of a substance with those of another, is not an essential property of a quantitative object. In fact, a thing could be imagined to have parts not related to the parts of other things, as would be the case if there existed only one body in the whole world. In such a case, namely, in that of a thing which was not related to any other thing because they were no others to contact, locate or *place* it, that thing would still retain its internal order of parts. The fact of the absence of other circumscribing bodies would not alter the fact that that thing was an individual substance having

parts which were distinct from one another; that thing would still retain its *internal* quantity although it would have no *external* quantity. Now it is the internal order of its parts, its internal quantity, which makes a thing individual and capable of existing as an individual, and not the external relation of those parts to parts of other things, or its external location in a place.

250. If therefore, by divine intervention, the relation of a substance to exterior place were suspended, we could still conceive that substance as a real and individual substance. This actually happens in the Holy Eucharist, where the body of Christ is not related to exterior things by its quantitative parts, but by those of bread. Consequently it has no place or position, as in the case of other material substances. Therefore in the Eucharistic Sacrament, the quantity of the body of Christ is present with all its parts; those parts, such as the head, neck and limbs, are distinct from one another and preserve the natural order of the human body, but their relation to external place and space is suspended.

251. This also happens in those miracles which involve the presence of two material substances in the same place, or the penetration of matter. *Impenetrability* of matter is a consequence of the external extension of matter in space. No two material substances can be related to one same exterior locating substance at the same time. But if their secondary or exterior extension were to be suspended by miracle, the nature of quantitative matter would still be preserved, and thus there would be no reason why two material substances could not occupy what would seem to be the same place; actually they would not occupy that place at all, since their relation to place would, in the hypothesis, be suspended. This happened at the Virginal Birth of Christ; when he rose from the closed sepulchre; and when he entered through the closed doors of the Cenacle.

252. These same remarks apply to *measurability*. Measurability is not of the essence of quantity, although normally all quantitative things are measurable. Measurability is essentially the relation existing between the parts of one thing and those of another thing, such as those of a ruler, which we take as a unit of measure. Therefore if, in virtue of a supernatural intervention, a thing ceased to be related to external place and to the objects located in that place, that thing would no longer be measurable. This is precisely what happens in

the Eucharist, in which the parts of the body of Christ bear no
relation to external objects and to external place; consequently the
body of Christ in the Eucharist is not measurable, and does not
possess the size which it would have under normal circumstances.

253. Neither is the body of Christ *divisible*. Divisibility results
from the possibility of actually separating the quantitative parts of a
thing. This possibility is not caused by the mere plurality of parts,
but from the relation they have to each other and to parts of other
objects. To divide is to dissolve the relation which one part
has to another part of the whole, and to relate it to part
of another thing with which it is made to come into contact. Thus if
a piece of wood is cut into two parts, the extremities whereby those
parts were previously joined together come into contact with the
environing air or ether or whatever else surrounds them.

Divisibility is therefore possible only because each part of a whole
possesses a distinct place of its own, as for example, the first half of
a piece of wood occupies one foot of space, and the other half
another foot. And since a foot of wood is indifferent as to whether
at one of its extremities it comes into contact with the extremities of
another foot of wood, or with the surface of the environing air, it
can be separated from the first foot of wood with which it previously
formed a whole. Separation therefore implies change of place, and
since the body of Christ is not in a place, it cannot be divided. It
is therefore entirely present in every one of the parts of the Host,
no matter how small these may be.

254. This is evidently not the natural way of quantity's existence.
It is a supernatural manner of existence, which resembles more the
manner of existing of substance itself than that of quantity. Substance,
in fact, is not directly located in a place, nor measurable, nor divisible,
since by itself it has nothing whereby it can be related to exterior
objects. It is only in virtue of its quantity that it is so related. We
therefore say that quantity, in this exceptional case, exists, not in its
own normal manner, but after the manner of substance, *ad modum
substantiae*.

CHAPTER 5

THE PRINCIPLE OF INDIVIDUATION

255. The fact that material things have an individual nature confronts us with a rather difficult problem. Indeed, substantial form is the differentiating and specifying element of material things. Form determines the species to which each essence or nature belongs, and thus makes the nature of one thing differ *specifically* from that of another. The nature of a cat, for example, and that of a stone differ specifically because each one has its own different substantial or specific form. It would therefore seem natural to conclude that all things differ specifically from one another, since each one has a substantial and specific form of its own. Yet it is a fact that all individuals do not differ specifically from one another; there are many things which belong to the same species, and only differ numerically. Thus, human nature is specifically the same in all men, and every piece of a broken stone belongs to the same species. It has therefore to be explained how this is possible, namely how several natures, each one having a substantial and specific form of its own, can nevertheless belong to one and the same species. We say that this is possible in virtue of what we call the *principle of individuation*.

256. This principle of individuation, in all things composed of matter and form, is the *transcendental relation* of primary matter to a definite quantity or extension. At first sight it would seem sufficient to say that quantity is the principle of individuation; in fact, quantity would seem to account for the numerical distinction of things because it has the characteristic property of making matter divisible into parts, and thus of causing each thing to have a distinct amount of matter which would seem sufficient to individuate it.

But this simple solution is not satisfactory because the individual form is the primary act of matter and is therefore prior by priority of nature to the secondary or accidental act of quantity. Therefore quantity cannot be the cause of that which it needs in order to exist. Neither can matter itself be the cause of its own individuality because matter as such is a pure potency stripped of all actuality, and cannot therefore be the cause of any kind of actuality or individuation. Therefore, although all scholastics do not agree on this point, we say that the principle of individuation is to be found in the transcendental relation of matter to quantity.

257. *Transcendental* relation is opposed to predicamental relation. A relation in general is the way in which one thing stands to another. *Predicamental* relation is an accident, one of the nine predicaments or categories; it is an acquired manner of being such as the relation of father to son. A *transcendental* relation on the contrary is an essential one, belonging to the very nature of a thing, to such an extent that without it that thing cannot even be conceived. Thus potency is transcendentally related to its act, without which it cannot exist; it cannot even be conceived otherwise than as the capacity of receiving an act. Such is the relation of primary matter to quantity. Matter cannot exist unless it be of a definite measurable amount; it has an intrinsic and essential need of a definite quantity in order to exist. This need constitutes the fundamental difference between material and immaterial substances; therefore we say that matter is essentially related to quantity. Such a relation does not add anything to matter, and must not be conceived as a property or an actuality of some kind, as is the case when dealing with predicamental relation. On the contrary it increases the potency and deficiency of matter; it is a kind of liability which increases rather than diminishes its need and imperfection, just as the addition of a negative number does not add to, but subtracts from a sum. Text-books express this relation by saying that matter is signed, *circumscribed*, ear-marked by quantity, *materia signata* (a) *quantitate*. This means that the individuation of material things is due to this need, to this necessity of matter to be circumscribed by definite quantitative limits.

258. The *substantial form* of itself would produce a specific difference; but when united to matter, it partakes of the conditions to which matter is subjected, namely of quantitative limitation and individuality. Form cannot exist without matter; it co-exists, that is to say it shares existence with matter. And because matter on account of its quantity, is divisible into parts, each one of these parts must be actuated by form. Thus form shares, not only the existence of matter, but also matter's quantitative and divisible mode of existence. In other words, form can only exist as the form or a definite quantity of matter; it is tied down to a particular mass of matter. And since one mass or part of matter is necessarily distinct from any other mass or part, the form of one mass cannot belong to

any other mass, and thus becomes an individual form, numerically and not specifically distinct from the form of the other masses.

259. Form therefore as such is indivisible, but it can be *indirectly divided* and multiplied by reason of the subject into which it is received. Primary matter, in fact, does not surrender the whole of its potentiality to every form that actuates it; the precise amount it does surrender depends entirely on the amount of extension allotted to each material object. Form can only actuate a definite amount of matter and thus become the form of an individual quantity; in other words it then becomes an individual form.

We could take a comparison from light. Light of itself is indivisible and one, yet the light of each one of several separately lighted rooms is distinct from that of the other rooms; we could put out the light in one of them without putting it out in the others. Or we could give the example already given when dealing with essence and existence: the air which fills several balloons of different sizes is one and specifically the same in each one of them; yet the air which fills the one is numerically distinct from that of the others on account of the distinct capacity of each balloon.

260. Since form can only be multiplied in the species by partaking of the multiplicity of the parts of matter, it follows that if a form exists without matter, it will necessarily differ specifically from all other forms. Therefore each angel is unique in is species. But the human soul follows the general rule of material forms; it is multiplied numerically by the multiplication of matter.

CHAPTER 6

NUMBER

261. Number is the *ratio* of two or more quantities, one of which is taken as a standard unit. To number or to count is to compare several individuals to another individual chosen as unit or as term of comparison, such as an inch or a penny. Number is the ratio or the proportion resulting from this comparison. Thus, to number a mul-

titude of trees, we take a tree as unit; we then compare it to another tree, and find that our unit is repeated exactly once, or that the ratio is one plus one. If the number were three, we should find that the total ratio is one, plus one, plus one. As this process would be rather long, we have recourse to what we call *figures*, and call the ratio of one plus one plus one, by the name of three. And so on with other numbers; we designate each one by a different and special figure, which we learn by heart when we are taught to count.

262. Since to count means to compare each unity of a multitude, one after the other, with the unit-measure, it is evident that we can stop this process whenever we like. We say that we have counted a multitude in part or in its whole, or have conceived a number, when we stop this process. Therefore number is specified by its last unity; it is the last unity that distinguishes one number from another. When we stop at a certain unity, we call the number a *rational* one, i.e. a number of which we can consider all the unities from the first to the last. If we do not fix and determine its last unity, the number is not real because it is not determined in its species, and is called *irrational*, incommensurable, indefinite or infinite, because it is not possible to consider all its unities, but only to indicate them by some mathematical sign. Such a number is not a real number but it is treated as such because it can serve as a basis to certain mathematical operations.

263. Number as such only exists as a concept; outside our mind, individuals or distinct unities exist, not numbers. Number is the result of an intellectual feat by which we conceive independent and whole unities as dependent parts of a series. There would be no number if there were no mind to discover this serial relationship and to perform the reflex operation of numbering and counting. Animals, for example, cannot count, but merely remember that one individual is placed after another; they can sense distinct unities, but they are incapable of conceiving them as a multitude or number. Uncultured and uncivilized people find it difficult to count even simple numbers.

If, instead of considering the serial relationship between the distinct unities of a multitude, we consider the unities themselves as being distinct from another and as forming the basis of the relationship, we say that we are forming the concept of a *numbered number*; whilst the concept of the relationship itself is called a *numbering number*.

264. We have just said that a number is called infinite when we do not determine its last unity. The question now arises as to whether such a number is only a mere imaginary one, or rather whether it can be said that an infinite number of things really could exist.

265. *Infinite* is that which has no limits. Now a thing can have no limits for two distinct reasons, namely either because it is so perfect that there is nothing outside it by which it can be limited, or because it is so imperfect that there is no limit to that which can be added to it from outside. We thus have two distinct kinds of infinite, the infinity of the one being an infinity of perfection, of essence or of actuality, that of the other an imperfect and potential infinity.

266. *Infinity of perfection* belongs to God alone. God has in himself all perfection; there is nothing outside his essence that is not contained in it. There are consequently no limits to the perfection of his essence, and nothing can be added to it. This is an infinity of unity, because only one being is infinite in this way. If, by supposition, there were more than one, none of them could have all perfections; they would have to share them, and thus none of them would be infinite.

267. *Negative infinity* is an entirely different thing. It is an infinity of imperfection, there being no limits to its deficiency, namely to the things it is wanting in, and which could be added to it. Primary matter is infinite in this sense, because there are no limits to its potential capacity and need.

268. Of course there can be no question as to whether a number can be infinite in the first meaning. But in the second meaning of the term, we can talk about an infinite number, or, to be more precise, about an infinite multitude. In this latter sense of negative infinity, an infinite multitude would mean one of which we could not reach the end by any known system of counting. Another unit could always be added to it. A number is characterized and specified by its last unit; until this has been fixed, a number is an indefinite one. Now a further unit can always be added to the last unit of any positive or negative number, and therefore a number can be thought of as incommensurably or infinitely great or infinitely small.

As to whether an infinite or rather an indefinite multitude of beings could actually exist, there would seem to be no serious objection to answering in the affirmative. Such a multitude would not be composed of so many unities that there would be none left to compose other multitudes, as this would be an infinity of unity and perfection. It would be infinite only in a negative sense, namely it would be a multitude which has unattainable limits, one that could always be increased by the addition of further unities. The greater the number of created things, the greater is their imperfection. Their multiplicity, in fact, proves that one or a few only are incapable of exhausting and holding the totality of created perfection. Therefore an infinite multitude of created things would only serve to demonstrate the greatness of their deficiency.

269. That an infinite multitude of individuals could exist, seems to be a logical conclusion from a theory of St. Thomas who proves that the world could have been created from all eternity, although we know that it was actually created in time. The possibility however of such an hypothesis includes that of an infinite multitude of created beings, since it would be impossible to number all the things which would have existed throughout an eternal duration. But whether an infinite multitude actually does exist is a problem which belongs to the domain of science and which will probably never be satisfactorily solved.

CHAPTER 7

PLACE AND SPACE

270. *Place* is the immovable surface immediately surrounding a body. To be in a place, in the most general meaning of the term, is to be present somewhere. Now there are five ways of being present, or five kinds of presence.

1. *Local* presence is that of a material substance which, by the contact of its quantitative parts with those of other substances, is located in a place.

2. *Virtual* presence is that of the operative power of a thing. Thus

a manager is present in the whole factory he controls, a king is present in a whole town that he visits. In this way angels are said to be in a place, because they are present wheresoever they display their activity; they are also said to be in a place *definitivé*.

3. *Formal* presence is the special presence of substantial forms in the matter they actuate.

4. *Omnipresence* is the ubiquitous presence of God who is present everywhere and in all things not only by his power, but also by his essence.

5. *Supernatural* presence, which is threefold: the presence of God in the justified soul by grace, the presence of a divine person in the human nature of Christ by hypostatical union, and the sacramental presence of Christ in the Holy Eucharist.

271. Local presence is the only one in which we are interested here, because it is that of a body in a material place. We have said that place is the surrounding surface of a body. Place must not be conceived as part of the objects which surround a body, but as the *containing capacity* of their surface which has no thickness; a surface in fact is indivisible in depth. Therefore the nature of the containing bodies is of no consequence with reference to place; it is their surrounding surface only which constitutes place by its immediate contact with the located body.

272. This surface must be immovable; this immobility is evidently only a relative one, since everything in this world moves. It is therefore taken with reference to some point sufficiently invariable to serve as point of comparison, such as the centre or the poles of the earth.

If the bodies which form the surrounding surface move, their movement will not affect the immobility of the located body, because their contacting surface is immediately replaced by that of other bodies which take its place. The nature or position of the locating bodies does not bear upon the place of the located body which remains in the same place as long as there is a contacting surface which does not move relatively to the centre of immobility.

273. This can be illustrated by the well-known example of the boat on a river. The boat is the located object, the surface of water immediately surrounding the boat constitutes part of the place the boat occupies, the rest being formed by the air which envelops its superior part. Although the river is flowing and the water round the

boat is changing, the boat remains in the same place. It would still be in the same place if all the water were drained, because it would then be entirely located by air.

274. Location, or the presence of a body in a place, is something real, one of the ten predicaments. It is a real accident or manner of being, not just a fiction of the mind. It is a modal reality. As an example, a letter in an envelope is different from one that is not in one, and there is a difference between a man sitting down and a man standing up, although nothing is changed in the nature or substance of either the envelope or the man.

275. *Space* is the distance between the opposite surfaces which surround a material substance. It could be described as the room taken up by the located bodies. Space is really only a different aspect of place; we arrive at the notion of space by abstracting bodies from the place they occupy. The dimensions of space are the same as those of the bodies which are, or could be, located in it. The limits of space are also the same as those of place; but in space these limits are considered, not in relation to a body which they might or might not surround, but in relation to the distance that separates those limits one from another.

Therefore the limits both of place and of space are constituted by the surface of the surrounded bodies because, as a surface is indivisible in depth, the containing surface of a locating body is not further away from a located body than the surface of this located body, and can therefore be identified with it. Therefore, if the whole universe were to be conceived as one single body, or if a body were imagined to be projected out of the universe, both the universe and that body would still occupy a place and a space, the local and spatial limits then being formed by the very surface of the universe or of the projected body.

276. The problem of the *infinity of space* is one which has always stirred the curiosity of the human mind. We would like to know what there is on the other side of the imaginary vault of heaven, and whether, if it were possible to fly so high as to go far beyond the moon, the sun and the remotest of stars, we should at last be halted by some mysterious boundaries, or whether we should be able to continue our upward journey for ever and ever.

Whether space is actually infinite, or whether there exist definite boundaries which limit it, is a question to which it will never be possible to give a peremptory answer. All we can do is to point out that there is no metaphysical contradiction in the concept of an infinite space. The only objection to its possibility would seem to consist in the difficulty of admitting the existence of an infinite multitude of bodies. Indeed, infinite space would not be space without boundaries at all, but space with infinite space boundaries, since space, by definition, is the distance between the surfaces of opposite material bodies. The material boundaries of infinite space would have to consist of an infinite multitude of parts. However, we have seen that the concept of an infinite multitude of bodies is not a metaphysical impossibility. Therefore from this point of view, we could conclude that space could be infinite.

277. On the other hand, if space is not infinite, we are faced with the equally difficult problem of absolute void beyond the confines of limited space. Indeed, if there are definite boundaries to space, beyond them there can be no bodies whatever, since if there were any, there would still have to be space to contain these bodies, and so on indefinitely. In other words definite space presupposes absolute void.

278. *Absolute void* involves the negation of all matter, place and space, namely of all material reality; it is a synonym of *nothing*. We generally try to conceive void as *something* existing beyond space; but in reality absolute void is just nothing at all, the negation of everything. Yet precisely because it does not exist and is not the object of an intelligible concept, it cannot contain a contradiction in terms. The possibility of absolute void results from the fact that the world was created out of nothing, and if it had not been created there would still be nothing.

279. *Relative void.* There is another problem connected with the consideration of space, namely that of relative void or *vacuum,* which could be described as an empty space. Such a space would be formed by real bodies, the surfaces of which would not however surround any other body. Now the conception of such an empty space does not seem to involve any contradiction in spite of the old adage that *nature abhors a vacuum.* In fact, there is nothing in the nature of space to require the presence of a body between its limits. Space is the distance between the opposite surfaces of locating bodies. Although in order to measure this distance, we have to introduce an intervening body such as a ruler, the distance itself remains the same

whether there is, or whether there is not, a located body enabling us
to evaluate the dimensions of that space. Space is not constituted by
the intervening body, but by the surface of the locating bodies; this
surface can be conceived to remain unchanged even if it does not
actually come into contact with a located body. An empty space
therefore implies no contradiction in terms.

280. The difficulty arising from the fact that there can be no
action at a distance, can be answered by saying that although there
would be no mass contact between bodies separated by empty space,
there could be a virtual contact between them.

Energy, being an accident, cannot exist or travel by itself; but there
is no reason to deny that an empty space could be temporarily and
partially occupied by some kind of carrier emanating from the source
of energy and travelling through that otherwise empty space. However, the problem of how energy is transmitted is hardly a philosophical one. Science may some day give a satisfactory answer. We
prefer to define an empty space as one empty of all known or perceptible matter.

CHAPTER 8

MOTION

281. We still have two extremely difficult problems to deal with in
Cosmology, that of motion or movement, and that of the measure of
motion namely time. We will deal with motion in this chapter and
with time in the next.

We are talking here of local motion only, which consists in a change
of position or place, or in a displacement of parts. Now local motion
is the strangest and most inexplicable of all phenomena. It is
mysterious because it faces us with the strange fact that things which
move are never in exactly the same state as they were before, although
they endure unchanged in their existence and individuality. They
remain what they were, and yet they are constantly acquiring new
manners of being which succeed each other in a continuous and
uninterrupted stream.

282. *Motion* is an extremely abstruse concept on account of the imperfection and incompleteness of its reality. In this, it resembles primary matter which is also difficult to analyse, precisely because it is so imperfect and incomplete. Motion, in fact, has no definite and permanent reality. It is neither a concrete thing, nor a definite or stable state of a thing, but consists in the fugitive and elusive fact of *acquiring* a state. It is a continual *becoming*, a fleeting reality; it disappears as soon as it has appeared. There is nothing real in it but a certain *indivisible* of motion, called the indivisible *instant* of motion. The whole reality of motion is centred in this flowing instant, although motion is not composed of instants; instants are not parts of motion.

As an example let us take the imaginary points joining the internal parts of a continuous line. These imaginary points can become real only if the continuity of the line is broken up, the extremities of each intersected part of the line thus being terminated by real indivisible points. These points would then be real, although indivisible, because the parts of the intersected line are real, and must therefore have real extremities. But, although real, these points are not parts of the line, because they only become real when the line ceases to exist as a continuous whole, namely as a line. If these intersected parts were again joined together, the indivisible points that terminate them would lose their reality, but would reappear again with the same reality as before by a new intersection of the line at the same place.

283. But motion has no real parts like the line. If it had, these parts would necessarily have to be either accomplished parts or unaccomplished parts of motion. But an accomplished part of motion is no longer motion at all, since the motion of that part has ceased, and an unaccomplished part of motion is not yet a motion, since the motion of that part has not yet begun. Now it is precisely because accomplished and unaccomplished motion are not real parts of motion like the parts of a line, that the indivisible instant which joins them does not possess the same kind of reality as the indivisible points of a line.

In fact, the instant of motion is always real, not like the point which is only real when the line ceases to exist as a whole, otherwise no instant of motion would exist unless the motion ceased, or, in other words, there would be no real motion at any instant of motion. The instant of motion also differs from the point of a line in that it is always fleeting and can never reappear like the point. It is never twice the same, but is constantly renewed, continually tending towards a fixed and permanent reality which it can never reach without ceasing to be.

284. Therefore the continuity of motion does not consist in a continuity of parts like that of the line, but in a continuity or in an uninterrupted succession of instants. The whole reality and continuity of motion is centred in the *fleeting and indivisible instant*.

285. As this fleeting and incomplete reality of motion is exceedingly difficult to conceive and to express, we have recourse to the helpful notions of potency and act, to throw some light on this obscure question. Act designates that which is complete and perfect; potency that which is incomplete and imperfect. An intermediary state of *becoming* complete and perfect, would therefore partake of both potency and act. Thus, whilst a wall is being painted white, it is not entirely, but only partially white. It partakes of the actuality of whiteness, but it also retains some of its former potentiality, and so is in an intermediary state between complete actuality and complete potentiality. Similarly, a stone describing a trajectory in the sky, is in an intermediary state between the actuality of its ultimate destination and the potentiality of its previous condition of rest; before moving, it was in potency with respect to movement; when it has ceased to move, it will be in act.

286. Therefore a thing is in a state of complete actuality when it has ceased to move, and is in a state of pure potentiality before it has started to move. Motion itself is the intermediary state between complete actuality and pure potentiality; in fact, it has some actuality since it is actually being performed, but it has also some potentiality since it has not yet been completely achieved.

And thus we are able to understand the classical definition which has been given of motion, namely: *the actuality of a thing which is still receding from its state of potentiality*.

287. Some old philosophers contended that there is no motion, and Zeno used to prove it by saying that at any given moment of an arrow's flight, the arrow is either where it is or where it isn't. If it is where it is, it cannot be moving, since if it were moving, it would not be there. And it is obvious that it cannot be where it isn't. The arrow therefore never moves at all. Of course it is easy to answer

that motion consists precisely in the fact that a thing never remains in the place in which it is, but leaves it as soon as it has got there. This happens not by disconnected jerks, but in a continuous and uninterrupted flow. Therefore the arrow always is in the place where it is, not in a fixed and stable manner, but in the imperfect and fleeting state which we call that of becoming, changing or moving.

288. Another instance of the same argument is that of Achilles who was never able to catch the tortoise which was given a start in a race. Whenever Achilles reached the point where the tortoise was, the tortoise had moved to a further point; and so indefinitely. A small distance always remained to be covered, because if the tortoise is supposed to be moving, it would always have left the place each time Achilles thought he had reached it. Motion is therefore an illusion.

Then there is what has been called the interminable half-hour. However little of it remains to elapse, that little is divisible into parts, each of which must elapse before the half-hour can come to an end. But each of those parts is also divisible, and so on indefinitely; the half-hour is interminable, since there are always further parts to elapse.

289. The answer to these two arguments, is that the space between two points, and the time between two moments, is a definite measurable quantity. Now a definite space or time is, and remains, an undivided whole; it has parts only in the considering mind, which is able to divide any integral whole into an indefinite number of parts. The difficulty arising from the indefinite number of its parts only concerns the mind, to which no limit can be set in its power of adding to, or subtracting from, a number. In reality, the distance separating Achilles from the tortoise, and that separating the hand of the clock from the half of the dial's circumference, is a definite measurable quantity, the end of which can be reached.

290. There are some who are of the contrary opinion, and who hold that everything moves to such an extent that perpetual movement and change are all that exist in the world. Things are but an illusion, since they are nothing but change. Old Heraclitus said that no one could bathe twice in the same river, because it is always running away and changing. It is however against common sense to say that because things are always changing, without ever ceasing, there is nothing in this world but becoming and change.

CHAPTER 9

TIME

291. If the nature of motion is difficult to grasp, that of time will seem perhaps even more difficult. *Time* is defined as: *the measure of motion conceived as having preceding and following parts.*

In reality motion has no parts, but consists entirely in an indivisible and fleeting instant, but we can imagine it as being composed of parts, as if it were a divisible whole. This concept is evidently a subjective one, not corresponding to reality; it is however necessary to form this concept in order to be able to measure or evaluate motion in numerable terms. It is only by mentally dividing motion into parts, that we are able to speak of a three hours' journey, of half an hour's work, of climbing half way up a ladder or giving a screw one third of a turn.

292. Now when we conceive motion in this manner, the parts which we conceive as accomplished and as preceding the indivisible instant of motion are called the *past*. Those parts we conceive as not yet accomplished and as following this instant are called the *future*. The instant itself of motion, considered both as uniting and separating those past and future parts, is called the *present*. The concept of motion as a whole composed of these three parts, past, present and future, is called *time*.

This concept of time is unreal and subjective, but time itself is real and objective. Its reality however consists entirely in the fleeting and indivisible instant of motion which we call present; the past is no longer real since it no longer exists, and the future is not yet real since it does not yet exist.

293. All, therefore, that is real in time, is the indivisible and fleeting instant of motion, which is extremely difficult and nearly impossible to conceive, since to do so we should have to make it stand still; but then it would cease to be a motion at all. And precisely because we are unable to conceive this fleeting instant in itself, we do the next best thing and endeavour to conceive it by a comparison between that which precedes it and that which follows. Instead of concentrating on the indivisible and fleeting actuality of the instant itself, and of vainly endeavouring to consider motion as an incompleted act on its way to the perfection of its actuality, we

take the far easier course of conceiving motion as a complete and perfect act, and then comparing it to a potential repetition of such an act.

In other words we conceive motion as having actual and potential parts, the actual parts being those which have already been accomplished and that precede the potential parts which have not yet been accomplished, but which we imagine will follow in due course. We are then able to form a vague concept of some kind of joining and continuing link between these parts, which also serves as a line of demarcation. This uniting and dividing link is none other than the *indivisible instant of motion.*

294. Time as has just been described, namely, considered by our mind as the measure of motion, is what is called *formal time.* Time in itself or *material time,* cannot be measured, since it consists in the indivisible and fleeting instant of motion.

295. It is because the reality of time is that of motion, that it is impossible to perceive time if we are not aware of motion. Thus, when awaking from sleep, we are not able to tell the time, because during our sleep we were not aware of anything moving. It is also because time and motion are one and the same reality, that the astronomer uses the same units to measure them both, by reckoning them in minutes and seconds.

296. With the concept of formal time we are able to evaluate in terms of measure the continual motion of things. Thus we arrive at the concept of *duration* and consider how long a thing lasts. Duration is the continued existence of a thing. It is a kind of relative concept, the result of a comparison between the existence of a thing and its motion conceived, not as a fleeting instant, but as a continuous whole. There are three kinds of duration, namely time, eviternity and eternity. The duration of time is the continued existence of material things which are always changing. Thus we say that we live in time, that time marches on, that time will come to an end. This is what we mean when we ask what time it is, that is to say, what is the measure of the clock's movement, or how many divisions of the dial the hands of the clock have passed.

297. *Eviternity* is the second kind of duration, and consists in the duration or continued existence of created spirits. It is a kind of imperfect eternity, an intermediary state between time and the eternity of God. It has no end like eternity; but it has a beginning

and is subject to succeeding and changing states, namely to accidental alterations. Angels are not subject to the changes of time and motion which are proper to material things, but on account of the continual succession of their intellectual and volitional acts, a kind of change is wrought in their spiritual faculties. To give this duration of successive spiritual functions a name, we call it eviternity, thus distinguishing it both from time and from eternity.

The *human soul* after death, even when re-united to the risen and spiritualized body, will also live in eviternity, not being subject any more to the changes of time and matter. In this world the human soul is indirectly subject to time on account of the body to which it is united.

298. *Eternity* is the third kind of duration. It is that of God himself and is usually defined as the perpetually enduring existence of the immutable and unchangeable God.

In God there can be no change or motion of any kind. Change implies a new manner of being; God cannot acquire any new way of existing, since he is the subsisting existence, and possesses in his infinite being all conceivable actuality. The concept of time, whether material or formal, is therefore entirely alien to God, and we consequently give a different name, that of Eternity, to the infinite duration of his unchangeable existence. Eternity can be defined as the perfect and actual possession of unending life or existence.

Time is an imperfect act, a fleeting and unseizable instant. Eternity on the contrary is an infinitely perfect act, always present and possessed in its entirety. If we could make the flowing instant of time stand still, and flow no more, if we could for ever stop a star at the very instant it contacts the hairbreadth on the pointer of the astronomer's telescope, if we could conceive an ever present and enduring indivisible instant, we might be able to form a vague concept of eternity. Eternity is a constantly enduring present instant, which has no past and no future.

299. When we talk of the eternity or of the eternal life of the soul after this life, and when St. Thomas maintains that the world could have existed from eternity, these expressions refer to the imperfect eternity which we have called eviternity. It is called eternity because it has no beginning or no end, and in this resembles the eternity of God. But it has a past, a future and a succession of present moments, and thus differs from the eternity of God, which has no past, no future, and no succession of present moments.

PART V

PSYCHOLOGY

INTRODUCTION TO PSYCHOLOGY

Psychology is a rational study of the psyche or the soul. We call it rational to distinguish it from experimental and modern psychology which rejects or at least ignores the rational principles on which the existence of the soul is established, and which has thus become a kind of psychology without a soul, which is a contradiction. Indeed, Psychology is treated to-day as a purely empirical science based on experimental research. Such an experimental psychology consists in the study of mental phenomena considered as the mere outcome of neurological reactions.

Now the Catholic psychologist has nothing to say against the remarkable findings of experimental psychology. Both Aristotle and St. Thomas would most certainly have made use of them if they had been then available. Yet it remains that only a return to the old traditional psychology and to the doctrine of the soul can supply the missing link of many modern psychological enquiries, and provide an explanation of otherwise inexplicable phenomena.

Psychology therefore must not be treated as a purely experimental science. It must be based on sound philosophical theories, and must include a profound study of the soul and of all the soul's vital and cognitive faculties. We usually divide it into three parts, the first dealing with the nature and origin of life and of the soul in general, as manifested through mere vegetal functions, the second with external and internal sense cognition, and the third with the human soul, with its intellectual and volitional acts.

LIFE

300. Life is the mode of existence proper to those things which perform immanent or self-completing actions.

Life is a special mode of existence. Each thing partakes of existence in a different manner, according to the requirements of its nature. Thus man partakes of existence in a more perfect way than a worm, on account of the greater exigencies of his nature; and since all living beings have a more perfect nature than those which are destitute of life, their existence is more noble and perfect, and is consequently given this special name of life. But because existence itself is something we cannot properly understand or define, it is not surprising that we cannot probe very deeply into the intimate nature of life. To fully comprehend it we should have to understand the nature of him who said: *I am the Life.* We therefore do the next best thing, and endeavour to understand the manifestations of life, namely vital actions. And thus we are led to say that life is the principle of immanent actions, in opposition to those that are called transient.

301. A *transient action* is the completion of an effect in an object other than the performing agent. Thus, burning is a transient action because the effect is completed, not in the fire which burns, but in the thing which is burnt. All non-vital actions are transient, because all physico-chemical forces produce effects in things other than those to which such forces belong. In fact, all forces of matter are forces of attraction or repulsion and tend in an outwardly direction.

302. A difficulty arises in the case of actions expressed by intransitive verbs, such as for example when we say that *stones drop, rivers flow,* the *wind blows,* or *particles shoot out* of radium. These actions cease with the doer, and do not pass to anything else. It would therefore seem that these non-vital actions were immanent and not transient ones.

To this we answer that an intransitive verb with a non-living subject does not indicate an action performed by the subject, but one performed in the subject by some other agent. The dropping of the stone is not due to any action of the stone, but to some other cause such as gravitation. Similarly, rivers do not flow themselves, neither does wind blow itself, nor particles shoot themselves out of radium. Matter is inert, it cannot move its own self, although its active power can move other things. Therefore, intransitive actions are not an exception to the general rule that all non-vital actions are transient.

303. An *immanent action* is the completion of an effect in the very agent which performs it. It is called a self-completing action, or an immanent one, because it perfects, and remains within, the agent. Thus, growth is an immanent function, because the living cell completes its own self by growing. All vital actions are immanent. Vital activity has an inward direction, a kind of reflexive orientation, and serves the sole purpose of perfecting the individual from which it emanates. This intrinsic design of vital activity is totally absent in the inherent powers of inorganic matter.

304. Yet an immanent action can be *accompanied* by a transient effect, namely an effect produced in something which is distinct from the performing agent. Thus the fructifying of a tree is an immanent action; yet it produces fruit, which is an object distinct from the tree. But these transient effects are only side-issues, and not the main effect of an immanent action. The action of bearing fruit primarily perfects and completes the tree itself, since a barren tree would be imperfect and incomplete, and only secondarily results in the production, let us say, of apples. Thus also, to sculpt is an immanent action which is the goal and completion of the artist's talent; the statue he sculpts is a secondary and accompanying effect, not absolutely necessary for the completion of the immanent action of sculpting. In fact, if an artist went through all the movements required to sculpt without actually holding a chisel, he would still be performing an immanent action. By doing so he would be perfecting and bringing to further completion his art, just as a boxer, whilst training, fights an imaginary foe; these movements are self-completing and are immanent actions.

305. There are *three kinds* of immanent actions and consequently three kinds or degrees of living beings, namely, Plants, Animals and Men.

Plants belong to the first or lowest degree of living beings. They have three kinds of immanent actions, namely, those of feeding themselves, of growing and of fructifying. These are obviously self-completing or immanent functions, since they perfect the very organism which performs them. But a plant cannot alternate these functions, since it feeds, grows and fructifies at definite and invariable times, and has therefore no command over the nature of the function it is to perform, or over the manner in which it performs it. These are fixed and determined, not by the plant itself, but by the force of biological laws to which the plant is utterly subject. In fact, plants begin to feed as soon as they are placed in favourable conditions, each plant reaching out in the same invariable way for its own special food. They grow steadily as if drawn by an irresistible force until they reach a fixed height and proportion, invariably the same for each kind of plant. And each plant produces a definite kind of fruit in the same manner and at the same times.

306. *Animals* have more perfect vital functions and belong to the second degree of living beings. They not only perform immanent actions, but the nature of the actions they perform depends entirely on them and is not, like in plants, fixed and determined by exterior forces. An animal does not always eat when food is placed within its reach; a cat will sometimes eat, sometimes play, and sometimes sleep. Furthermore it not only varies its actions, but directs them towards a great variety of objects. In all this it differs essentially from the plant. But the animal always performs these actions in the same way. A book can be written about nest-building or about the behaviour of ants or bees: they never vary. A dog does not plan, does not invent new ways of living, does not do anything to better its conditions.

307. *Man* belongs to the third degree of living beings. He is superior to the animal because the whole perfection of his actions depends on himself; he is not governed by any fixed law or dependent on any outside influence in the choice of his actions, or in the manner of performing them.

CHAPTER 2

THE ORIGIN OF LIFE

308. We must now consider the origin of life, on account of the famous theory of Evolution, and establish what must be the views of the Catholic philosopher concerning this widely known problem. *Evolution* in general is the origination of one species from another one. There are two kinds of evolution. Inorganic evolution or *Transformism* is concerned with the structural formation of the earth, and is connected with what is generally known as the Nebular hypothesis. *Organic* evolution deals with the origin of life, and maintains that living beings were developed by natural means from less perfect forms of existence. It is generally associated with the name of Charles Darwin, but others before him had outlined a similar system. The system is based on variations produced in the species by natural selection, struggle for existence and survival of the fittest, but no conclusive proof has yet been produced as to the existence of these variations and developments. Evolution can be denied with as much justice to facts, as that which led to its assertion.

Indeed, if there are great resemblances between certain types of living beings, there are also great differences which would seem to imply that they did not derive from each other. Present experience shows us that species hold fast to their type; there is no example of evolution in the species of our days. The stability of all present species is an incontestable fact, no example of evolution having ever been observed. Plants, animals and human beings of our times are depicted in historical documents exactly as we know them. The discovery of fossils in ancient strata only points to the extinction of certain types of organisms. There is no proof that they evolved into higher beings. And all attempts at variations of living species, or at the production of permanent new ones, have failed. Moreover, the evolution of life from matter or spontaneous generation, is against all known scientific laws, and never occurs to-day.

Why should evolution have ceased for the last several thousand years? If evolution is an effect of natural laws, we ought to be able to witness at least a partial evolution in some of the present types. There is however no evidence of this fact.

309. But evolution is not in contradiction with Catholic thought. Provided the evolutionist is not led to the rejection of the three

following fundamental principles, he is free to draw his own conclusions as to whether or not there are a sufficient number of experimental facts to corroborate his theory. It is a purely scientific concern. Neither the Church nor Philosophy has anything to say in the matter.

310. The first principle concerns the divine *origin of matter*. We must hold that the whole mass of matter as it exists to-day in the universe was created by God. Scientists agree unanimously that the mass of matter composing the universe is a constant factor, that no new matter is made, and that none is lost. The only effect of physical forces is the transformation of pre-existing matter. This is true not only of the present, but of all times. Neither man, nor the elements, can produce an atom of matter. This requires no proof, it is an accepted fact.

We are therefore faced with the inevitable conclusion that since no power of this world can produce matter, its existence must be due to the action of someone who could produce it. We call this supreme agent God. We are forced to admit that such an agent exists, by the very fact that, since everything must have a cause, matter must also have one. The cause of matter cannot be found in this world, therefore it must be sought for outside. Since there was no matter before it existed, God could not have made it by transforming previous matter; he therefore had to give existence to something that did not exist before. We say that he *created* matter, or made it out of nothing.

311. The second principle concerns the divine *origin of power*. The First Cause gave to matter all its physical and vital properties. There is nothing in this world which can endow matter with energy. We accept the fact that the various things of this world have properties and energies. But man did not put them there. Therefore we maintain that the all-powerful Agent did so. It was he who gave to fire the power to burn, who made acids corrosive, metals hard, and who gave to organic beings their vital activity. There may be several ways of explaining how he did it, but the fact remains that these properties and energies cannot be accounted for unless we attribute them originally to God as to their first cause.

312. The third principle concerns the divine *origin of the human soul*. We must admit that God creates each individual human soul. The soul is not transmitted to the child by its parents, as the

Traducianists said. The human soul is spiritual and exists independently of matter. It cannot therefore be generated by the parents whose function is simply to transform matter; a spiritual substance cannot proceed from a corporal principle. Neither can it derive from the soul of the parents, since their soul, being spiritual, has no parts and is indivisible. It is therefore impossible for any particle which we might conceive as a spiritual germ, to be detached from the soul of the parents to form the soul of the child.

We must therefore again look for this cause outside the universe, and recognize that the only possible cause is God, who produces the soul, not from pre-existing matter, but from nothing, by *creation*. Each time an organism has been suitably disposed by the parents for the reception of a soul, God causes a spiritual soul to exist in that organism.

313. *Conclusion.*—Evolution would seem to be a safe theory with regard to the mineral reign, that is to say with regard to non-living beings. Scientific discoveries unanimously point to a slow evolution of the present order of things from a primitive state of chaos. Geology is quasi-conclusive on this point. The Bible itself says that the earth was in the beginning in a chaotic state, and that the last four days or periods of creation, were set apart for the work of orderly arrangement; thus it agrees very closely with the hypothesis which assumes the whole mass of the universe to have been in the beginning nothing but a huge rotating nebula.

314. Regarding life, if we keep in mind what has just been said, namely that not only the mass of matter, but also its properties and energies must have an adequate cause which can be no other than God, there is no reason to deny that life could have evolved from matter. Life made its appearance upon earth long after the existence of the mineral reign. Whether, when God created the material elements, he gave to some of them the power to slowly evolve into living beings, or whether, after a certain period of time, he made completely new living beings by a special act of creation, we do not know.

If therefore, by evolution of life, we mean that certain material elements gradually began to show signs of life through a latent power God had previously given to them, there is nothing to prevent us from professing evolution. Evolution as a theory is unacceptable to the Christian only in as much as it is foreign to the idea of God's direct or indirect intervention, and tries to explain the existence of matter, power and life, as a fortuitous event.

315. With regard to man, there is no reason to deny the evolution of his body, like that of other living beings. Man's body *could* have evolved from inferior organisms. When it is said in the Bible that God made man from the dust of the earth, it is not said that he made him instantly. The work could have taken a very long time, time enough for the gradual evolution of his body to take place through many successive stages, from a primitive cell or atom. Or God could have taken the body of a superior animal such as an ape, to fashion it into that of man, because an ape is also made of the slime of the earth. But there is no evidence of this. The reasons which make us hesitate to accept the evolution of other living species, militate far more against the animal origin of man.

316. Even with regard to the human soul, it is not out of place to remark that St. Thomas professes a certain type of evolution, by maintaining that man begins life with a vegetative soul, which disappears to give way to an animal soul as the organicity of the embryo increases. When further development has been reached, the animal soul in its turn disappears; God then creates the spiritual soul. In his opinion therefore, man is not conceived with a human soul, but receives it at a relatively late stage of embryological process. This question, namely whether the human soul is infused at the first moment of conception or later on, is one that will probably never be satisfactorily answered. Modern physiology definitely favours the view that animal life is present at a very early stage, and the Church deals with the most imperfect embryo as if it might be a human being.

CHAPTER 3

THE SOUL IN GENERAL

317. The problem of the soul is much more than a mere question of names. We can call it a psyche, an entelechy or anything else we like, provided we agree on the meaning of these names. What is

fundamental is to acknowledge the existence of a principle of life essentially different from the physico-chemical forces of matter. That such a principle must exist is obvious from the characteristic differences between living and non-living beings.

318. The heterogeneous structure of the *living organism* is made up of microscopic cells which are highly complex in their constitution. A cell can incorporate foreign matter into itself; it can grow and develop into an extraordinary complicated variety of tissues and organs, all perfectly unified according to a definite type, and for specific functions. These tissues and organs have the extraordinary power of repairing any wear, tear and damage inflicted upon them. Thus the tongue never wears in spite of its continual work, a wound will heal, a tissue will grow again when torn away. And finally, the living cell has the power to reproduce an entirely new organic being similar to itself. Some living beings have the still higher and more striking characteristics of cognitive, emotional and motor activities.

Non-living beings have none of these functions. A stone, for example, does not grow by intussusception of outward substances, or by converting them into itself. It can only increase by mechanical accumulation or juxtaposition. It has no organs or heterogeneity of parts, each part being, and remaining, homogeneous in structure. It is incapable of modifying or repairing itself, and it cannot produce other individuals of the same species. Neither has it any of the higher cognitive or emotional vital functions, nor any self-motion.

319. Now unless we prefer to adopt the unscientific attitude of ignoring the cause of these vital phenomena, we are bound to recognize that they cannot be accounted for by the ordinary forces of matter, otherwise all material beings would be endowed with them. We are therefore led to the conclusion that the special phenomena displayed by living beings are due to a higher principle which we call *soul*. We are not dealing here with the special problem of the human soul, which differs from that of plants and animals in that it has an existence of its own, and is not dependent on matter for its existence and for its intellectual operations. But as far as its union to, and its presence in, the body is concerned, it resembles that of plants and animals.

320. Therefore, considering the soul as a principle of life common to plants, animals and men, although modern parlance rarely

refers to the soul of an animal or to that of a plant, we can define it thus: *The substantial form of a body which is able to perform vital functions.*

By calling the soul a *substantial form,* we first of all imply that it is, like all other substantial forms, known to us only by intellectual abstraction, and not by the senses. Secondly we imply that the soul is the principle of all the vital functions of the body, in the same manner as the substantial form of radium, for example, is the principle of radio-activity. Hylomorphism teaches us that a substantial form is the *first actuality* of an essence, making that essence belong to a particular species and investing it with specific properties. Among these properties are the active and functional powers of living beings. Now, in virtue of its substantial form, a thing has not only specific properties, but many other qualities which it shares with other species of things. A piece of oak-wood has several properties which are common to other kinds of wood, and to many other substances; it has also a few special characteristics that are not found in any other thing, its particular hardness, for example. But one and the same substantial form of oak gives it, not only its specific, but also its generic properties. In other words, there is in each thing only *one* substantial form which is the principle of all its properties and activities. In fact, there could not be two or more substantial forms in a thing, otherwise that thing would belong to two or more species at the same time.

321. Therefore in plants there is only one substantial form which gives to them not only their specific vital properties, but also those they happen to share with inanimate things, such as shape, colour, height, and so forth. For the same reason, animals have a single form or soul, which makes them able to perform not only the functions of animal life, but also those belonging to the vegetal reign; one and the same soul is the principle of their organic, cognitive, emotional and motor activities. In man also, there is only one soul, which virtually contains all inferior substantial forms, and by which man lives organically, moves, feels, sense-perceives, reasons and deliberates.

322. Since substantial form is an act of the essence, without which the essence would be a pure potency incapable of existing, it follows that there can be no part of the body not actuated by the soul. In other words, the soul is everywhere in the body, in every single part

of it. We must not think of the soul as dwelling in the body like the marrow in the spine, or the pith in the tree. Although the example is inadequate, we could compare the presence of the soul in the body to that of light in the air, or of heat in a furnace. The body is not just matter, as we often imagine it to be; but matter and form, body and soul. The flesh and bones of the body are composed of body and soul; organicity is not something belonging to the body alone, but to the body and soul. Therefore no part of the body can continue to live when separated from the rest of it, or when the soul, by death, has parted from it. In fact, physiologists tell us that disintegration of the organic structure sets in immediately after death.

323. Now as soon as the substantial form of a thing disappears, another form takes its place; thus, if wood is burnt, its form is immediately replaced by that of ashes. If we were to smooth out the contours of a marble statue, the form of the statue would disappear to give place to that of marble. So when the soul departs from the body, or from one of its parts, by separation from the whole, another substantial form takes its place. The new form will be an inorganic one; in fact a corpse or an amputated limb is just a mass of inanimate matter.

324. Since each part of homogeneous matter, namely that of non-living beings, has the same nature and structure as the whole, if a block of marble, for example, is broken into pieces, new forms of exactly the same nature as that of the whole immediately take possession of each piece. There is no limit to this multiplication of the form of inanimate matter except that of the physical possibility of dividing it. Animate matter on the contrary is not homogeneous, but organic. *Organicity* is the arrangement of the parts composing a living body, or the inner design by which the special functions of the several parts of the body are interdependent and co-ordinated in view of the unity and perfection of the whole. Organicity is a fundamental phenomenon and condition of life. It implies two things. The first is that no two parts of the organism are exactly the same in structure. The second is that all the different parts are interdependent to such an extent that all their energy is directed towards the preservation of the whole. That is why we call their activity, not by the name of simple actions, but by that of *functions;* this word meaning an action performed for someone or something else. This unity of function in spite of the multiplicity of the forces at work in

the organism, is the main characteristic of living beings. The parts are essentially subservient to the whole.

325. Obviously this organicity will disappear if the unity of the living being is destroyed by dividing it into parts. And since organicity is an essential condition of life, neither life nor its principle, the soul, can continue to subsist in these parts. In fact they are no longer parts of a living body, having neither the heterogeneity of structure, nor the unity of function which constitute an organic being. If a leg is amputated from an animal, the rest of the body preserves sufficient unity and organicity for the functions of life; but if an important organ, such as the head, is amputated, this unity and organicity is completely destroyed, and life with its substantial form disappears. There is no real life in a tissue, muscle or heart which has been artificially preserved; although it may continue to manifest for a time some of the symptoms of life, these activities are not organic functions, since they do not contribute to the preservation of an organic whole. Very simple organisms, such as those of worms, can be separated into living parts, precisely on account of the simplicity of their structure; each part retains a sufficiently perfect organism to function as a whole, and so, in these, as in the case of mineral forms, the soul is multiplied by the multiplication of the parts.

CHAPTER 4

ANIMAL LIFE

326. *Animals* are living beings which occupy an intermediary place between plants and man. The extraordinary behaviour of certain animals is thought by some people to be a sign of intelligence. This however is only a manner of speaking, as few people really intend to convey thereby that animals can reason and deliberate like human beings. They usually draw a line between animal and human behaviour, and the whole question is really one of terminology. By intelligent behaviour they simply mean that certain animals some-

times perform unusual and marvellous actions, which, however, even at their best, have only a distant resemblance to some elementary form of human behaviour. Animals, in fact, have no intellectual cognitive powers; their highest form of cognitive ability is embodied in an interior sense which we call the power of estimation; this is the best way to translate the Latin name of *aestimativa*. Moderns prefer to call it instinct.

327. To act with intelligence means to pursue an object which is considered as being more suitable than others when compared with them. This is what we call to act for a purpose. Since all things have some good points, any one of them can be conceived as suitable if these good points are taken into consideration and abstracted from all others. Hence intelligent beings, on account of their power of abstraction, have a wide range of objects from which to choose, and can select now this one, now that one, according to the particular aspect under which they actually consider it. It follows that they can substitute one thing for another, and are thus led to new discoveries and inventions, and to an immense variety of ways in which to perform their actions.

328. Now it is precisely because animals never vary the manner in which they perform their actions, that we are led to conclude that they do not act for a purpose, and that, consequently, they do not act intelligently and are not endowed with intelligence. They differ from plants in that they are not compelled to act in predetermined circumstances. Plants have no control over their functions, but animals are not compelled, for example, to eat when food is placed within their reach. A cat will sometimes eat, sometimes play or run, and sometimes sleep, but it always performs these actions in the same invariable manner, and always selects the same identical things as objects of its pursuit. Neither do animals make new discoveries, they do not invent or progress, the evident reason being that they cannot conceive goodness in the abstract, but are only able to perceive the particular goodness or usefulness of a certain number of things, and are thus incapable of substituting other things which might turn out to be just as good.

329. In fact, the alimentary requirements of an animal are limited to a small variety of foods; birds build their nests in exactly the same way as they did thousands of years ago; the marvellous activity of bees and ants is absolutely regular and invariable in all its details; a

spider will rebuild its cobweb in the same place, although it has been swept away time and again. Evidently, therefore, although animal behaviour is marvellous, it is not intelligent. Animals do not plan, do not invent, and do nothing to better their condition.

330. Nor can animals count. To count is an abstract intellectual operation. They do not conceive several distinct unities or objects as a multitude or as a number; they simply perceive them as particular objects distinct from one another, and remember that one is placed after the other.

331. But although animals do not pursue any deliberate purpose in the performance of their actions, it does not follow that there is no purpose in their behaviour. That there is a definite *plan* and *purpose* in the whole cosmic labour is an obvious fact. This fact, rejected by some as a consequence of the evolutionary theory, is exaggerated by a few, who maintain that animal behaviour includes the consciousness of a goal and the choice of the means leading to it. But this is not the case. The existence of a detailed plan behind the vast scheme of the universe is consistent with the fact that this plan is not known by all those who execute it. A gigantic business enterprise can be brought to a successful conclusion even if the greater part of those engaged in that business are in complete ignorance of the general plan. The plan of the universe is known in its entirety by the First Cause who is its author, and in a restricted way by created intelligent beings. All other beings of a cognitive or non-cognitive nature conform blindly to this plan of which they have no knowledge whatever, because they have not been endowed with the intellectual powers which would enable them to understand purpose and design.

332. Animals are composed of matter and form. Now the substantial form of vegetals, animals and man is called a *soul* in order to distinguish it from that of non-living beings. Therefore in a philosophical sense, animals have a soul. Modern usage however generally reserves the name of soul for that of human beings. Consequently when it is said that animals have a soul, this in no way implies that it is spiritual and immaterial like that of man. It is produced from, and returns to, the potency of matter, in exactly the same way as the substantial form of all inferior beings.

CHAPTER 5

COGNITION

333. One of the most important manifestations of animal life is sense-cognition. Both animals and men are able to contact the exterior world by cognizing it. Here we will endeavour to explain what exactly cognition is, with reference especially to sense-cognition; however, it will be seen later on that most of what we shall say here about the nature of sense-cognition equally applies to intellectual knowledge.

334. Sense-cognition is the act of acquiring knowledge by means of one of our five exterior or one of our four interior senses. The knowledge it gives is that of the exterior appearances or accidents of individual objects, such as their shape, size, colour and so forth. Intellectual cognition is the act of acquiring knowledge by means of our spiritual intellect; it makes us know the nature of things abstracted from their individual characteristics.

Cognition is performed by means of a *vital representation* or reproduction of an exterior object in the cognizing faculty. To understand this, three basic principles must be grasped.

335. The *first principle* is that in every act of cognition the cognizing faculty undergoes a modification. This needs no proof, since the passage of a cognizing faculty from the state of potential cognition to that of the actual cognition of an object, is evidently a modification. This modification consists in an impression made upon the faculty, such as that made upon the eye, the hearing apparatus, the faculty of imagery, and so forth.

336. The *second principle* is that this modification is produced by the cognized object. If it were not, there would be no necessary connection between our knowledge and the things we know; knowledge would be subjective, since, if the modification were not produced by the known object, there would be no alternative but to ascribe it to the cognizing subject, and thus we should not know a tree, for example, or a man, as they are in reality, but as they were made to appear to us by the unstable modifying factors of our organism.

It is precisely because our faculties are not the active agents of their cognitive modification, but are subjected to it through the agency of the object of their cognition, that they are called *passive* faculties. This however does not imply that cognition is a mere passive state. Cognition is a vital function, and consequently a real immanent action. The faculties are therefore *also* active, because they have the active power of transforming this passive impression into a formal factor of cognition. Although, for example, wax can receive the passive impression of a seal, it cannot cognize the seal which modifies it, because it has not the active power of using this impression as a principle of knowledge.

337. The *third principle* is that the object produces this modification by impressing its likeness upon the faculty. This principle is merely an application of the general metaphysical law that an effect always bears a resemblance to its cause. Indeed a cause is able to produce a particular effect only because that particular effect is contained potentially in that cause. There is evidence of this in the fact that a thorough knowledge of a cause can reveal all its potential effects. An effect can be called an explicit expression of the pent-up energy contained in its cause. That is why a child resembles its parents, and the style and nature of a work of art unmistakably point to its author.

338. Now the likeness of an object impressed upon a cognizing faculty is a special kind of likeness, on account of the special nature of the faculty. This happens in all representations; a cause impresses its likeness upon an object according to the different nature of the object upon which it is impressed. Thus a painting, a statue, a photograph and a reflection in a mirror of the same person, represent that person in a different manner. No representation reproduces all that is contained in the represented object, a picture of a man for example, does not reproduce the components of his organism or his physical substance, but only his exterior features, his figure, colouring and so forth. Otherwise a picture would be a real living duplicate of that man, and not a mere picture.

Therefore, neither does cognition represent a thing in its physical reality or in its material individuality. The image or likeness varies with the different cognitive faculties; thus a sound image differs from a visual one, a picture of the imagination is not the same as an abstract concept. But in all cases a likeness of the object is impressed upon the faculty.

339. Because this cognitive likeness is of a special kind, a special

name has been coined to designate it. It is called an *intentional* or *impressed species*. The word *species* is used here as an equivalent of image. Sense-representations are often called images, for example visual or mental images. But the term *species* is preferred in order to embrace both sense and intellectual representations. The term *intentional* is not taken in the meaning of something done with a purpose or an intention, but simply to imply the aloofness from matter of the cognitive representation and to distinguish it from mere physical or material impressions.

The actual process of cognition is, however, and always will be, shrouded in mystery. This is not astonishing, since it is extremely difficult for us to understand the nature even of the primitive functions of organic life, or of the physical and chemical reactions of inanimate objects.

CHAPTER 6

FACULTIES AND SENSES

340. We have said that living beings differ from non-living ones on account of the vast diversity of their active manifestations. Because living beings are capable of actions superior to those of non-living ones, their power to perform these acts has been given the special name of *Faculty*. A faculty is the immediate or proximate principle of a vital act. Faculties are also called active potencies or powers of the soul. They are divided into *organic*, *sensory* and *rational* faculties. Organic faculties are those of reproduction, nutrition and growth. Sensory faculties are of three kinds. The first kind are the cognitive ones, namely the five external senses, and the four internal ones of consciousness, imagination, instinct (in man, particular reason), and memory. The second kind of sensory faculties are the orectic or appetitive ones, namely the feeling and emotional ones. The third kind is the motor faculty, embodied in the muscular system. The rational faculties are the intellect and the will. In all there would therefore be 16 faculties.

341. This scholastic classification of faculties is of great help in

the systematic treatment of vital functions. As to what these faculties really are, we know very little, and can only refer to them as capacities, abilities, or powers, to perform certain functions. Indeed it is only through the functions or vital acts which we perform that we are able to know what we are capable of doing; our knowledge of our faculties is limited to what we know of their functions. This however does not tell us much, just as saying that fire is the power to burn does not explain the nature of fire.

342. Yet we do know that the power to act is something distinct from the function which results from it, as an effect is something distinct from its cause. There must be a difference between the vital functions and the ability to perform them. In fact, living beings are not constantly exercising all the functions of which they are capable, neither do they always perform a function to the full extent of their capacity; thus an animal does not always eat, nor does it always eat as much as it could. This would not happen if the power and the function were one and the same thing. Indeed, it is obvious that the power to feel or to think is not the act of feeling or of thinking, because when we are not actually feeling or thinking we still retain the power to do so. In this, a vital being does not differ from inorganic matter; elements also have latent powers which they do not always display, and which consequently are distinct from their actual reactions under certain circumstances.

343. Therefore faculties are not mere names to label certain classes of similar functions. They are real powers, something quite distinct not only from their functions, but also from the substance of the being to which they belong. Otherwise it would be impossible to explain the specific variety of these functions. The act of smelling for example and that of hearing, that of walking or understanding, or that of remembering and eating, are so diametrically opposed that, besides the one and only individual nature or substance to which they ultimately belong, there must be several proximate specifying agents which we call faculties.

344. On the other hand, faculties must not be conceived as separate *parts* either of the soul or of the body. The soul has no parts, and those regions of the body where certain functions are manifested, such as the exterior sense-organs, are only instruments of sensation. A sense-organ is not a faculty. The moving power behind the organ, in other words the vital faculty, is rooted in the entire living organism,

in the body and soul as a whole; each vital faculty belongs to the whole being or suppositum.

345. This *suppositum* is endowed with several distinct active properties which we call faculties or proximate principles of action. Although some of these properties are manifested in separate bodily organs, we must beware of conceiving them as separate realities, acting side by side, independently of each other. The functions of each faculty are more or less influenced by those of the other faculties; we cannot perform an act resulting exclusively from one faculty without the concurrence of at least some of the others. Even the intellect and the will are influenced in their spiritual functions by each other and by the organic and sense-faculties. Many equivocations would be avoided if we remembered that although the intellect and the will are theoretically independent of matter, and will in fact be independent when the soul is separated from the body, in this life, it is impossible to use them independently of either the internal or external senses. Every vital function is performed by the whole living substance, and belongs to the whole suppositum or person.

346. The senses are the material faculties of cognition. There are four interior senses rooted in the nerve matter of the brain, namely the Sensus Communis, also called internal or fundamental sense, and often simply Consciousness; the Imagination; Instinct which in man is called power of estimation, cogitative faculty or particular reason; and finally Memory. There are five exterior senses, namely sight, hearing, smell, taste and touch.

347. Our senses are reliable; we have no reason to doubt that we perceive exterior things as they really are. Our senses were made for the definite purpose of perceiving external reality, and it would be against common sense to say that they were incapable of doing so. The eye was obviously made to see, the ear to hear, and so forth; if they could not do so, there would be no object in using them at all.

The senses however have certain limitations; they are only meant to work in definite circumstances. An appropriate position, distance and proportion of the object, are indispensable if the senses are to be correctly stimulated. Our senses are tuned in a special way; they will not respond if the object is not equally tuned. For example, the eye cannot judge the colour of an object if the light is too weak or too strong, its size if it is too near or too distant, or its shape unless the object is placed in the proper position.

Healthy and normal condition of the senses is also a necessary requisite for reliable sense cognition. Diseased organs cannot function normally. Abnormal conditions of the cognizing subject, such as intoxication, hallucination or sickness, also affect the proper functioning of the senses.

But if the senses are in a healthy condition and are used in a normal and proper way, they do not err. A thousand men could measure the height of a steeple without finding the slightest variation in their results. Precision instruments are produced daily, and are verified and tested by several people, whose results must all tally perfectly unless the instrument is to be rejected.

348. This does not mean that we are not sometimes led into error. We are sometimes deceived by optical illusions such as mirage, conjurors' tricks, the fantastic shapes assumed by familiar objects in the twilight, the moving pictures of our cinemas and so forth. But real deception is an exception. The illusion is either deliberate as in the cinema, where we know that the figures are not really moving, or else it can easily be detected and corrected. The powerful discriminative and co-ordinating agency of consciousness soon disposes of any momentary deception, by careful investigation, and by the help of our other cognitive faculties.

349. Furthermore there is a fundamental truth underlying the question of knowledge which is too often overlooked, namely that knowledge is an act of the Ego, of the complete person, not the result of one or the other separate sense or faculty. No single faculty is meant to give us a complete knowledge of any object. Each faculty contributes, by co-operating in its own way, to the final effect. Mistakes and errors can occur if we content ourselves with the result of a single experience; to know a thing, we must not only look at it, but feel it, and perhaps hear, taste and smell it, we must think about it, compare it to other things, and so forth. The ultimate act of knowledge is thus performed, not by any individual faculty, but by *me*, through the ministry of many or all of my faculties. If performed under appropriate conditions, the final result will be reliable and trustworthy.

CHAPTER 7

CONSCIOUSNESS AND PERCEPTION

350. It would be beyond the scope of scholastic Psychology to deal separately with each exterior sense. For this purpose reference to a good manual of experimental psychology is to be strongly recommended, since a general knowledge of the nerve and muscular reactions of the senses and of the brain is conducive to a better understanding of our cognitive process. We shall limit our study to the four interior senses, the first of which we call consciousness.

351. *Sense-consciousness* is the fact of being aware of our own acts, mental states, tendencies and existence. It is the practical recognition of the internal events of our own sensitive nature. Now it is most remarkable that, in spite of the constant activity of our organism, the conscious events of our life are comparatively few. Most of our bodily movements consist in automatic and conditioned reflexes which are performed quasi-mechanically and pass unnoticed. Nor do we always realize the various emotional states to which we are subject; thus, we are not always conscious of the comforts we are enjoying, or of the pleasure or pain caused by the daily occurrences of life. As to cognition, although the number of things which are continually besieging and stimulating our senses is remarkably great, there are proportionally few sensations of which we are aware; most of the time our senses register in a merely passive manner the impressions they receive. Some people are more observant than others, but every one is subject to innumerable unobserved sense-impressions, which nevertheless produce real physical stimuli upon their sense-organs. Thus we can stare at a person, gaze intently at a thing, or hear traffic all day long without noticing what we have seen or heard. Examples of total or partial absence of observation can be multiplied, especially concerning the details of objects with which we are in daily contact. We are not aware of these impressions at the time of receiving them, but sometimes we react to them later on; the sense-impression is stored away for some time, until a new stimulus happens to re-awaken it. For example, we are sometimes able to say that the clock struck a certain number of times, although we took no notice of it when it did strike; we remember a fact or a tune to which we paid no attention at the time. It is consciousness that makes us thus aware of what is happening in us.

352. But consciousness is not a state of mere passive awareness; it makes us realize what it is we are aware of, it implies a definite act, the act of *discriminating*.

The numerous acts of our sensitive life, our sense-stimuli, our muscular movements and our emotional conditions, set in motion a multitude of nerve-currents which cross and recross each other in all directions, and result in a maze of interconnections. Each new act thus becomes involved with all the others, and in order to be conscious of it, we must carefully disentangle it and distinguish it from the others. This is the function of consciousness, which could be compared to a Post-Office sorting department, or to a central telephone exchange, since it discriminates, recognizes, labels and redirects the various messages to and from our senses. It makes us aware that we are seeing and not hearing, or that we are seeing something white and not something black, that we are feeling pain and not pleasure, or that we are walking on a slippery road. It makes us realize what we are doing, feeling, thinking about, or what is happening to us.

353. It also makes us able to select at a given moment any particular sense-message and to keep in the background others which would tend to force their way into the field of our consciousness. It consequently makes us able to *co-ordinate* several particular sense-impressions into one single perception, as for example when we notice the size of an object by looking at it and feeling it at the same time, and also to synthesize certain sensory and muscular stimuli in order to perform actions such as writing, playing the piano, driving a car and so forth.

354. Although these functions of sensitive consciousness seem fairly obvious, the nature of the sense-faculty to which they belong is a matter of much discussion. It is usually called *sensus communis*, and is classified as one of the four internal senses. It has also been called simply the internal or the fundamental sense. This sensus communis would not seem to be localized in any special part of the body, but seems rather to consist in the general sensitivity of the whole organism. We can conceive it as an intrinsic power belonging to the sense-organism as a whole, and ready to function in its observing, discriminating and co-ordinating rôle whenever it is called upon to do so.

355. *Perception* is not the act of a distinct faculty or sense, but

designates the special co-ordinative function of our faculty of consciousness. It is however also used in a more general and vague
manner to designate any kind of cognition.

356. Perception does not simply make us aware of what we have
sensed; it is a far more complex and comprehensive operation. It
enables us to know things that do not impress any particular sense,
or do not fall within the exclusive range of any of our peripheral
organs. Many, if not all, of our sensations, are in fact complex rather
than simple. Each sensation awakens a kind of vestige of the preceding ones, adds its impression to them, so that it builds up into
something new, like a canvas which changes at every stroke of the
painter's brush. Many sensations shade into each other, so that what
we are generally aware of is something rather complex, the object of
our actual sensation being accrued by all we have previously experienced in connection with it. This explains how we can perceive
things we cannot, for example, actually see, like the spherical form
of a circle.

357. There is also another kind of consciousness, namely intellectual consciousness. The obvious place to deal with this would be
when explaining the intellectual functions of the mind; but it seems
more practical and useful to speak about it here under the general
heading of consciousness.

358. *Intellectual consciousness* is twofold: direct and reflex.
Direct consciousness consists in the fact of being aware of what we
are conceiving in our minds. In every act of intellectual knowledge
we are implicitly conscious of the act we are performing, *in actu
exercito*, as we say. As an example let us suppose we form the intellectual concept *man* or *being in general*; we are simultaneously conscious of the fact that we are doing so. In other words there can be
no unconscious intellectual act, the reason being that the object of the
intellect is abstract, and the formation of an abstract concept requires
an actual effort and application of which the intellect would not be
capable if it were not conscious of what it was doing. This does not
mean that we are always actually realizing that we have formed an
abstract concept, but that we are always actually aware of what we
are thinking about.

359. *Reflex* consciousness is a deliberate return of our mind upon
itself and upon its act, an explicit consideration of the very act of
knowing. For example, after having formed the concept of *man* or

being, if we make this concept the object of a new act of the mind, and thus discover that *man* is an abstract concept or that *being* is a transcendental notion, and so forth, we are making an act of reflex consciousness.

It is obvious that the seat of intellectual consciousness is none other than the intellect itself, which is cognizant of it own acts and its own self, either in a direct or in an indirect and reflex manner. Consciousness however differs from the ordinary act of knowledge, in that its object is restricted to the personal states of the thinker, whilst the ordinary act of understanding embraces any intelligible object.

CHAPTER 8

IMAGINATION

360. Another of our internal faculties is known as the imagination. It consists in the power to perceive exterior objects after the sense-stimulus has ceased. Our exterior senses can only perceive those objects which are actually stimulating them. Now it would be rather unsatisfactory and inconvenient if we could only know things that were actually stimulating our sense-organs, which come and go as each object disappears from our field of perception with the advent of a new one. In order to perceive the smell of a flower for example, it would be necessary each time to be in the presence of a real physical flower. We have therefore been endowed with this marvellous faculty of imagination which enables us to retain the passing impressions made upon our sense-organs, in the form of internal representations or images, and thus to perceive exterior objects in the absence of the stimulus they produced. Because the imagination is also, although in a loose sense, called mind, the images it produces are called mental images, or even thoughts and ideas; the scholastics however prefer to call them phantasms, which term is not taken in the normal English sense of *illusion* or *phantom*.

361. A *phantasm* is a mental image of a thing or of a sensation previously experienced, but actually absent. A phantasm always pre-

supposes a previous sense-experience; a man born blind cannot have mental images of colour.

Some phantasms are exact copies of things or sensations, in which case we speak of reproductive imagination. But some do not represent things exactly as they are or as we have experienced them; they are the result of mental associations, and are said to be the product of our creative imagination. When these latter are fanciful and extravagant and have no practical scope, they are fantasy images, and are generally formed without any conscious control: they are frequent when asleep or half awake; we are then said to be dreaming.

These fantasy images represent things as partaking of shapes and qualities belonging to other objects. The material or stuff of these fantasy images is gathered from previous sense-experience, but it is arranged in a manner which is a pure creation of the mind. Thus we think of a centaur by joining together in our mind a man and a horse; we imagine we are flying by attributing to ourselves the property of flying which belongs to planes or kites.

362. Phantasms play an important and necessary rôle in intellectual cognition. Our cognitive faculties, that is to say our exterior and interior senses and the intellect itself, are not independent agents, but partial factors of cognition. They all collaborate to make cognition possible; in fact, the final act of cognition is not performed exclusively by one or the other of our faculties, but by the person to whom they all belong. I can see, remember and understand; we do not say that our eyes see, our memory remembers, our intellect understands, but that we see with our eyes, we know with our faculties which are instruments of the global act of cognition.

363. With regard to the formation of phantasms, the collaboration between imagination and intellect is so great, that the one never works independently of the other. The highest acts of abstraction and intellection are always accompanied by, and involved in, phantasms, and the contents of our phantasms are amplified and enhanced by intellectual concepts. Concepts and mental images are theoretically two very distinct things; but in the act of cognition we make use of them simultaneously in such a manner that it is extremely difficult and almost impossible to be clearly conscious of what is pure concept and what is only mental image.

364. Phantasms are absolutely necessary for the formation of concepts; this necessity arises not from the nature of intellectual

cognition, but from the present state of union between body and mind. The intellect abstracts from phantasms the *material* or *stuff* of its spiritual concepts. Furthermore, in the very act of knowing or of understanding, the intellect turns again to phantasms and keeps them ever present, at least in a vague and indistinct manner, as if it fears it will lose sight of the concept if it cannot turn to the material phantasm from which it has formed the concept. It is something like a public speaker holding his script all the time he is speaking, giving it an occasional glance or at least conscious that he is holding it in case of a lapse of memory. Thus, whilst discussing or reflecting, we continually have recourse to concrete examples to illustrate our abstract concepts.

365. It is on account of this intimate collaboration that the mind feels the repercussion of any lesion of the cortical organ of imagination. For the same reason, physical fatigue and bad health make intellectual cognition more laborious, and during sleep, when the imagination is incapable of functioning in an orderly manner, the intellect also is handicapped.

366. Although we reject Innatism, namely the doctrine which holds that we can have mental images that are inborn and that do not owe their origin to sense-perception, it does not seem in opposition to scholastic teaching to maintain that some kind of innate thought is possible. Since the power of imagination is strictly dependent of brain structure, there would seem to be no reason to deny that heredity can influence image-formation, because the structure of the brain is inherited like the rest of the organism. This might explain certain natural ways of thinking and the special mental propensities of certain individuals. Musical, artistic, poetically minded people usually inherit their mental tendencies. Dullness and insanity are also inherited. Whole families and nations decay mentally. It is therefore quite possible that we inherit certain imaginative tendencies which incline the mind to a definite type or trend of thought, endowing us with what could be called *archetypes* or primordial ideas which pervade the general trend of thought throughout our life, giving to some a morose mind, to others a trivial one, to others a clever mind and so forth.

367. Mental images must not be confused with what are known as after-images. An *after-image* is the continued experience of a sense impression after the outward stimulus has ceased. It is due to

a certain inertia of our sense-organs, and is more pronounced in some senses than in others. For example, after a choir conductor has sounded his tuning-fork, he continues to hear the sound thus obtained long enough to be able to give the opening note to his singers. The prolongation of that note in the conductor's ear is an after-image. But if he gave the note without a tuning-fork, he would then be using, not an after-image, but a real mental image of a sound he has learnt in the past by repeated experience. Likewise, if we suddenly close our eyes, we are able to see for a few seconds certain objects we were looking at. Smell and taste often produce after-images; in fact we speak about an *after-taste*.

368. A mental image on the contrary is a permanent reproduction of a passing sense-impression. It is a copy of a past sensation. Thus we can mentally see a rose with our eyes shut. These images are copies of sensations previously experienced; people born blind can never think of colour or have any visual image, people born deaf can have no sound images, and so forth.

369. As a rule the term image is used only with reference to visual images which reproduce the colour and shape of things. But in a philosophical sense it is used for any kind of mental reproduction such as that of a tune or of the smell of onions. There are many kinds of images:

1. *Visual* images, such as those of the colour of a flower, or of the contour of a map.

2. *Sound* images, such as those of a tune, or of someone's accent in speaking.

3. *Motor* or muscular images, those for example we form when we mentally beat the time to music, silently pronounce the words we are reading, or imagine being taken down in a rapid lift, or cat-climbing a steep building.

4. *Smell* images, for example the thought of the smell of a rose.

5. *Taste* images, produced by thinking, for example, that we are enjoying our favourite dish or drink.

6. *Touch* images, when we think that we are touching, let us say, silk with rough fingers, or imagine that a spider is crawling up our leg, or when we hear someone say that he is itching.

7. *Temperature* images, which make us shudder at the thought of cold, or make us feel cold if the fire goes out, even if the room is quite warm.

8. *Pain* and *pleasure* images, which speak for themselves; pain images greatly increase the ordeal of a visit to the dentist, pleasure images often produce greater joy than the pleasant experience itself.

9. *Verbal* images, which are complex. They are composed of visual, sound and muscular images. We visualize the written word, although a blind person or one who cannot read would form no visual image of the words he is pronouncing; then we hear in our mind the sound of the words we think about, and finally we imagine the appropriate muscular movements of our speech organs without however pronouncing the words aloud. When we read, a kind of inner speech takes place in us, to such an extent that some people cannot refrain from whispering the words, or at least making with their lips the movements required for exterior speech.

CHAPTER 9

MEMORY

370. Memory is another internal sense and consists in the ability to recall past events and to recognize them. After the impressions produced on our imagination by the stimuli of our peripheral senses have been sorted out and collected by consciousness, they are transmitted as permanent impressions or images to this sense or faculty of memory; we say that they are *committed* to memory or memorized. Memory keeps them under control by enabling us to recall them in an orderly fashion. In fact, without this controlling power, cognition would be a rather unsatisfactory process. Our mental images would overwhelm us by their number and variety. By the laws of association or ideas, these images would all be constantly present to the mind, every thought would be submerged by an enormous variety of other thoughts, and thus cognition would be utterly muddled and confused.

371. Remembering a thing implies more than the mere thinking about it. In fact we can think of a thing without remembering it. To remember, it is necessary to recognize it. To *re*-cognize is to have a kind of second knowledge, to recall not only the image itself of a

thing, but to *place* that thing by reconstructing the circumstances, the background, and in one word, the associations which accompanied its previous formation in our mind. This recognition is most essential. Obstruction and confusion would be inevitable if a waiting crowd, for example, were to be admitted all at once through a theatre door. The superintendent admits them one by one, after recognizing them either personally, or by the number, for example, or price of their tickets.

372. To recall our mental images we follow the same rule; we recall them one by one as we need them. To do this, we must recognize, as it were, their claims to admission. This we do by retracing their origin, by identifying them as being the result of some particular past experience. If they do not tally with this identification test, we reject them. This is what we call *recognition*. To recognize means to connect our image with the object which occasioned it, to recall how, or when, or where, we made that image; in other words, it means to identify our images as having been produced by some definite former sensation or experience.

Thus, if we were asked the date of the battle of Hastings, and could not remember it, it is within the sphere of possibility that we might answer at random that it was 1066; we might hit upon that figure just by chance; in this case we would be actually thinking of the date, without however remembering it. So also, we say that we remember someone if we are able to recall when or where we met him, or some other detail that makes us recognize that person. To remember the lines of a piece of poetry, we must recall the position in which the words are placed, and recognize them as those written in the book.

Recognition, and consequently remembering, requires an effort at first; but it is accomplished spontaneously after a few efforts. Thus we recognize and remember the letters of the alphabet with the greatest ease on account of the frequent use we make of them. When beginning to learn Greek, on the contrary, we have to stop at many letters in order to recognize them. Repetition is therefore an important factor of memory.

373. The importance of *association* as a factor of memory is obvious. The more associations we consciously make when forming mental images, the easier will it be to remember these images. Associations act as the cues of memory; several are better than one,

because if one is not available, we can have recourse to the others. Great care must be taken in the choice of these associations; they must be as natural as possible, and must be easier to remember than the thing itself with which they are associated. All mnemonic systems are based on associations; they are methods of establishing associations in order to assist the memory. But without having recourse to any mnemonic system, we naturally make associations when we endeavour to learn. Looking at printed words, listening to someone pronouncing them, pronouncing them aloud ourselves, are visual, auditory and muscular associations which help us to remember a lesson. In order to remember the name of a thing in a foreign language, we associate it with the picture of that thing, the place where we have seen it, the uses to which it is put, and so forth.

374. In normal and healthy people, memory is much more efficient than is generally supposed. We do not usually forget things on account of poor memory, but because of some defect in our image-making process. Memory is impaired by age, bad health or defective constitution; but its inability to perform is not more frequent than defective intelligence is. Poor memory must be generally taken in a relative meaning. Thus people who, for example, cannot learn poetry by heart, usually have an extraordinary facility for something else, such as dates or names. Some never forget a face or easily remember colours, although they usually forget an appointment or a duty to be performed.

If we except extraordinary and rather infrequent cases, memory is rarely incapable of performing the functions we have a right to expect from it. The real and most frequent cause of forgetting is the fact that we do not take enough trouble to impress sufficiently the thing to be remembered upon our imagination; it consequently fades away and cannot be recalled. One of the reasons why a thing does not impress our mind, is our lack of interest and attention in the act of learning. We generally remember the things which interest and concern us, those, in a word, which we want to remember, although of course when plotting the curve of retention, we must take into consideration many factors such as native brain structure, the subject to be remembered, the background of study such as place, time, environment, health, fatigue, posture and the like.

375. Retroactive *inhibition* is another cause of our inability to remember. Subsequent images somehow tend to disintegrate and

impair preceding ones. It is as if the new patterns formed in the brain matter were disturbed by the new intruders before proper consolidation. This is called interference or interpolation in experimental psychology. There is also the fact of deliberate inhibition of which we know very little except that it enables us to check the natural flow of total recollection of our memory images. In fact, memory is a native power not only of recalling at choice certain images in preference to others, but also of temporarily forgetting other interfering and unwanted images. Forgetting is not always a disadvantage; it is a natural and necessary factor of the selective activity of our memory.

When dealing with the sense of memory, we must bear in mind that it is greatly assisted in its functions by the intellect and the will. The intellect is also a power of retention, recall and recognition, and it is not always possible to draw a line of demarcation between the functions of these two faculties. Furthermore the will is also an inhibitive power; that is to say, it can deliberately keep in the background images of which we have no actual need. It thus greatly assists memory in its controlling functions. We can deliberately forget, as has been said above.

CHAPTER 10

INSTINCT

376. We still have one more internal sense to deal with, namely instinct. This is a faculty common to both man and beast; but man's instinct is responsible for many actions far above mere animal life and is in such close contact with his intellectual faculties that it has been given a special name, that of *particular reason* or *cogitative faculty*. Since this superior type of human instinct is very different from ordinary animal instinct, we will deal here exclusively with instinct as it is found in irrational animals and in man only inasmuch as he acts like animals.

Animal instinct is an impulse to perform certain actions without any previous experience, and arises from the knowledge of what is useful or harmful to the organism. It is a characteristic of cognitive beings. The greater part of an animal's life is governed by instinct; man also frequently acts by instinct. Instinct is not a simple phenomenon, but consists of three distinct elements, which however are well-blended ingredients and do not prevent us from conceiving instinct as a single well defined phenomenon. These elements are an *impulse*, a *cognitive factor* and a *motor response*.

377. A natural *impulse* or tendency is the first factor of instinct. All things exist for a definite purpose in this world; they all have specific functions. Something from within inclines them to perform these functions. For want of a better word, we call this inclination a tendency or impulse. The physical attraction and repulsion of the elements, their natural properties and energies, their chemical affinities and reactions, growth and reproduction in the vegetal reign, are examples of the natural inclinations and tendencies common to all things. These tendencies are expressions of the latent forces of the things to which they belong, and consequently they vary according to the nature of those things. Thus a stone has no natural tendency to float in the air like smoke, because it has not the power to do so, being of a different nature.

378. The natural inclination of a thing is therefore directed to performing those functions of which its nature is capable. Some things have higher tendencies than others. The properties known as radio-activity for example, are of a superior sort to those of ordinary fire; the tendency of plants to reproduce themselves is on a higher plane than that of a chemical's reactive energy. The term *impulse* is generally used only in connection with the tendencies of cognitive beings, which are superior to those of non-cognitive ones. Therefore by impulse we mean the natural tendency of a cognitive being to perform the functions of which it is capable, for the betterment and advantage of the organism. A cognitive being is capable of functions which are not the mere outcome of physical, chemical or organic forces, but also of the cognitive energies. In other words, in cognitive beings, there are not only physical and organic tendencies, but also mental impulses. Therefore, although a cognitive impulse is but a special instance of the general inclination of all things towards the production of their natural effects, it has the very distinctive feature of being guided and

directed towards its object by thought, and not compelled to act by mere mechanical forces. Thus a stone thrown in the air is compelled to fall by the law of gravitation, whilst a dog's impulse to bark is governed entirely by the nature of the thoughts it entertains.

379. *Cognition* therefore, or the knowledge of the object towards which the organism is inclined, is the second factor of instinct. There is no doubt that instinct postulates this knowledge factor, which extends beyond the range of ordinary sense-stimulus. Thus the newly born kitten at once proceeds to the rather complicated action of sucking, not through direct sense stimulation, but because it instinctively knows that action to be a useful one. The mouse instinctively flees at the sight of the very first cat it sees, not because of the outward appearance of the cat, but because it has the instinctive knowledge that cats deal roughly with little mice. The study of animal behaviour reveals a most amazing possession of skilful knowledge. We call this knowledge the power of estimation, which is a translation of the Latin *aestimativa*. It makes the subject estimate the value of exterior things in terms of usefulness and harmfulness. This power is ranged alongside the other three internal senses.

380. Therefore animals have been endowed by nature with the power to know and appreciate the usefulness and harmfulness of the objects they perceive. But we must not exaggerate this cognitive factor. However marvellous animal behaviour may appear, there is no reason to believe that animals have any knowledge of the reasons directing their behaviour, and they certainly have no choice as to the means leading to their goal. Their knowledge does not extend beyond the usefulness or harmfulness of a few particular objects which they are able to pursue or reject according to circumstances.

381. *Motor response* is the third factor of instinct. The animal organism is supplied with special inherited arrangements of the nervous system, whereby it is able to perform a certain set of actions. These ready made schedules of action are known as patterns, and consist in pre-arranged nerve connections which are automatically set in motion at certain moments. They are fixed and invariable mechanisms ready to function in a pre-established manner as soon as the organism is suitably aroused. They could be compared to the mechanism in modern organs which enables the organist to change the whole arrangement of his stops by pressing a button, thus setting in motion a whole new series of stops selected by him before starting

to play. The execution and specification of animal behaviour in accordance with these pre-arranged patterns, is made possible by the driving factor of instinct, that is, the power of estimation. A hen does not go broody on account of pure mechanical drives; it does so in response to an impulse aroused by the inherited knowledge that it is useful for her to do so; nothing will induce her to do so if she does not care to. You cannot make a donkey move or force a cat to eat food it does not care for.

CHAPTER II

EMOTIONS AND REFLEXES

382. Besides cognition, there are two other manifestations of animal life, namely emotion, and muscular reactions or reflexes. *Emotion* implies much more than a mere physical impression or feeling such as the bodily sensations of hunger and fatigue. Emotions are termed *passions* by the scholastics. Modern phraseology reserves the name of passion for emotions of an intense or violent degree. A *sentiment* is also an emotion, but usually denotes a more refined kind of emotion.

383. Now although we all know experimentally what it is for example to be happy, excited or embarrassed, it is extremely difficult to describe an emotion. We will propose the following as a tentative definition: *An adaptation of the organism to a conscious physical reaction.* We say that it is an adaptation. In fact, it is a sort of tuning of the organism, something far more subtle than a mere organic modification. It is an attitude or state produced in our organism by certain conscious reactions. Thus the emotion of fear is a response of the organism to our apprehension of danger; joy results from the tuning of the organism to the conscious perception of some agreeable object.

384. Emotions are always accompanied by an organic modification such as acceleration of the pulse, heavy breathing, variations in

blood pressure, restlessness, fatigue, thirst and the like. Sometimes they are even manifested by specific overt behaviour and by motor responses such as shouting, dancing, or pacing up and down, gesticulating, flight, and so on. Facial language which includes smiling, laughing, sobbing, and a large number of facial movements, especially of the eyes, is another expression of emotion. To these must be added vocal expression or inflexions of speech, and of course the language of gestures.

385. But it is important to remark that emotion does not consist in this bodily alteration. To feel angry is something quite different from shouting or clenching the fists, fear is not the same thing as the trembling and the sudden cessation of the digestive process. Indeed it often happens that the pathological changes generally coupled with an emotion are manifested in circumstances when no such emotion is present. Thus some of the symptoms of fear are registered during the physical excitement experienced after a long race, or after running up the stairs. On the other hand, man is sometimes able to control his emotions so completely that hardly any of the habitual organic symptoms are observed or take place. This points to a difference between a feeling or emotion and the bodily change produced by it.

386. The number of our emotions is enormous. A complete list of them would be long and tedious. Some of them have many varieties not easily distinguishable, such as surprise, amazement and wonder, or aversion, disgust, loathing and hate. Attempts have been made to classify emotions, but none seem to be entirely satisfactory. St. Thomas enumerates eleven principal emotions which he calls passions, namely: love and hatred, desire and aversion, joy and grief, hope and despair, courage and fear, and finally anger.

387. *Reflexes.*—Animals are able to perform certain actions by instinct—as we have already seen—and man is capable of many deliberate movements and actions by the sheer power of his will. But besides these actions, there are others which are called *reflexes*, and which are reactions of the muscular system to certain stimuli of the nervous system. They are of two kinds, automatic or unconditioned, acquired or conditioned reflexes.

388. *Automatic* or unconditioned reflexes are those muscular movements of which we are not conscious at all, or at the most, only after the fact, as, for example, changes in the circulatory, respiratory

and digestive functions due to external stimuli, sneezing, coughing, blushing, blinking, accommodation of the crystalline lens, the motion of the arm to protect the head from a falling object, the knee-jerk when knocked, the withdrawal of the hand from a burning object, the closing of the eye at the contact of a foreign body, and so forth.

On account of the multiple interconnections of sensory and motor fibres of the nervous system, these simple automatic reflexes often merge into more complex responses. One stimulus can produce several reactions; thus a loud bang can make us jump, exclaim and breathe quickly. On the other hand, the same reflex can be produced by different kinds of stimuli; thus the reflex of turning round can be caused either by being called, or by being tapped on the shoulder, or by a sudden flash of a light.

389. *Acquired* or conditioned reflexes are movements previously learnt, and are produced by a stimulus which has no immediate apparent connexion with them, and which, of its nature, would normally be the cause of some other kind of reaction. Thus for example, to beat the time with one's foot is not a direct organic response to the auricular stimulation produced by the hearing of music; the casual muscular movement of picking up a pin from the floor whilst engaged in conversation, is not neurologically related in a direct manner to the sight-stimulus caused by the pin. A great many of our daily actions are acquired reflexes, and often develop into habits.

Acquired reflexes are called conditioned responses because they are the result of various stimulated conditions in which the organism has previously been placed. They differ from purely automatic reflexes such as the knee-jerk, and from the deliberate actions performed intentionally by man, and have to be learnt by sense-experience. The infant cannot perform them until it has learnt the possibility and the manner of performing them.

390. There are different ways of learning to perform these acquired reflexes, that for example of watching and observing, even unconsciously, other people. In this way we learn to accomplish most of the routine work of our lives such as dressing, writing and so forth. Apprentices become clever craftsmen in this way. Practical demonstrations are given for this purpose. Some reflexes are acquired by random movements of our limbs which we are inclined to repeat if we find that they result in an agreeable experience. In this way we generally acquire our characteristic manner of sitting, standing and

so forth, and many personal mannerisms. Some reflexes are produced by what psychologists call the trial and error method, others by interior or exterior sense stimuli not directly connected with them. In this latter manner a dog is taught to beg by giving it a piece of sugar, and we assume facial expressions corresponding to our internal emotions.

391. *Habits.* Acquired reflexes generally become habits. In fact a habit can be defined as an acquired reflex or muscular movement performed easily and even unconsciously. Habits are acquired by the frequent repetition of the same act and would seem to be due to grooves formed in the structure of the organism, especially in the plastic matter of the nervous web. Frequent sense-stimuli leave permanent traces in the organism and form, so to say, trodden pathways, ingrown and sometimes indelible impressions, as a name carved on a tree will grow with it and become part of its structure.

392. But if this physiological explanation would seem sufficient to account for many manual and motor habits such as walking, dressing, writing, and so forth, intellectual and volitional habits cannot be interpreted as mere products of reflex behaviour. These habits are rooted in the spiritual soul which possesses a native tendency to perform in a more natural, efficient and orderly manner those acts which it often repeats. Thus intellectual and volitional habits originate through the deliberate repetition of intellectual and volitional acts.

393. *Two remarks* must be made. The first is that the will is in command of most of our reflex behaviour. The will is therefore theoretically responsible for all our habits, in the sense that it has the power to inhibit those actions the repetition of which engenders the habit, and those also which would naturally flow from a habit already acquired. It is therefore in the power of the will to acquire, to strengthen, to inhibit and to eliminate all habits.

The second remark is that although the will is spiritual, there is no such thing as a pure volitional act as long as the soul is united to the body. Just as the intellect requires the help of sensory cognition to perform its act, so also the will does not act independently of the reflex mechanism of the body. The will can only pursue an object inasmuch as it is presented to it by the intellect, and the intellect can only apprehend that which is presented to it by the senses. Strong mental and bodily habits can therefore sometimes indirectly overpower the will. Mental habits do so by rendering the intellect incapable of presenting to the will suitable objects of pursuit, bodily habits by making the task of controlling them so strenuous that the will often breaks down under the effort. They cannot of course force the consent of the will, but they can prove too rebellious for the will to uphold its command. It must be remembered that body and soul are so intimately united that there is no such thing as purely bodily or purely spiritual functions of any kind; both body and soul concur in all our functions; whilst united, the one cannot act without the other. To eliminate a habit, an act of the will is not sufficient; the nervous system must co-operate and to do this it must actually destroy in its own self the pathways created by the repeated impressions made upon it. This often becomes a task which is beyond its power.

CHAPTER 12

THE INTELLECT

394. We must now tackle the problem of the human soul and that of its specific faculties, the intellect and the will. We shall deal first with the intellect, because a thorough knowledge of the intellectual act is absolutely necessary in order to explain the nature and the characteristics of the intellectual soul.

The intellect is a spiritual faculty capable of knowing the nature of both material and immaterial objects. By calling it spiritual we mean that it is not a material faculty like our bodily organs and senses; this negative manner of describing it does not really tell us in what the intellect itself consists, but it is all we are able to discover about the nature of a faculty which soars high above all others.

395. The intellect is often called *mind*. This however is an equivocal term, and the indiscriminate use which is made of it is the source of numerous misgivings in psychology. Indeed, mind can refer either to the spiritual faculty of the intellect or to the power of imagination which has its seat in the brain matter. Great care must therefore be taken to avoid this ambiguity when using the term mind, by specifying in which of these very different meanings we are speaking of it.

396. Mind and intellect are also sometimes used for the soul itself. Although the soul is distinct from its faculties and consequently from the intellectual mind, it is only natural to designate the soul by the name of its noblest faculty, since it is only through the knowledge of our intellectual acts that we are able to arrive at the knowledge of the soul itself.

397. *Spirituality* of the intellectual mind. We prove that the intellect is a spiritual faculty in the following way. The intellect, like all other cognitive faculties, must be altered or modified in order to perform its act, as we have seen when explaining the nature of cognition. Now the factor which thus modifies it is an abstract concept, and an abstract concept cannot possibly modify a material organ. Therefore the intellect cannot be a material organ, or in other words, it is spiritual.

398. When matter is altered, it is evident that it must be altered in a definite manner and degree. If for example, a billiard ball is altered, the alteration must assume some definite form; the ball cannot be changed to a vague and indetermined size, shape, colour, and so forth. Alterations wrought in matter are always of a definite extent and measure, since they consist either in an increase or decrease of its qualities, or in a direct change of its quantitative dimensions.

In fact, matter is so intimately tied up with quantity, that it cannot exist without definite quantitative dimensions. It has a transcendental or essential relation to quantity and cannot even be conceived without it, to such an extent that matter has been wrongly identified by some philosophers with quantity. The reason is that matter owes to quantity the individuality of its concrete existence. Matter cannot exist unless it has an individual existence, and it cannot have an individual existence without quantity, as we have already seen in Cosmology. Therefore any alteration of matter must necessarily affect the quantity which circumscribes it.

399. If the intellect were a material organ, it could hardly be conceived as being located elsewhere than in the brain. Now it is an undisputed psychological fact, that brain-matter undergoes a modification in the process of image-making. Mental images are accompanied by nerve and cell mutations in the cortical matter, and, like all other material alterations, this cortex modification must be of a definite measurable nature. This altered state must differ from the previous one in a concrete and individual manner. If science were in

possession of sufficiently advanced means, it would be able to measure and tabulate the exact degree and mode of brain alteration in each one of its cognitive acts, in the same way as the impressions caused in our exterior senses can, to a certain extent, be expressed in measurable terms.

But if brain matter is altered, there must be a cause to produce this alteration. And since each alteration has a definite individual character, its cause must also possess definite individual characteristics. Thus a seal which impresses in wax the shape and details of an image, must necessarily possess that same shape and those same details; that image could not be made by a seal of a different shape and of different details. Likewise, the exact manner in which the cortex is altered depends entirely on the individual characteristics impressed upon it by the concrete objects of its cognition via the stimuli these produce on the sense-organs. When brain-matter is modified, an exact pattern of the sense-perceived object is produced in it, something like that produced in a photographic camera. We can therefore conclude, and the conclusion is of the greatest importance, that it is the individual characteristics of the cognized object which cause cortex alteration and consequently brain cognition in the form of mental images. There is no other way of explaining the individual character of brain alteration in the formation of mental images.

400. Now it requires no special effort to go a step further, and to argue that an object which has no individual and dimensional characteristics could not possibly modify brain-matter, and consequently could not be known by the brain. But no abstract concepts, by definition, have any individual characteristics of matter; they abstract from all dimension, intensity and degree of matter. There is therefore nothing in them that can determine the individual character or pattern of brain modification, and consequently they cannot possibly be impressed upon brain matter, which by its very nature, can only be impressed and altered by something having definite individual dimensional characteristics and features. Since mental images act as a seal which stamps upon the delicate plastic structure of the brain its shape and its details, it is obviously impossible for brain matter or any other matter to receive the imprint of images which have no shape and no individual dimensional features. Consequently, as it is indubitable that we have abstract concepts, there must be in us some other faculty or power which has

not the material impediment of matter, and which can be impressed by an object abstracted from all its material features. We call this faculty the non-material or spiritual mind or intellect.

401. *Reflection.* The foregoing remarks are an attempt to explain the axiom quoted in text-books in order to prove the spirituality of the soul, namely: *Whatsoever is received, is received according to the nature of the recipient.* There is, however, yet another way of proving the same truth by considering our power of reflection. Matter cannot reflect, whilst the intellect is capable of the deepest and most penetrating reflection upon itself and upon its own acts.

Each part of matter, on account of its quantitative individuality, necessarily excludes every other part. Precisely because matter has distinct parts, there can be no fusion or community amongst these parts, each one having its own special individual quantity which it can share with no other. These parts are joined together, but they have nothing in common with each other except the indivisible extremities by which each of these parts is joined to the following. These common extremities, however, are indivisible and unextended, and are consequently not parts of the divisible whole. Therefore, although one part of matter, let us say for example, one part of a piece of paper, can be applied over or upon another part by folding the paper in two, yet one part cannot be folded over its own self; the part over which it is folded is different from that part which is folded over it. Therefore, because it is material, the brain cannot reflect, that is to say, it cannot return upon its own self, and consequently it cannot introspect its own actions, any more than the eye can know the nature and the laws of visual perception.

But the intellect can penetrate into the inner recesses of its own nature and reconsider its own acts. It can reflect on its own self and on the very act by which it is reflecting. There is nothing in its own self that it cannot scrutinize and penetrate.

402. We are therefore entitled to conclude that a mind capable of a reflective act must be spiritual. Precisely because it is not material, it has no parts, and is not encompassed by quantitative dimensions. Consequently the whole of it is entirely wherever it is; it is completely present to its own self. And thus we can conclude that the mind is not material in its composition, not only because it can form abstract concepts, but also because it is able to reflect upon these concepts and to introspect its own intellectual acts.

CHAPTER 13

THE AGENT INTELLECT

403. Besides the intellectual mind of which we have spoken in the preceding chapter, there is what is called the *agent intellect,* which is our intellectual power of abstraction. The purpose of the agent intellect is to transform phantasms or mental images into intelligible ideas or concepts by presenting them to the intellectual mind without their material individual characteristics.

A *concept* is the mental representation of the nature of a thing abstracted from all the individual characteristics of matter. It is the result of the process of abstraction, and is often referred to as an abstract concept, although of course all concepts are abstract. The thought of a triangle simply as a figure bounded by three lines and containing three angles, without specifying its size or shape, that of an animal without reference to any particular kind of animal, whether it be a horse, a fly or a sea-monster, are concepts. Thus also the concept *man* does not represent any particular person, but just man in general, whosoever he may be: tall or short, king or beggar, white or black; it just bears upon that by which man is a human being, and not a tree, a tiger or a house.

404. Great care must be taken to distinguish such abstract concepts from mental images. It is a distinction of great importance since the proof of the soul's spirituality is based upon it, as we have just seen. Yet the utmost confusion reigns on this subject. Most people include under the general terms of idea or thought, the very distinct products of our imagination and of our intellect.

An *idea* in its strict scholastic interpretation, is an *archetype,* that is, a mental representation of something to be made or accomplished. But it is often used in a much more general meaning to designate both an intellectual concept and a mental image or phantasm. Therefore this term, like that of *thought,* must be interpreted in the light of the context, because both of them are susceptible of the twofold meaning of concept and mental image.

405. Concepts represent things in a different way to that in which these things exist in reality, namely without their individual features. In fact no representation reproduces all the physical reality of a represented object; the most faithful representations made for example

by paintings, photographic plates, television screens, or even by the senses, let us say by the eye, do not reproduce objects in their material reality. The eye does not perceive the whole of an object; it perceives or *abstracts* its colour, without any of its other qualities such as its heat, weight and so forth. The things we see are not reproduced in the eye with their material reality, but with a kind of spiritual, or as we say, *intentional* mode of existence. Each of our senses selects, and *abstracts*, so to say, the particular quality it is meant to perceive.

406. We must however beware of thinking that concepts represent things as really existing without their individual features. Concepts are true and faithful representations. The abstract concept of *man*, for example, does not make us conceive man as not having any special height, weight or other individual features, but it simply makes us think of a man without thinking of these features. Thus we define man as a rational being and are not concerned with his height, colour, or his particular features. When we conceive *colour* in general without referring to any particular colour, we do not imply that an object could be actually coloured in a nondescript manner without any special colour at all.

407. Abstraction therefore simply divests an object of its physical dispositions or qualities such as colour, resistance and so forth, and also of its mathematical or quantitive conditions, namely size, weight and so on. The concept thus abstracted is objective and corresponds to reality, because its object, which is the nature of things, really exists outside our mind and is contained in the sense-phantasms. Abstract knowledge is therefore not illusory or false.

408. Now abstraction is performed by what we call the *agent intellect*. This mysterious agent intellect is therefore nothing else but our innate power of performing the difficult operation of abstraction and thus of forming abstract concepts. And although abstraction requires an effort, it is certainly easier to perform than it is to endeavour to form concepts of things that are already abstract, namely of immaterial things such as spirits, which have no material characteristics from which to abstract. The materiality of things, which can be sense-perceived, provides us with a kind of spring-board or starting point which the cognition of spirits does not give us. This is why material things, and not spiritual objects, form the primary and direct object of our intellectual knowledge.

409. It is difficult to express in clear and cut terms exactly in what the process of abstraction consists, but some kind of insight can be obtained by describing the agent intellect as a light, and its abstractive operation as an illumination. This is much more than a mere comparison, because the agent intellect really is a kind of light, and is in fact commonly called the *light of reason*. When confronted with a problem which we fail to understand, we say that we are in the dark; we talk of dark terms, obscure passages and sayings; light on the contrary is a synonym of understanding and knowledge, since we ask to be enlightened on a subject, or for light to be thrown on an obscure quotation, and so forth. Bright minds are those gifted with superior power, and we use almost indiscriminately the words *to see* and *to understand*.

410. Abstraction is therefore a kind of intellectual and spiritual illumination which makes the hidden nature of things contained in phantasms visible to our intellect; this it does by giving to them a spiritual and intelligble appearance, just as the switching on of a light in a dark room makes the room visible to the eye, or as a microscope or an x-ray reveals objects otherwise invisible. Indeed, phantasms are constantly offering to the intellect an enticing bait, namely objects possessing an intelligible nature. The intellect however cannot grasp this bait, it cannot reach it, on account of the manner in which it is presented, namely because this nature is hidden by the individual and material characteristics which encompass it. The function of the agent intellect is precisely to discard these hindering features and thus to reveal the nature behind them.

411. Unless we deny that we have abstract concepts, we must admit the existence of the agent intellect. In fact, if we admit that we are able to form abstract concepts of things which in their extramental reality are concrete, we must logically admit that we have the power to make them abstract. This power to abstract is all that the name agent intellect is meant to convey. The main objection lies, not so much in the difficulty of admitting the existence of the agent intellect, but in that of admitting it to be a distinct faculty of its own.

412. But when we talk about this duality of intellects and say that we have two intellects, one the agent, the other the passive intellect, we do not mean that we have two intellectual minds. There is only one thinking mind, only one intellect which understands and comprehends, namely the passive intellect. This passive intellect upon which

are impressed the abstract images or concepts of things, is the intellect proper which performs the actual operation of understanding the object presented to it by the agent intellect. The passive intellect comprehends, the agent intellect makes a thing comprehensible. The passive intellect grasps the meaning of a concept, the agent intellect forms the concept. The agent intellect is called intellect simply to distinguish it from the senses, and to indicate that it partakes in the global act of understanding by preparing the way for this intellectual operation. In other words, it is easier to grasp what is meant by the agent intellect by saying that our intellectual mind has two distinct functions, namely the power of understanding and the power of illuminating phantasms in order to make them understandable.

CHAPTER 14

THE INTELLECTUAL SPECIES

413. We have just said that the agent intellect abstracts, and thus reveals to the mind the hidden nature of things. The result of this abstraction is called an *intellectual species*. Now there are two kinds of intellectual species, called the impressed and the expressed species, and it is of the utmost importance to understand exactly what we mean by these terms.

414. The *impressed species* is the spiritual appearance or form given to an object by the agent intellect. The object of intellectual cognition is the universal nature which exists in individual things. This nature is contained *fundamentally* in the concrete object and in the phantasm; but it is not *formally* there, namely not as a universal. It has to be made formally universal by the agent intellect and is then called a species. To become intelligible, an object has to be denuded of all its individual characteristics and quantitative properties by the agent intellect, which spiritualizes the material phantasm, thus transforming it into something actually intelligible and capable of impressing the spiritual mind. This spiritualized phantasm is called a *species* from a Latin word meaning appearance. It is called an *impressed* species because it is actually impressed upon the intellect

when the act of knowing takes place. An impressed species is also called a concept or an idea.

Therefore an impressed species or concept is the means by which our spiritual mind is able to know material things, since it presents, or *re*-presents, to the mind in an intelligible manner an object which has already been presented to the senses in its exterior reality. It is evidently not the species or the concept which we know, but the object represented by the species; the species is only the medium of cognition.

415. When we say that the species is impressed, we must cast aside any material interpretation of the term impression, since there can be no question of a physical mark imprinted upon a spiritual mind. It would be perhaps more helpful to think of the meaning the word conveys in phrases such as *he made a good impression*, or *I was impressed*. The real meaning intended here is that the mind is stirred or aroused from its passive state into action, just as an impression generally arouses in us some kind of functional activity. In what precise manner the mind is impressed and stirred, we do not know. We can conceive an entirely spiritual impression of this kind only by analogy with the physical impressions made on the senses.

The sense-species is, in a certain manner, also a spiritualized species. No one would maintain that a known object is impressed either upon the sense-organs or on the brain matter in all its material reality. Something happens to it; it is shorn of part of its materiality. In point of fact the picture of a tree on the retina of the eye, or on the brain in the form of a mental image, is not as big as the real tree, neither is it, for example, unyielding or moist. It abstracts from these qualities, and, thus denuded of their gross materiality, it acquires a kind of immateriality or spirituality. However, it reproduces the quantitative proportions of the object, although in a different manner to that in which they exist in that object; this fact suffices to enable the material organ upon which it is impressed to be modified by it. But the intelligible species abstracts even from the quantitative proportions of matter, and can therefore only be impressed upon an entirely spiritual faculty.

416. This impressed species, by stirring the mind, becomes the cause, the formal cause, which makes the mind know one thing rather than another; it is a spiritual form which informs the mind and specifies the act by which it knows. We would be making more than

a comparison if we likened it to the substantial form which makes a thing that which it is and different from other things. It is for this reason called the *formal* and specifying cause or factor of intellectual cognition. It is like the mould or pattern which brings into existence particular figures or images.

The impressed species is therefore the *means* of intellectual cognition. This does not mean that our cognition is *indirect*, as if we knew first the concept and then the object it represents; in such a case knowledge would not be objective, since we would not know the object as it really was but only as the concept made it appear to us. On the contrary, the species is the means of cognition in the sense that we know first of all and directly the object as it is in itself through, or rather in, the intellectual species as in a mirror, which however, as has already been explained, does not distort or falsify our knowledge. The species or concept representing the object is only known indirectly by a reflex act of the mind.

417. The impressed species is also called an *intentional* species. Intentional here is simply a synonym of spiritual. The concept itself is said to have an intentional, namely, a spiritual existence, and is often referred to as an intention. Thus we speak of concepts of the first and of the second intention.

418. A concept of the *first intention* represents that which the mind intends primarily and directly when conceiving the concept. For example, if we form the concept *man*, we primarily intend and wish to think about the human nature of man. A concept of the *second intention* results from an ulterior act of the mind, a second act, by which, after having arrived at the knowledge of human nature, it begins to consider and reflect upon the nature, not of that which is represented by the concept, namely the human nature, but upon the nature of the concept itself which it has formed.

419. Now the characteristic property of concepts of material things is their universality; a concept of the second intention is therefore one which represents the universality, that is to say the logical extension of these concepts. Thus we form a concept of the second intention by considering *man* as one of the species of the genus *animal*. To sum up, a concept of the first intention, which is also called a direct, metaphysical, categorical or predicamental concept, is that which represents the abstract nature of something belonging to one of the ten predicaments. A concept of the second

intention on the contrary, which is also called a logical, indirect or reflex concept, represents the universality of a concept, that is to say, one of the five predicables. It is important to observe that the primary act of cognition is not reflection, or an act by which it conceives reflex concepts of the second intention, but the direct knowledge of concepts of the first intention.

420. The *expressed species* is the manner of being of, or the appearance assumed by, the mind when it cognizes a thing through the medium of the impressed species.

The mere act of abstraction accomplished by the agent intellect when it forms or conceives an impressed species, does not complete the act of intellection. All that it does achieve is the presentation to the mind of an abstract nature that can be impressed upon it and understood, and which we therefore call an *intelligible,* not an *intellected* species. The function of the impressed species is to stir the mind into action. The mind consequently reacts, and this reaction constitutes the act of intellection, an act quite distinct from that by which the agent intellect abstracts and illuminates. Intellection is the act by which the mind actually considers the nature of an object made intelligible by the spiritual appearance or manner of being, given to it by the impressed species. When the mind looks at this clarified or spiritualized appearance of an object, it sees through or in it, the nature of the object itself. This vision of the object thus spiritualized by the species, is called the expressed species.

The expressed species is therefore the nature of an object actually considered, not in its physical reality, but in the representative or abstract mode of existence given to it by the impressed species. It is an interior expression of the concept in the intellect itself, and is also called *word* of the mind, often expressed by words of the imagination and of speech. No instant of time separates the formation of the impressed and expressed species, but the one is not the other. The expressed species is the result or product of the act of intellection; the impressed species is the result of the act of abstraction.

421. We have said that the expressed species is the appearance assumed by the mind itself when the mind is modified by the impressed species. The mind in fact then becomes actually knowing, and has a different intellectual appearance than when it is simply able to know, without actually knowing. All knowledge is a modification; intellectual cognition is no exception. Furthermore all know-

ledge is a modification which assimilates and unites more or less the knower to the known thing. Knowledge consists in grasping, holding, taking in, the known object; the intimacy or this inward reception increases with the perfection of knowledge. Intellectual knowledge is the highest of all immanent actions, namely of actions which modify the agent itself. Transient actions modify not the agent, but an outside object; fire for example, does not modify itself, but the burnt object.

422. Now in intellection, the union of the known object to the intellect is so intimate, that the object becomes one with the intellect; the modification it produces affects the knowing intellect so greatly, that the intellect is transformed into the known object, to such a degree that we say that the intellect considered as actually knowing an object, is identical with that object considered as being known. It is like a red hot poker united to the red glow of the furnace in which it is heated.

423. Now it is this appearance of the knowing intellect which we call the expressed species; it is the term, the aim and final result of the grasping and comprehending of the known object, the completion of the mind's reaction to the impression made by the impressed species. Whilst the impressed species is the pattern or the mould, the expressed species is the resulting image and pattern produced by the mould. Therefore the impressed species is a spiritual modification of the *phantasm* which renders the phantasm an intelligible representation or image of the object. The expressed species on the contrary is a modification *of the mind* itself, which makes the mind spiritually resemble the object it knows, thus producing in its own self a perfect image of that object.

424. This distinction between impressed and expressed species is hard to grasp. It is difficult enough to understand exactly what is a species or an intellectual image in general; to grapple with distinctions between species would seem to be beyond the reach of the human mind. The difficulty arises from the fact that we are forced to have recourse to material symbols and examples, whilst in reality there are none of a spiritual species. The important thing to realize is that the existence of both species is an entirely intellectual one since a species only exists in the mind; therefore any difference between them must be an intellectual or mental difference. The impressed species differs from the expressed species because it has a

different manner of existing in the mind, the impressed species representing a thing simply as cognizable, the expressed species, on the contrary, as actually known by the mind.

CHAPTER 15

DIRECT AND REFLEX KNOWLEDGE

425. There are two kinds of knowledge according to which of two distinct kinds of concepts we draw it from. We primarily and directly know the nature of the material things that surround us; indirectly and in a reflex manner we are also able to know our own acts and other spiritual things. Hence we divide knowledge into direct and reflex.

426. *Direct* knowledge is either discursive or intuitive. Discursive knowledge is the particular kind of knowledge proper to man alone, and is acquired by a kind of mental discourse. He acquires knowledge step by step, by proceeding from the knowledge of one thing to that of another. In spite of their spiritual nature, our intellectual functions are subject to time, because, whilst the soul is united to a body, its spiritual acts are dependent on phantasms which are acquired in time. This is why judgments are necessary, because simple apprehension or formation of concepts does not give us full knowledge; we have to join these concepts by adding each new concept to one we have previously conceived and in the comprehension of which we perceive it to be contained. Thus a judgment is a process performed in time, and is called a discursive process.

That we should have to acquire our concepts in time through sense-cognition has been denied by those who maintain that we have been endowed from birth with what they call *innate* or inborn ideas. That we have no innate ideas results from the following facts. Firstly, there are no ideas the sense-origin of which cannot be accounted for; even the origin of transcendent ideas can be traced to phantasms drawn from sense-cognition. Neither is it possible to recall or to use a concept without having recourse to an individual image or a concrete example. Secondly, the child starts life with the knowledge it gradually obtains via its senses; if it had inborn ideas, these would be the first to be manifested. Thirdly, the privation from birth of one of the senses such as sight, automatically deprives a man of all and any ideas which originate in that sense, the concept of colour in the case of blindness.

427. *Reason* is the special name given to our discursive intellect. It points to our particular manner of acquiring knowledge which is gradual, each step being linked with the next one by a common thought, as the consecutive chords of a harmony are generally united by a common note. This common concept forms what is called in Logic the middle term of a syllogism. The syllogism typifies the act of reasoning. This does not mean that each time we reason we must make a syllogism in the strict form laid down in Logic. Yet the words we use in any type of reasoning could be re-arranged in syllogistic form. If they cannot, we can rest assured that there is some flaw in our reasoning, since there can be no exception to the elementary laws of good reasoning laid down in the treatise on syllogisms.

428. Discursive knowledge is opposed to *intuitive* knowledge which consists in being able to see all at once everything that does or does not belong to a thing. Intuitive knowledge would enable us to know all there is to be known about trees, for example, without having to study at all, as soon as we had conceived the idea of tree.

429. Evidently this is not our usual way of acquiring knowledge. It belongs to the superior spirits which we call angels. However, we have an intuitive knowledge of the first principles, since they form the starting point of our reasoning process. But apart from the knowledge of these principles, our knowledge of all other truths is discursive, that is to say it proceeds from the knowledge of principles to that of conclusions which we have to demonstrate. Thus we gradually build and increase our knowledge, whilst Angels understand all there is to be known by one simple glance at the infused ideas they possess, without any effort or study. Therefore in Angels, not only first principles, but all conclusions are self-evident truths.

430. The concepts we have dealt with so far are concepts abstracted from the material things which surround us. In fact, it is the hidden nature of these material things which constitutes the primary and direct object of our intellectual faculty. This object comprises both the nature and the component elements of the nature of material things, such as matter and form, essence and

existence; it also includes all the attributes and accidents of these things considered in an abstract manner.

But the abstract cognition of the material world does not exhaust the potential capacity of the intellectual mind. In fact, the intellect is by nature able to know anything that is intelligible. Now there are many intelligible things which are not material, such as the concepts themselves by which we know the nature of things, the act of abstraction, of intellection, of reflection, and also of spiritual volition, not to mention others such as speculative and moral judgements. Furthermore the human soul, the disembodied spirits called Angels, and the Supreme Spirit called God, are eminently intelligible, since they are by nature abstract, and consequently, in themselves more intelligible than the nature of material objects which have to be painfully abstracted from their materiality.

431. These spiritual and abstract objects however, do not constitute the primary and direct object of our knowledge, because our mind is primarily made to know the nature of those things the cognition of which can be shared by its bodily senses. Spiritual objects are therefore called the secondary or indirect object of the mind. They are known by an indirect act of the mind, an act which is also called a *reflex act*. We express this by saying that the mind knows the abstract nature of material things by a direct act of the *first intention*, or as it were, by a first glance, whilst it knows immaterial things by a reflex act, a second glance, or an act of the *second intention*. This act is called reflex because it consists in returning over, or re-inspecting, concepts we have already formed, by reflecting upon our own intellectual acts and thoughts by a new intellectual act.

432. The first objects of reflex knowledge are our concepts and our intellectual functions. These do not represent the primary and direct object of our knowledge because we primarily know the nature of things represented by concepts, not the concepts themselves or the act by which we know them; in fact there are many people who have not the faintest idea of the nature either of their concepts or of that of the functions of their intellect. It is only by deep reflection that we are able to form a vague idea of what a concept really is, and of the manner in which our intellect functions.

433. The second object of reflex knowledge is the essence or nature of our soul. We arrive at this knowledge by scrutinizing the abstract nature of our intellectual functions, and thus conclude that

there must be in us an abiding principle, independent of matter, and spiritual in nature.

434. The third object of reflex knowledge is the disembodied spirit which we call Angel. This knowledge is not only reflex and indirect, but also very imperfect. We can only have a generic idea of Angels. We know that they are of the same generic kind as our own spiritual soul, but we do not know in what they differ from our soul, except in a negative way, namely that they have no bodies. The fourth object of reflex knowledge is God himself. We have not even a generic knowledge of God, but only an imperfect analogical one.

CHAPTER 16

THE INDIVIDUAL CONCEPT

435. In this chapter we have to face a rather serious difficulty in view of the fact that we have insisted that all concepts are abstract and represent the universal nature of a thing, and not the concrete individual as it exists outside our mind. Yet it is an undeniable fact that we frequently do make judgements of the following kind: *Peter is intelligent, you are hungry, this is a book.* Terms such as *Peter, you, this book,* are indubitably particular and non-distributive, representing individual and not universal concepts.

Therefore it must be possible to form not only universal, but also individual concepts. In fact there are immaterial substances, Angels for example, which cannot be conceived as universal, since no two Angels have a common nature; they cannot therefore exist or be known otherwise than as individuals.

436. We must point out first of all that it is not the individuality as such, but the materiality of a thing which prevents it from being actually intelligible. Universality as such is not an essential but an accidental attribute, added to the concept by a second or reflex act of the mind which many people, all in fact except philosophers, hardly make at all. The immediate purpose of the act of abstraction

is to abstract from the materiality of a thing, and thus an abstract concept is always spiritual, but of itself it is neither actually individual or universal; it is, so to say, indifferent as to whether it represents an individual or a universal nature. Concepts of material things are indeed potentially universal and can become actually so by reflection, that is to say by a further act called a reflex act, which is a kind of indirect or second glance of the mind and which is for this reason called a second intention. By this act we consider the abstract nature represented by the concept as belonging to many individuals, namely as a universal, if in fact it does belong to many; if however it happens to belong only to one individual such as Peter or this stone, it is evident that even by reflecting upon such a concept we cannot make it universal.

437. Therefore there is no contradiction involved in saying that an abstract concept is individual, since abstract is not opposed to individual, but to material. This is why we can use a concrete word as the subject of a proposition, and say *Peter* is intellgent, *this book* is interesting. As a matter of fact, all concrete words used as the subject of a proposition primarily refer to individual objects. We say that they have an individual or personal supposition. This means that when I say that Peter is intelligent, I am visualizing abstract human nature as existing in this individual man *Peter*, although I could think of it as belonging to many other men.

438. It will be objected that although theoretically it be possible to form an abstract concept of an individual, practically it is impossible to do so with regard to material things. Their individuality, in fact, is tied up with their materiality in such a way that we cannot abstract from the one without abstracting from the other, because it is precisely their material features that make them individual; their individual features are necessarily material ones, so that it would seem impossible to abstract from their materiality without abstracting from their individuality.

To this we answer, that although the spiritual mind cannot immediately and directly grasp the material features of a thing, it can do so indirectly, because it can form an abstract concept of *material features* in general, and apply this concept to the concept of human nature. Thus it can think of Peter as existing with, and robed in, materiality.

439. But what is more to the point is to remember that our cog-

nitive faculties are not isolated agents, but partial factors of one final act of cognition. Properly speaking, and this is a fact too often over-looked, it is not our cognitive faculties that know, it is not the eye that sees, the hand that feels, the imagination that pictures absent things, the memory that remembers, or the intellect that forms abstract concepts; it is the complete person, the I or the Ego, which performs these functions by means of the joint operation of all our faculties, which hardly ever act separately, all having a special part to play in every cognitional act. We seldom, if ever, apprehend an object purely by sight, touch or any other exterior or interior sense, or by the intellect acting by itself. All our faculties are continually furthering each other's functions, and this deep collaboration makes it impossible to say that at any one moment we are working with either our intellectual or our sense-faculties alone; this is especially true with respect to our power of imagination. Each act of cognition is a sort of medley of abstract concepts and of mental images. No clear-cut line of bifurcation can be drawn between the individual and the universal elements of any cognitional act.

440. In fact, phantasms are not merely added to the concept; they are intimately connected with it, so intimately that their formation is an integral, although instrumental, part of the very act of intellection. The act of intellection is undoubtedly distinct from that by which we form mental images; but these two acts are so indispensable to each other, that on the one hand we never produce or recall a con-cept without forming a mental image, and on the other hand, it is nearly impossible to form a mental image without at least a back-ground of abstract thought.

441. We can therefore say that we rarely in this life form purely abstract concepts. By this we mean that the objects of our concepts are never presented to the mind in a purely abstract manner, but are always intermingled with the phantasmal elements from which they are abstracted, and in which they are actually seen. The con-cept bears, so to say, an imprint of the phantasm from which it is drawn. Thus when I think of man in general, although I am abstract-ing from the individuality of man, I am nevertheless visualizing human nature as I know it to exist in some man or other. If I were asked to describe human nature in the abstract, I should have in mind the human nature of some individual man, and my description would be tinted, so to say, with the individuality of that man.

442. Therefore the question as to whether and how we can have an intellectual concept of the individual Peter, can be answered by saying that the information about Peter's individuality is supplied by the individual elements of the complete act of cognition, the joint-result of which is expressed by a concrete term. By a final act of cognition, I know both the abstract nature of Peter, and his individuality, although several distinct faculties contribute to this final act. As the soul is united to the body to form with it one single substance, the sense faculties to the intellectual ones to form one single cognizing subject, so phantasms are united to concepts to form one single cognitive product.

443. In conclusion, we can say that it is not only possible to know the individual, but that the knowledge of the individual is far more common, natural and easy than that of the universal. The problem of the universals is indeed one of the most abstruse in metaphysics. There is evidence of this difficulty of apprehending the universal in the numerous and lengthy discussions which the theory of the *Universals* has produced in the history of Philosophy.

CHAPTER 17

PARTICULAR REASON

444. After having briefly explained all there is to know about our intellectual faculties and functions, we must now explain what is meant by that very special faculty of man called his *particular reason* or *cogitative faculty*. We will at once define it as a special sense-faculty of man which elaborates and prepares the material of his abstract concepts.

To understand this definition, we must remember the rôle played by the senses and especially by the imagination in the act of intellectual cognition. Our intellectual knowledge has its origin in sense cognition: if we could not perceive anything with our sense-organs, we should have no intellectual concepts. Now the information gathered by the exterior senses is first of all transmitted to the imagination under the form of phantasms or mental images, some of which are committed to memory. They are then taken over by the faculty of instinct. Animals instinctively divide these phantasms into two big classes: images of useful and images of harmful things, or actions to be done and actions to be omitted. The mental images of animals have no other use.

But in man, phantasms have another and nobler scope, namely to present him with the material for his intellectual concepts. In man also, phantasms are taken over by a faculty, which on account of its superior functions, instead of being called *instinct* as in animals, is given the name of *power of estimation, aestimativa,* cogitative faculty, or particular reason.

445. The superiority of this faculty in man is due to the fact that all the faculties of man are continually ministering to the needs of the spiritual mind which, on account of this uncessant contact with them, exercises over them a profound influence. Man's exterior senses do not all benefit to the same extent by this contact; sight, for example, hearing and smell are sometimes more developed in animals, though they are always more refined in man. But his interior faculties are indubitably greatly perfected by their contact with his intellectual soul; his consciousness is more discriminating and alert, his memory is more orderly and retentive than those of animals; his power of imagination also greatly benefits under the guidance of reason, and reaches untold depths of observation and comprehensive description.

446. But when we turn to his instinctive faculty, we find that it attains such a perfection that it only preserves a remote resemblance to animal instinct. Its functions are and remain organic reactions of the neural system; they are however so closely associated with the intellectual process, that they seem to imitate in a certain manner the discursive and reasoning methods of the intellect. That is why this faculty is called particular reason or cogitative power. Undoubtedly it can only know individual objects, and not the universal nature of things like the intellect; as in animals, it only results in mental images of those particular objects which are useful or harmful. Nevertheless it is a kind of synthesizing faculty; it enables man to form patterns of the data gathered by the imagination and recalled by memory. The sum total of this information forms what is known as *experience.* It forms the basic stock of a useful and practical sense-knowledge which increases with time. It is from this stock

that the general and universal ideas of intellectual knowledge are directly drawn. It is to this unified product of sense-knowledge that the intellect turns in order to abstract its concepts, and to recall concepts previously formed.

447. Therefore, although it has no knowledge of the universal, particular reason extends, by its power of comparison and classification, to much more than the simple perception of particular objects. It rises above the level of ordinary sense-cognition, and forms the borderline, the point of contact, between the material and the immaterial. Since the intellect abstracts its concepts from material and individual images, there must be a point of contact between these and the immaterial intellect. At some moment or other the spiritual intellect must come face to face with a bodily organ upon which it can perform its abstracting operation. The faculty which has the privilege of thus contacting the spiritual mind, is particular reason or the cogitative faculty.

CHAPTER 18

THE HUMAN SOUL

448. The human soul is the substantial form of man. In the mind of many philosophers until quite recent times, the notion of physical reality was identified with that of concrete matter, and matter in their opinion meant a tangible and visible mass, such as a piece of coal, a pin, air, water, or anything else that could be sense-perceived. Of later years, however, there has been a decline in this gross materialist conception of reality. Matter is no longer considered as a tangible mass that can be seen and felt, but something composed of ethereal and intangible units or particles which escape all direct sense-observation, floating in a new kind of medium called space-time, and conditioned by the laws of relativity. The very continuity of matter, which was at the basis of previous experiences of masses of matter, has been questioned. In one word, the modern view of reality seems to be approaching rapidly towards an interpretation which is far less material than it used to be, and is ready to admit the existence of a reality which cannot be sense-perceived, but only logically inferred.

What is however more to the point as far as we are concerned, is that the infinitesimally small particles discovered by science are endowed with an active power out of all proportion to their size. The energy of particles much smaller than the atom exceeds that of any known mass of matter. Hence, we are forced to search elsewhere than in the mass of matter for the cause of these prodigiously active phenomena. The physicist, unable to point to this hidden cause, calls the potential energy of his particles by various scientific names; the metaphysician attributes it to what he calls *form*.

449. According to the theory of hylomorphism, all material things are composed of two elements called matter and form. Matter is a potential element, the potential capacities of which become actual by its union to form. Form is that which gives actuality to the potentiality of matter; in this philosophical meaning, form has not been adopted in our English language, in which it stands for shape or figure. Here we are using it as meaning the principle or cause of the active power and properties of matter.

But although form is the cause of all the active manifestations of a substance, it cannot act without matter. Matter is the medium by which it carries out its active powers. Thus the active power of radium is due to the form of radium, but it can only be carried out by means of the matter of radium. So, on the one hand, matter depends utterly on form, and on the other, form depends utterly on matter. They cannot either exist or act without each other; they can only do so in as much as they are substantially united in the complete individual substance.

450. Man also is composed of matter and form; the matter is his body, the form his soul. Indeed there must be in man another element besides the inert mass of his body, namely a form, to account for his vital energy. It is not more extraordinary to postulate the existence of this form which we call the human soul, than it is to maintain that there must be in an atom of radium some active principle distinct from its mass, which endows it with an energy out of all proportion to its infinitesimally small size.

451. Now in inorganic beings, the active power which radiates from their substantial form is spread uniformly over the whole mass, every part of this mass being equally active. Every part of an acid is corrosive; every part of radium, however small, is radio-active. The activity of an organic being, on the contrary, does not belong to the

entire mass; it is located in particular organs or regions of the body, although of course the rest of the mass contributes more or less to its execution. But the organs alone are not responsible for this activity; they can only act in virtue of the soul. Now just as the substance resulting from the union of the body and the soul is designated by the special term *man,* an organ actuated by the energy emanating from the soul is called by the special term *faculty.* Faculty is derived from the Latin *facere,* meaning *to do,* and designates both the bodily organ and the active power given to it by the soul.

452. Man has many faculties, the faculties of sight, touch, memory, imagination, and so forth. These are material faculties, because they depend on organic matter for the performance of their functions. But the formation of abstract concepts is not carried out directly by means of material organs like the rest of man's activity. The mind therefore which produces these concepts is not a material faculty, but a spiritual one. This means that whilst in all other things, matter is entirely dependent on form and form on matter, in man matter is dependent on form, but form is not dependent on matter, because his soul, besides being the active principle of all his material faculties, is also capable of functions which exclude any intrinsic co-operation of matter.

453. Now if the soul does not depend upon matter in the actual use of its intellectual faculties, it is logical to conclude that the mere separation of the body from the soul would not impair its activity and prevent it from performing its intellectual functions. And since nothing can function unless it exists, in the hypothesis of such a separation, the soul, in order to be able to function without the body, would have to continue to exist in this state of separation. In other words, if the soul is independent of matter in the use of its intellectual faculties, it must also be independent of matter for its existence. A soul which did not continue to exist when separated from the body, evidently could not continue to function.

454. To say that the soul has an independent existence, means that it does not need to be supported by matter in order to exist. Therefore whilst in all other things, neither matter alone nor form alone can exist, in man the body cannot exist by itself, but the soul has an existence of its own, which it communicates to the body. In other things, the existence of the individual substance is merely the result of the

union of matter to form; in man on the contrary, the individual exists by partaking of the existence which belongs properly and primarily to the soul. We call all other forms material forms, because they depend on matter; the human soul is said to be spiritual, because it does not depend on the body for its existence.

455. The soul is a *substantial principle*. It is united to a body in order that man might take his place in the visible creation; without a body, the soul would be an incomplete species. But although an incomplete species, it is a complete substance, on account of its independent existence. Substance in fact is defined as that which can exist by itself, that which does not need to be supported, as it were, in existence by anything else. In this sense it is opposed to accidents and qualities such as colour, heat, strength, and so on, which exist only in so far as they are supported by some existent subject; that is, they exist in, and belong to, something else which bears them and keeps them in being. Action belongs to this latter class; it is an accident or mode of being, and cannot exist by itself. Whether a chemical reaction, an organic function or an act of intellection, action is always dependent on some existent subject; it must be the action of something or of someone.

456. Now it is impossible for the subject of an action, or of any other attribute, to be in its turn dependent upon another supporting subject which in its turn would again be dependent upon another, and so on indefinitely. This would constitute an infinite series of dependent subjects, which is a contradiction in terms; for an infinite series would imply that there would be no last subject upon which the others depended, and therefore the series itself would not be dependent but independent. Thus in a series of dependent subjects, there must be an ultimate one which supports the attributes and especially the activity, of the others. And this subject must be self-supporting, able to support itself; in other words, it must be a substance, not an accident or a property.

This supporting subject, in all things except man, is the complete individual substance composed of matter and form. But in the case of man, the complete individual cannot be the subject of all its activity, the reason being that man is capable of certain spiritual functions which exclude any direct co-operation of the body or of bodily organs. Therefore, it remains that the only subject to which these spiritual functions can belong is the soul itself, which must consequently be a complete and independent substance of its own.

457. This subject is often referred to as the *ego,* a modern term corresponding to what the scholastics call the suppositum, which last term can, in the case of man, be rendered by the more understandable term *person.* Person however is not taken here in the meaning of personality or character, but as the permanent principle or subject of all exterior and interior human actions. It is in this sense that we say that actions belong to the suppositum or person. By *ego* therefore we mean the root of all our psychological and physiological phenomena, the subject that feels, sees, hears, knows and so forth.

458. But we must distinguish carefully between the ego as the substantial subject or principle of our actions, and the ego considered as a concrete whole made up of all the states, experiences and relations of which the ego is the cause. In other words we must distinguish between the ego or person itself, and its inward and outward modes of expression. The modes can vary, the ego cannot. Changes of habit, disposition, character and so forth can be explained by variations in the display of our psychic forces, and the fact that a changed personality is sometimes not conscious of the preceding one, only points to a lack of memory and not necessarily to a rupture of the ego. Many of the alleged facts which are ascribed to a subliminal self or to a sub-conscious ego, are natural psychological phenomena known as reflex or automatic responses. Dreams, somnambulism, artificially induced sleep such as hypnosis, and all other automatic processes, are due, not to a self which is split off from the natural ego, but to the one and only ego which is, however, not always aware or conscious of all the psychological phenomena to which it is subjected.

CHAPTER 19

INDEPENDENCE OF THE HUMAN SOUL

459. The doctrine of the spirituality of the human soul would seem to contradict certain undeniable facts. The first is that all our knowledge originates in our senses; we cannot have a concept of any kind unless it is abstracted from a phantasm of our imagination, and

unless it is actually accompanied by a phantasm each time we reconsider it. If a man could be born without any exterior senses whatsoever, his mind would be a complete blank; he would have no intellectual knowledge. Man neither acquires nor uses his intellectual knowledge without the help of his bodily faculties. Furthermore, the degree of his intellectual capacity is intimately connected with, and subjected to, the conditions and variations of the nervous system and the brain matter of his body. Mental power varies in proportion to the size, the conformation and the health of the brain; compression or concussion of the brain invariably produces diminution, aberration and even total cessation of intellectual activity, and it is quite certain that bodily sickness and disease affect our mental powers. These facts would seem to destroy our assertion that the soul is independent of the body in the exercise of its intellectual functions.

460. But we must remember that the soul is made for the express purpose of animating a body. Although a spirit, the soul is not a disembodied spirit like the Angels, but, in the mind of God who created it, it is destined to exist with a body from which it was originally never meant to be separated. It is therefore only natural that the body should somehow share in all the soul's functions. The soul could of course have been given an abundant store of inborn knowledge, and thus not have been obliged to contact the outer world; but such a manner of acquiring knowledge would have been a discordant note in the harmony of nature's perfect order. If man could have known the world without the use of his bodily faculties, there would have been no reason for him to have had a body at all. Such an hypothesis could not be reconciled with the universal teleology of the rest of creation. But its mere possibility points to the basic independence of the soul.

461. That the soul should actually make use of the body in the acquisition of knowledge, does not however destroy its independence, because the body and its senses have no part in the *actual performance* of intellectual functions. They administer to the mind, they present the material from which its concepts are abstracted, but the process of abstraction itself, and that of actual intellection, are exclusive operations of the soul. The senses and the brain are instruments by means of which the soul contacts the outside world. They play a part in the preparation of suitable material for the higher operation of intellection. One cannot cut a loaf of bread without a

knife, perform a surgical operation without a scalpel, or paint without a brush, yet no one would attribute these actions to the instruments which are used in their performance. The mind transforms the data provided by the senses into something which material faculties cannot grasp, and in a manner in which they not only do not, but cannot, have any part.

462. As a matter of fact, the mind could not form abstract concepts unless the senses had previously supplied it with the necessary information about individual objects. We could not form the concept of colour in general if we had never seen any colours. It is precisely from the data gathered by the senses that the intellect abstracts its universal concepts. If these data were missing, the intellect would have nothing from which to abstract. The abstract nature considered by the intellect is only to be found in the individual and concrete things of the world, not floating around in the air. To get at it, the intellect must have recourse to the senses which are the sole means of contact with these exterior objects.

463. So also, because intellectual thought not only originates in sense-perception, but makes use of phantasms by performing upon them its delicate operation of abstraction, it follows that variations in our nervous and organic system can affect our intellectual activity. Concussion of the brain can distort the mental pictures we form of exterior things, and prevent the proper functioning of the association process; consequently the intellect, not having sufficient or truthful data to work upon, will itself be subject to diminution, aberration, or even total cessation of its activity. It is for the same reason that the size, weight and shape of the brain can affect intellectual activity, although this is not the general rule.

To put the whole question in a nutshell, we say that the intellect depends upon matter and organic functions *extrinsically*, but not *intrinsically*. This means that this dependence refers to those previous stages of intellectual activity that are outside the real intellectual performance, not to the inner sanctum where the real act of intellectual abstraction and intellection is performed.

464. There is another difficulty called the problem of *interaction*, namely, that of conceiving how an immaterial and independent substance such as the soul, can contact, and act upon, the body, and how the body can react, as it certainly does, upon the soul. That two things so widely different as mind and matter, which obey laws of

such a different nature, are able to *get* at each other, would seem to indicate some kind of mutual dependence.

This interaction is a fact beyond dispute. The mind is continually acting upon the body, as for example, if I make up my mind to perform an irksome job, my nervous and muscular system automatically sets to work. If I think of a funny story, I may well burst into laughter. If I think of the cruelty of an enemy I shall probably clinch my fists. A mere act of the will can move my little finger. On the other hand, the body acts upon the mind. Thus if I am sick or tired, I shall probably have gloomy thoughts, or perhaps not be able to use my intellectual powers at all, while if I drink a glass of wine I shall have kind and friendly thoughts.

465. The answer is a simple one. The soul is the substantial form of the body; we have insisted on this point. For this reason the soul is the source of all the activity of the body. Matter of itself is inert; form is its only source of energy. Therefore not only intellectual activity must proceed from the soul, but also all sense and organic power. Now form contacts matter in such a way that it is present in every part of that matter. Matter as we know it, the matter of an existing thing, is not pure matter, but matter and form. The human body is not body alone, but body and soul. The soul contacts and animates every single cell, which otherwise would not be alive. Matter and form, body and soul, when united, are not two distinct beings in close contact with each other, but one single substance. The question of contact and consequently of interaction, properly speaking, is out of place. There are not two substances acting upon each other, but one single substance performing the actions for which it was made.

466. Those who fail to understand how the body and soul *get* at each other, do so because they are at a loss to realize that material or mass contact is not the only manner in which two things can be united. The substantial union of matter and form explains the whole question. The soul is united in this way to the body. And although it is a form which has the exceptional privilege of performing certain functions in which the body has no direct part, it is nevertheless a form made for the express purpose of enabling the body to carry out its organic functions. But if we still cannot see how this is possible, we should reflect on the manner in which a flame for example spreads to a piece of paper, or an electric current takes control of a piece of

wire. We do not know exactly how these phenomena happen, but we do know that the flame and the electric current were made for those special purposes, and that consequently they are able to fulfil them.

467. Concerning the mutual influence of body and soul, it is important to remark that the extent of the influence of body upon soul is much inferior to that of soul upon body. The influence of the body on the soul is only indirect, because, theoretically at least, the soul is always able to assert its independence and to refuse to be influenced. However violent may be the pressure exercised by bodily organs, the soul can deny all co-operation; however tired we may feel, we can, by an effort of the will, continue our mental work; however upset we may be, we can still entertain happy thoughts.

CHAPTER 20

IMMORTALITY OF THE HUMAN SOUL

468. From the fact that the human soul is able to exist by itself on account of its intrinsic independence in the performance of its intellectual function, it is natural to conclude that when the organic life of man ceases to function, the soul will be able to continue its intellectual and spiritual activity. Death is the cessation of the functions of the heart and brain, of the circulatory, respiratory and other organs, but does not directly affect the spiritual operations of the soul.

469. It will be objected that the body and the senses are required as instruments to gather information for the mind. But the necessity of this instrumental share of the senses in the act of intellection arises only from the fact that the soul is united to the body, and that the soul is consequently meant to know primarily the material objects of this world which it contacts by the senses. This is the normal and actual, but not the only possible manner it has of acquiring know-ledge, even whilst united to the body. We reject the hypothesis of , inborn ideas, not because it militates against the nature of the spiritual mind, but simply because it is against facts, and because it

would destroy the objectivity of our knowledge of this world. The sense-origin of our ideas is not required by the nature of the intellectual act itself.

470. So long as the mind can have species or ideas impressed upon it, it is able to function, no matter where these ideas come from. In other words, the necessity of sense-co-operation is a fact arising solely from the actual union of the soul to the body, and not an intrinsic condition of intellection. Consequently if, when separated from the body, it is possible for the mind to acquire ideas in some other manner, the absence of sense-co-operation will form no intrinsic obstacle to the performing of its act. That it is possible for an intellectual spirit to acquire knowledge in a different manner to that in which our mind usually acquires it in this world, is evident from the fact that God and the angelic spirits possess a knowledge far superior to ours without any material and organic help and understand better than we do all the things of this world. St. Thomas therefore maintains that the separated soul will acquire knowledge by means of ideas infused into the mind by its Creator in the manner he sometimes gives supernatural knowledge even in this world to a few privileged souls. The soul will thus be in a state similar to that in which it would have found itself if it had never been united to a body, and in which the angelic spirits themselves exist. The mind will therefore not have to abstract ideas from material objects, but will be provided with ideas that are already abstract. Furthermore, the mind will preserve all the ideas which it acquired when united to the body, and these will increase the stock of its knowledge.

471. The possibility of the soul's survival is therefore beyond all doubt. But the fact of its survival still remains to be shown. This can be done by eliminating all the possible causes of its non-survival. If the soul ceased to exist after death, it would be either by destruction, by annihilation or by simply disappearing like a light which goes out.

472. The soul cannot destroy itself, because nothing can destroy its own self; for if the agent of destruction were the very thing which was being destroyed, that agent would have to continue to exist until it had carried out the destruction, and thus still exist after it had been destroyed.

473. The soul cannot be destroyed by another agent, because the only way in which this could be done would be by disintegration. Now

disintegration is the resolution of a thing into its parts; but the soul is simple and has no parts. Only matter has parts on account of its quantitative dimensions.

474. The soul cannot be annihilated. *Annihilation* is but a convenient word, used to denote a sudden disappearance which we are at a loss to explain. There is really no such a thing as annihilation. One of the most fundamental laws of science is that nothing is utterly destroyed. When we say that a thing has been destroyed, we simply mean that it has passed from one state to another. To annihilate in the proper sense of the word, is to reduce to nothing, and this would require energies greater than those possessed by anyone or anything in this world.

475. God could annihilate. But if we introduce God into our philosophical discussions, we can assume that we believe in him. God is not someone to be introduced just for convenience sake, when we find no other issue to our problems. If we believe that there is an Almighty God, we are at once faced with other issues, and one of these is that God has spoken to us in Holy Writ. Now in the Scriptures it is clearly stated that the soul will live for ever. Furthermore, God is not only Omnipotent, but also infinitely Wise. It would be contrary even to human wisdom to make a thing for a definite purpose and then not to use it for that or for any other purpose. Now by making the soul independent of the body in its intellectual functions, God made it able to think and to exist without the body; but to make it able to go on living without the body, and then by a very special act of his Will, to deny it the means of existence by annihilation, could hardly be called an intelligent action.

476. And finally the soul cannot disappear like a flame which goes out. Something like this happens in the case of inferior forms, especially those of animals: the soul of an animal just ceases to exist. But this happens because the soul of an animal has no existence of its own. In all beings inferior to man, it is the composite which exists; matter and form do not exist by themselves, because they are not complete substances; they only exist because they partake of the existence which belongs exclusively to the complete substance composed of matter and form. So when the individual ceases to exist by the removal of a condition necessary to its existence as a whole, the cessation for example of some vital function, both matter and form cease to partake of the existence which they possessed only as parts of

that complete individual. Matter is transformed into something else, form just disappears, as the shape of a bronze statue does when the statue is melted down. Neither matter nor form can properly be said to be destroyed. Matter in the common opinion of all scientists is indestructible. Form is not destroyed, since destruction implies the loss of existence and form has no existence of its own. It is therefore the individual which is destroyed, not its elements.

But the human soul is a complete substance; it has an existence of its own. It does not partake of the existence of the individual as other forms do, but the individual partakes of the existence of this spiritual form. The soul therefore cannot disappear as the colour, the shape or the size of a stone, for example, vanishes when the stone is broken up and is disintegrated.

477. There is another proof of the immortality of the soul, called the *teleological* argument. The natural tendency of things towards ever increasing perfection is one of the cherished principles of philosophy. All agree that natural causes must be able to fulfil their purpose and arrive at the end for which they were made. It is in this way that the gradual development of man's abilities is explained. There is no reason why this law should not be verified with regard to the intellectual soul. Its aspirations must somehow be satisfied. Yet man never seems to attain complete satisfaction in this world; the existence of a future life is a necessary postulate for its realization. In fact, the more man develops his intellectual faculties in this world, the greater becomes his conception of ideal happiness and perfection, but at the same time, the more he realizes how far he is from their acquisition. There is perhaps no one in this world who could say that he is entirely satisfied with his lot. Some try to be content with what they have because they know how useless and even harmful it would be to do otherwise; but they know they could have been happier than they are, their cravings are far from being satisfied. This is a strange fact when we consider that dumb animals are perfectly content, that they live in an atmosphere of beatitude.

It would be very abnormal for man, the king of creation, to be unable to attain true happiness and satisfaction. Without a future life in which his aspirations are gratified, life in this world becomes not only a mystery, but a nonsensical farce, a blot upon the rest of creation, where all is order, where all fulfils perfectly and completely the end for which it was made.

478. The *ethical* argument is drawn from the sense of morality, duty, honesty and justice which is inborn in every one of us. Although situations may often arise where faithfulness to this sense of duty brings misery and material damage upon us, we still cling to it. The great majority of people would be reluctant to tell a deliberate lie, or to harm someone unjustly, even at the cost of personal harm. And those who put aside the dictates of their conscience and violate this sense of duty, are perfectly aware that they are doing wrong, even if the habit of doing so has blurred their feeling of remorse. It is rarely the hope of material advantage, or fear of material hardship that urges us to do what we know to be morally right, and to avoid what we know to be morally wrong. We do it instinctively without any hope of reward or fear of punishment. There is a kind of blind instinct in us that makes us realize that the pleasures, honours and riches of this world, are not the only things that count.

479. Moreover our sense of *justice* requires the reward of virtue and the punishment of vice. Now virtue is seldom justly rewarded and vice is seldom punished in this life. This rational and natural feeling of justice cannot be frustrated for ever. The acceptance of a future life solves the problem; after this life virtue and vice will receive their just retribution.

480. The *historical* argument is taken from the testimony of practically all nations and people throughout history. Everywhere we find anchored in nature the universal belief in a future life. This belief is one of those truths which it would be against common sense to deny.

CHAPTER 21

THE WILL

481. Man is endowed with another spiritual faculty besides the intellect, namely the will, which can be defined as a *rational impulse towards that which is good and useful*. The good and useful as

apprehended by the intellect is called a *purpose*; therefore we can call the will an impulse to act for a purpose.

The functions of the will are not mere sublimated forms of material energies or of brain activities, as some would make believe, but functions of a spiritual and immaterial order, like the faculty itself from which they proceed. All things have a special raison d'être, some special function to accomplish, and are equipped with the power to perform it. This power constitutes the specific property of each thing, such as the resistance of a metal, the corrosive power of an acid. Each thing has a natural tendency or inclination to act or react in a definite manner, or, as we say, to perform some specific function.

482. Now cognitive beings are endowed not only with mere physical energy, but also with cognitive power. Therefore their specific tendencies are not the mere outcome of blind physical forces like those of non-cognitive beings, but they are controlled by the cognitive factor of their nature. In other words they are conscious tendencies, and are called impulses. There is indeed an obvious difference between a dog's reaction to an exciting smell, and the mechanical movement of a stone falling to the ground.

But since man's knowledge is of a far superior nature to that of an animal, his impulses must evidently be of a more elevated nature. Animals only pursue the particular goodness of concrete individual objects, whilst man perceives goodness in general and is attracted towards individual good things only because he perceives them to partake of the general nature of goodness. His impulse is therefore not limited to any particular thing; he can substitute one thing for another. This particular impulse of man is called the will, and sometimes a rational appetite or instinct, or a *conative* faculty.

483. The impulse of the will towards good in general is a compulsory one; man is not free in this respect; he cannot choose an object which he conceives as evil. In this he resembles the rest of creation. Nothing can be naturally inclined towards that which is harmful to, or destructive of, its nature, because the nature of a thing, which by definition is that which makes a thing what it is, cannot possibly cause that thing not to be what it is. Although some things such as fire, acids and so on, would seem to bring about their own destruction, a closer examination shows us that fire, for example, does not consume its own self but other things, and that what is

burnt is transformed into something else, not in virtue of its own inclination, but through the agency of an exterior cause. A knife is not naturally inclined to be blunt. Neither do animals engage in deadly fights because they want to be killed. A martyr, a soldier, goes to death because he conceives death as a good and noble thing.

This compulsory volition of goodness in general is not strictly speaking an act, but more in the nature of a *habit* of the will. It is an innate disposition of the will; a basic and irresistible force which underlies and directs every one of its acts.

484. The will is, like the intellect, an *immaterial* faculty, because its act is of a spiritual nature. In fact, the act of the will is in the highest degree of remoteness from materiality. Its complete independence from organic activity is especially obvious when we consider that its acts are frequently in absolute conflict with the natural tendencies of bodily functions, as when we abhor sin whilst feeling a strong inclination towards it, or when we rejoice in the midst of tribulations which would naturally tend to make us sad.

485. The act of the will is of such a spiritual nature that it can be performed without the help of words to express it, a feat which is practically impossible even to the spiritual intellect. Unless we frame it with a word, the expressed species cannot be properly and completely formed; but to perform an act of the will, we need only turn our will towards its object without any physical or mental effort whatsoever. To express this extreme spirituality and immanence of the will-act, it is called an *intention*; it is also called an *elicited act*, that is to say an act that is *drawn out* from its latent state. It is extremely difficult to understand in what exactly this movement of the will consists, and how we form these spiritual and interior acts of volition. But we must remember that it is no easy matter to understand even how the impulsive movements of our organism called emotions, are accomplished. We know that we feel physically attracted towards a thing, but we would be at a loss to explain in what exactly this attraction consists.

486. It is important to observe that the abstract concept of goodness originates, like all other concepts, in sense-knowledge. Consequently the senses and the rest of the organism, which have a part to play in the formation of this concept, can indirectly influence the very act of the will. It is the privilege of the will to be able to control the senses; the will can never be forced. But it can fail in its duty

because it is led astray by distorted phantasms and by erroneous judgements. Still its most evil acts are always performed because they are thought to lead to something good.

487. But besides the pure volitional intention or elicited act, there is also what is called a *commanded act* of the will. The will in fact is not an isolated faculty; it is in continual contact with all the faculties which are rooted in the same soul as itself. Neither is it simply in contact with them; it has been endowed with the power to make them feel its influence by moving and directing them in the acquisition of its goal. Thus the will is the directing factor of man's activity, and practically all his faculties obey its command.

488. A commanded act is therefore that by which the will, after having made an elicited act or intention, commands the other faculties to contribute towards the attainment of its purpose. To write a letter, I first intend and resolve to do so, and then I set in motion my mind and my nervous system in order to perform the job. As to how the will can issue orders which are faithfully and completely carried out, is, and always will remain a mystery. The mere fact that our little finger will instantly obey a purely interior act of the will, is a marvel that surpasses any feat of the most clever engineering.

489. Our intellect is under the control of the will. We can only form an abstract concept by deliberately intending to do so. The act and the object of intellectual cognition depend entirely on the will's decision. Imagination and association of ideas are also subject to the will; the will can compel our imagination to stay at its work, and can interfere with its train of thought and create another one by directing the powers concerned into different channels. Association of ideas is not necessarily the mechanical result of a pure neurological process; man is capable of deliberate associations which are due to the will's command. This command is not however always a smooth one; matter resents the interference of the will. This often results in a struggle between the imagination and the will, and it is only with great effort that the will is able to overcome the strong impulses of sensory activity.

490. Unconditioned reflexes and automatic processes performed by the involuntary muscles, are not directly subject to the will's command. But all other reflexes and movements, all manual

actions, posture, facial and vocal expression and many other actions which in animals are purely instinctive, are under the absolute control of the will.

CHAPTER 22

FREE-WILL

491. We have just said that the impulse of the will towards good in general is a compulsory act, since we cannot deliberately choose that which we consider evil. But with regard to particular good things man is endowed with absolute freedom of choice. He can select amongst all the things he knows that which he considers the best means to attain the final end and aim of his will, namely good in general. We therefore say that man is endowed with free-will, namely with the power of acting for a purpose or for an end in whatever way he chooses.

There is a purpose behind the intricate and accurate behaviour of the Universe. There is nothing random and haphazard about the regularity and constancy of natural laws and effects. That inanimate things and plants, having no cognitive powers, are unable to know this order and design, and to act accordingly, is not an argument for denying that such a purpose exists, since they are blindly guided towards the special end for which they were made by the Agent who made them for that special purpose; man alone acts for a purpose.

492. Now if a thing attains the precise purpose for which it was made, it is said to be *good*. Even defective and faulty objects have their use, which is not however that which more perfect objects were intended to have. In fact, all things are exactly as they were meant to be by their Maker, and are endowed with sufficient power to fulfil their purpose, whatever this may be. There is a scholastic tag which sums this up by saying that *all things are good*. This is perfectly true in a philosophical sense. All things can be put to some useful and good use.

493. Yet precisely because things are made only for one or several particular purposes and are of no use for any other, they are not entirely and universally good. They have only a small share of good qualities, of ideal and universal perfection and goodness. For this reason, they are called *particular* goods, in opposition to the universal and absolute good. The universal good, full and complete goodness, only exists in our mind which abstracts from all individual short-comings. In Ethics, it is shown that this ideal and universal goodness can be found as really existent, if we raise up our thoughts to the Maker of all things who gave them existence and all the other per-fections that make them good.

494. Now particular good things, as they exist in their concrete individuality, cannot be the object of the spiritual will, any more than individual objects can be that of the spiritual mind. The will is attracted towards them only inasmuch as their abstract nature is judged by the intellect to be good and attractive. The goodness which constitutes the object of the will is not the individual goodness of a thing, but the goodness which is revealed by a judgement of the mind. And because there is no complete and absolute goodness except in God, any judgement concerning the goodness of other things is necessarily restricted to the limited share of goodness they possess. The mind is even justified in judging them not to be good at all, since they are so far remote from the ideal it has formed of absolute goodness.

Now the will follows only those judgements which affirm that things are good; it chooses these and rejects the others. This does not imply that the things which form the subject of the rejected judgements are bad, but simply that the mind does not present them to the will as sufficiently good to be chosen as actual objects of pursuit. Thus the act of the will depends upon an act of the mind, and the will is called a rational impulse, *liberum arbitrium*, precisely because it is guided by a rational judgement of the mind. On the other hand, the object or purpose of the will is called the *reason* for which it acts, this word meaning a judgement at which we arrive by reasoning.

495. But although the mind, in virtue of its judgements, is respon-sible for the will's choice, the choice itself is entirely free and independent. The mind sets a bait or goal for the will, pro-vides it with a suitable object of pursuit, but the will itself is the

only reason of its own choice. Choice is a proper and specific act of the will alone. The will has to follow the particular line of action set by the mind, but in setting it, the mind is dependent on the will. Indeed, the will is in full command of the intellectual mind. The intellect can only function by order or consent of the will and in the precise manner directed by the will. The will arouses the intellect to action, assigns the particular task it is to perform, and controls its operations from beginning to end. Thus, not only the intellectual act itself, but its object also are pure matters of the will's own choice.

496. At first the mind is allowed to roam, wander, and form a multitude of judgements concerning a particular channel of thought the will itself has chosen. The will then makes the mind reconsider some of these judgements, or sometimes even interferes, by diverting the mind into other channels of thought. This exercise of the mind is called the act of deliberation. Finally, at a stage chosen by itself, the will imposes silence on the mind and puts an end to its delibera- tions. It causes the mind to cease its operation, simply because, at a certain moment of its own choice, it decides that the judgement just made by the mind shall be the last as far as that particular trend of thought is concerned, and that this judgement points to a suitable line of action. Although some other judgement might have been equally, and perhaps more, eligible, the will, by an act of free-choice, decides in favour of this one, which thus becomes final and decisive, and is called the *last judgement*.

497. Deliberation is an act by which the intellect judges of the goodness of a particular thing and of its suitability as an object of the will's pursuit. In the case of conflicting motives the intellect would remain in a state of equilibrium like that of Buridan's ass, which died of hunger and thirst, because it was incapable of decid- ing whether it should eat or drink when food and water were placed at equal distances from it. The will terminates this indecision of the mind by selecting one of the lines of action proposed by the intellect, thus making one of its judgements the last practical judgement.

498. The decision of the will is something like that of an umpire who gives a final judgement on matters which, after further reflexion, he might have viewed in a different light. Whilst the judgement of the mind could be compared to the irrevocable sentence of a last court of appeal, the will fulfils a rôle similar to that of the judge who pro- nounces that irrevocable sentence. A comparison to a motor-car's

headlights illustrates rather neatly this twofold action of mind and will: the motorist follows the road shown by the lights, but at the same time he directs the lights precisely along the road he wants to follow.

Therefore, although there is always a reason for the will's choice, there is also perfect freedom in this choice. The reason for the choice is provided by the mind; the freedom of the choice has its roots in the nature of the will itself. That is why we call the will by the name of free-will. In other languages, in order to point out how the will freely chooses the judgements presented to it by the mind, it is called, perhaps more logically, free-judgement, *libre arbitre*, *liberum arbitrium*.

499. The freedom of the will results from the following proofs. The fundamental proof is the fact that the natural inclination of a thing, precisely because it is a natural inclination, makes that thing tend towards the objects which are in reach of its natural powers. Since cognitive beings have the natural power of knowing things, they are naturally impelled towards the objects of their knowledge. Therefore man has a natural impulse towards the objects of his intellectual knowledge. This impulse is called the will. But because the intellect perceives things in the abstract, and is thus not limited in its knowledge to any particular object, it follows that the attraction of the will is not restricted to any particular object. Consequently the will is free to select any object of its choice. Freedom of choice, or free-will, is thus a logical consequence of the abstract nature of intellectual knowledge.

500. There is another proof of the freedom of the will which appeals to some people more than the preceding one, and which can be called the *moral proof*. It is drawn from the sense of obligation and duty that is deeply rooted in all men. There is no other possible explication of this fact, than to suppose man to be free, because, if he were not, the notions of right and wrong would be void of all meaning. Remorse and repentance, merit and desert, the idea of justice and responsibility, are inconceivable unless based on the fact that man is free to act as he likes, and therefore answerable for his actions. We know that these notions are not mere words, but sentiments graven on the mind of man, and embodied in the teachings and customs of all nations. Such widespread notions cannot be obliterated. We cannot deny their existence just because they do not fit in with theories that do not admit of human liberty.

501. And finally the conviction that our will is free can be proved from our own personal experience; this is the *introspective proof*. Voluntary attention to one thing rather than to another abundantly proves that we are free to turn our minds to whatsoever we like to consider. No one, or nothing, but ourselves guides the trend of our thoughts. Furthermore we are the sole cause of our decisions. We take counsel and deliberate; but when it comes to the final act, we make up our own minds without any exterior interference. No one can force us to change our decisions or our choice. We feel and we know perfectly well that we are the sole masters of our acts. Under the greatest interior or exterior pressure we can be obstinate in our resolutions. Such an attitude is entirely inconceivable if we deny the freedom of our will.

CHAPTER 23

THE INTENTION OF THE WILL

502. The act by which the will desires and chooses something that the mind presents to it as a suitable means of obtaining its end and purpose is called an *intention*.

503. In this the human will differs from animal instinct which pursues particular objects only inasmuch as they seem attractive; an animal eats or sleeps simply on account of the satisfaction it finds in performing these actions. The *material* object of free-will and of animal instinct is therefore identical, namely the individual objects of sense-experience. But that which we call the *formal* or specifying object, is altogether different. Whilst animals pursue these things because they are stimulated to do so by the mere instinct of self-preservation, or for the pleasure they find therein, man on the contrary pursues these same objects because, by reasoning, he discovers that they will help him to fulfil a definite purpose, and will finally make him attain his last end.

504. Therefore, although the real object of the will is goodness in general, we nevertheless deliberately desire and pursue particular

good things, not for the goodness they actually contain, but for the goodness they will lead to. Thus, with my will, I can decide to eat; but if I behave as a man, as a reasonable being, and not like an animal, I shall decide to do so not because the food is nice and gives me a sense of pleasure, but in order to increase my energy for the fulfilment of my duty. That the will is meant to act in this way, is evident because we can decide to endure pain or to eat something distasteful, simply because we know that in the end it will do us good.

The real object of the will is therefore specifically one only; it is called aim, purpose, design, motive and so forth. And since this object draws the will and induces it to make a decision, it is also called a cause, namely the *final cause*.

505. From what has been said, we can define the will-act as an act performed for a purpose. This act is started and achieved in the will, without any outside help or interference. It belongs to those acts which are called immanent. It is the supreme form of immanent action. The intellect has to contact the exterior world by abstracting its concepts from phantasms. But the will has no immediate contact with the outside world; its object is immediately present to it; there is no previous abstracting or preparing the object. To perform the act of willing, the will has simply to turn to the mind to find there a suitable object of pursuit in the form of a concept already abstract. Volition is therefore more immanent than intellection; the act of resolving for example to carry out next year plan A instead of plan B, is performed entirely by and in the will, and illustrates the immanency of volition.

506. It is on account of this immanence that the will-act is called an intention. This derives from the Latin *tendere in* and differs from attention which comes from *tendere ad, to tend to*. Thus by calling the will-act an intention, we imply that the will, instead of having to look for its object, so to speak, outside itself, has simply to turn towards an object which it finds in the intimacy of its own being. This does not mean that the will does not turn to exterior things; but, as has just been said, it does not turn to them on account of themselves, but only inasmuch as they are comprised in the interior concept of goodness in general. As an example, an insignificant and perfectly useless object is sometimes bought at a very high price purely for its sentimental value, and not for its own worth.

507. An *intention* is therefore the will-impulse towards that which the mind apprehends as good. Theoretically, this impulse has no repercussion on anything but the will itself; the will-act is accomplished entirely in the will; it is *elicited* by and in the will, and is therefore called an elicited act. The execution of the will's command by other faculties requires a further act of the will, a commanded act. Thus, for example, to hope that an invalid will soon get better, to pardon in our heart an enemy, to resist interior evil suggestions, or to pray to the Almighty, are pure intentional and elicited acts, simple intentions of the will unaccompanied by any act of other faculties.

508. The fact that the will-act is independent of any other faculty, has useful applications in moral matters. The moral act, good or bad, is totally achieved in the will. The exterior act, often consequent on the intention of the will, does not change the morality, that is to say, the nature of the will-act itself. For the same reason, we can understand how the intention can change the nature of an action, as for example in the administration and reception of a Sacrament, or in the performance of good works.

509. There are three main types of intention, according to the manner in which we make use of our will.

The first type concerns the free *exercise* of our will. Thus we can intend to act or not to act, to make a decision or not to make it, to pray or not to pray.

The second type of intention concerns the free *specification* of our will-acts. This is the type of intention by which we intend to make an act of praise of God instead of, for example, an act of thanksgiving, or by which we hope that a certain candidate will be elected rather than another.

The third type of intention is what we call a bad or *evil* intention. It is a gross abuse of the act of free-will. It consists in intending to sin, by deliberately pursuing with our will those objects which are forbidden and which we know will prevent us from attaining our last end, but which, by a perversion of judgement, we decide will do us good.

510. A *virtual intention* is a remote one, one that has been made previously and has not been retracted, and which, by its determining tendency, controls a whole set of actions which follow it. It is really

an actual intention, the influence of which, besides being felt at the moment of making it, persists through whole series of actions which at first would appear to be uncontrolled and spontaneous. This virtual intention can be placed amongst the most important factors of our life; it controls the greater part of our daily actions. Walking, speaking, carrying on with our work or play, are not purely mechanical actions or habits; they are all controlled by a virtual intention which was actual when we started to perform them; they are consequently deliberate acts. Thus, if we make up our mind to drive a car to the right instead of to the left of the road, or to converse in a foreign language which we know, we do not have to renew our intention of doing so once it has been made, but can carry on without thinking about it, under the influence of a virtual intention. There is no limit of time to the duration of a virtual intention. It persists until definitely retracted by a contrary actual intention. This is evident in promises, which contain an intention of doing or not doing something; although a promise may have been made years ago and never renewed, we still feel that we are obliged to keep it.

511. An *habitual intention* is hardly an intention at all, since it has no influence on the act which is being performed. It is an intention which is interrupted by the state of unconsciousness or by anything which makes us lose, even temporarily, the use of our reason. An habitual intention would be that of a man who carries into effect, whilst sleeping, that which he had resolved to do before falling asleep. This previous intention can of course affect his nervous system and his imagination and thus be the indirect cause of the reflex movements necessary to produce that action. He is responsible for having made that intention whilst awake, just as if he had performed the action at that moment; but whether he does or does not perform the action whilst asleep, adds nothing to his responsibility, because an habitual intention has no direct influence on the action since it is interrupted by his state of unconsciousness.

But if we are not in a state of unconsciousness, even if we happen to be distracted and are not actually taking any notice of what we are doing, our actions are still under the influence of a virtual intention if we have previously conceived one; as a matter of fact, if questioned and thus brought suddenly back to reality, we would be able to say at once what we were doing; an unconscious man would not be able to do so.

CHAPTER 24

THE WILL-ACT

512. *Desire* and *love* are other names for the will-act. These terms in general designate the inclination of a cognitive being towards something apprehended as good and useful still out of reach. We are not talking here of the desire and love of objects known merely by sense-perception, but of those known by the intellectual mind and presented to the will as worthy of its pursuit. There is a rather interesting and practical conclusion from this remark as regards supernatural goods. To desire and love them simply means to turn our will towards them and accept them as good and desirable, or, in other words, simply to make the intention of acquiring them, although nothing in our emotive life makes us feel we want them.

513. *Fruition* is the relief felt by the will when, after deliberation, the mind arrives at a final judgement. By the fact of making a deliberate intention or decision, the will consents to the acquisition of that which it desires. This consent automatically puts the will in possession of the object it has freely coveted and chosen. Then, by a final act, which could be better described as a state, the will rests in the possession of that intellectual object. This state is one of quiescence, complacency and satisfaction. It is a state productive of joy and contentment, and is called fruition. It is the natural consequence of a deliberate intention, and consists in the relief felt at the cessation of deliberation, hesitancy and indecision. It follows that the presence or absence of fruition is a definite and absolute test as to whether we have consented to a thought or to a judgement.

But fruition is not a physical or emotional pleasure; it is a purely spiritual satisfaction. Some have maintained that beyond the feeling of comfort produced by the gratification of our physical need of pleasure, there is no other satisfaction. Introspection however testifies to the existence of real satisfaction which is not of a material or emotional nature: a satisfaction which is the natural result of having attained an aim, of having fulfilled a purpose, such as having mastered a difficult problem, or having vindicated one's honour. This satisfaction of the will surpasses all others; we forgo all other pleasures for the sake of this one. It is unknown to animals which can enjoy a feeling of comfort and security, but which derive no joy from an accomplished duty or a fulfilled purpose. We, on the contrary, can enjoy not only having performed an exterior action, but can also rejoice in the functions of our intellectual mind and in the performance of our volitional acts.

514. *Will-power*. It is undeniable that the will, by simply intending to do so, can make the other faculties obey its command, even though we find it difficult to understand how a spiritual faculty can transmit its orders to the material cells of the organism. But on the other hand, the will is not always able to reign with absolute supremacy over the other faculties. Some people, in fact, do not seem to have as much will-power as others, especially in certain painful and difficult circumstances.

515. It is however more consonant with reason to say that the only proper way of referring to strength of will is in terms of convincing values, and to compare the will-act, not to the stroke of a hammer which varies in strength, but to the closing of a switch which sets in motion a uniform current. This means that the apparent variations of will-power do not point to a variable intensity of the will-act, but to different subjective values or impelling motives.

The will continues invariably in its determination, as long as the mind is sufficiently convinced that it is useful and good to do so, and that the closed switch must not be re-opened. If some people do not seem to have sufficient will-power to carry out what they know they ought to do, it is because their conviction is not strong enough, and that they manage to lessen in their own opinion the blame attached to their conduct. To break their resolutions or not to make them at all, they have recourse to excuses, that is to say, to motives which seem to justify their behaviour and make them believe that it is not of such extreme and urgent importance to carry out their resolution.

516. Intellectual power on the contrary varies in intensity in each individual, much as vitality, reaction capacity, sensitive, imaginative and emotional powers change from one individual to another. The reason for this is that the field of intellectual, sensitive and muscular activity is made up of an unlimited number of objects of great variety which cannot all be pursued by each individual; some people are able to pursue more of them than others. But there is only one object of the will, namely abstract and universal good. The will pursues many particular objects not on account of their particular value or attraction, but only and always on account of one and the

same motive, that is, because the mind is convinced they will lead us to our final goal. The will-act consists in deciding to pursue the course of action which the mind considers conducive to the final goal, or not to pursue it, in saying yes or no. There is no intermediary act between making up one's mind and not making it up.

517. Therefore the will-act of deciding, resolving or commanding, is one only, admits of no degrees, and cannot be more or less strong. If we are not sufficiently convinced that we must act, we remain at the mercy of conflicting motives, and either do not resolve, or after having resolved, give way later on to considerations which make us withdraw our resolution.

518. This theory would explain certain facts otherwise unexplainable; it would explain why people who are able to perform great acts of courage seem helpless on minor occasions which they do not consider worthy of such a display of energy; they are capable of heroic acts, and yet unable to conquer certain little habits they have contracted. Others on the contrary are called weak characters and are said to have little will-power, and yet, if the occasion arises, they suddenly perform great deeds because they become suddenly aware of the necessity of putting an end to the waverings of their mind.

519. The value of our convincing motives does not however depend exclusively on the considering mind; habits, physical dispositions and temperament, emotions, environment and so forth, can play an important part in our decisions by influencing our trend of mind, by making important motives appear negligible and worthless, or vice-versa. A whole complex of individual characteristics is indirectly responsible for the final decision of the will. The final victory or defeat of the will in following the dictates of reason, is thus an expression of individuality, personality and character, rather than a manifestation of strength of will-power.

Therefore when we break a resolution, it is not for lack of will-power. It simply shows that the motives which impelled us to make it were not strong enough to conquer our emotions and sense-stimuli; at the moment of breaking the resolution we lose sight of the importance of the impelling motive, or perhaps do not think of it at all. Deep reflection and persuasion are the driving factors of the will; we cannot force our will to do what we are not irrevocably convinced we must do.

CHAPTER 25

THE ANGELS

520. The subject of the present chapter should really belong to theology. But there are certain philosophical points of view concerning the Angels which illustrate the nature of the human soul and to which we wish to draw the student's attention. We shall therefore presume the existence of these pure spirits as being proved elsewhere, and proceed at once to draw a few rational conclusions from this fact.

521. Angels have no body, their essence is not composed, and consists solely of form; they are pure forms or quidditative acts. They differ from the human soul in that they are complete substances, not only in their essence, but in their species; whilst the human soul, although complete as a substance, is not complete as a species unless it is united to the body. Consequently each Angel differs from another specifically, each one is a distinct species of its own. In other words, all differences between Angels are specific, since they are due to form, all formal difference being necessarily specific. Human souls, on the contrary, are all of the same species, and differ only numerically, this numerical difference being due to the individual differences which originate in the matter to which they belong, or to which they are destined to be re-united.

522. It also follows that Angels cannot occupy place or space as material things do; to be in a place or space are exclusive properties of material substances. But since Angels have a certain amount of power over the material world, they must be present in the place in which they exercise that power. Their presence in a place can be compared to that of the human soul, which is also a spirit and is not, strictly speaking, in a place, but is tied down to the limits of the place in which it manifests its activity. This kind of presence is called a virtual presence, a presence which results from the limited sphere to which their activity is confined. Angels are therefore said to be in a place *definitivé*, that is to say by the definition or limitation of their power. This applies to the good and to the bad Angles, and also to the human soul when separated from the body.

523. Angels do not gather their ideas by means of external perception as we do, since they have no corporal organs or senses.

They have no agent intellect like ours, the sole object of which is to abstract from the materiality of our sense-images. Angelic cognition derives from ideas directly infused by God in the act of creation. Thus they have a stock of inborn natural knowledge, to which God adds further ideas in a supernatural manner.

Neither does the Angel reason as we do. Its knowledge consists solely of direct intuition. It knows directly, without any need of demonstration, all that is contained in the comprehension of each idea, rather as we understand the first principles. Apart from the knowledge of these first principles, the rest of our knowledge is discursive, that is to say that we proceed from the knowledge of principles to that of conclusions which we have to demonstrate. Thus we gradually build and increase our knowledge. Angels on the contrary understand all there is to be known by one simple glance at the infused ideas they possess, without any effort or study. Therefore in Angels, not only first principles, but all conclusions are self-evident truths.

524. Our knowledge of the Angels is reflex, that is to say, we know them only indirectly. Granted that we know of their existence through revelation, all we know about their nature is by comparison to our own soul, by discovering that they belong to the same generic nature of spiritual beings. But we cannot know anything about their specific differences, and hence our knowledge of them is very imperfect, since to know a thing is to know its specific difference. Our knowledge is rather negative than positive; we know that they have no bodies, and can deduce some general conclusions from this fact. but not much more.

VOCABULARY AND INDEX

The numbers refer to the paragraphs.

A

ABSOLUTE. Independent. God is independent because he does not owe his existence to any cause; substance, because it does not require a subject to support it, 163; quantity because it does not depend on any other accident, 181. See absolute mode, 185, absolute distinction, 166-167. The Latin term *absoluté* is used to signify that a word is taken in its straightforward meaning, in opposition to *relativé* or *respectivé* which means that a word is taken in a relative and restricted sense.

ABSTRACTION. Process by which the agent intellect isolates the hidden nature of things from their material characteristics. 407 f.

ABSTRACT WORDS. Expressions of abstract concepts. Concrete words often have an abstract meaning, according to the rules of supposition. 3, 13 f, 20.

ACCIDENT. Manner of being which does not exist by itself as substance does, but only in and by a substance which it modifies. It is also called a secondary act or form with regard to the essence, *in linea essentiae,* and a secondary potency with regard to existence, *in linea existentiae.* 175 f.

ACT. That which perfects and completes. The entitative act, or act of being, is existence; the quidditative act, or act of the essence, is the substantial form. 139 f. Accidents are secondary acts, 177 f. See Potency.

ACTION. Execution of a movement or change. There is no real difference between the action of an agent and the passion, that is, the immediate effect or change produced by the agent. 190 f.

ACTU. In act. That which is no longer in potency or in a potential state with regard to the act it is meant to have. Primary matter is in act when united to substantial form, essence when united to existence. A nature is universal in act or formally when conceived as such by the mind, otherwise it is potentially, fundamentally or materially universal. An efficient cause is *in actu secundo* when it is actually producing an effect, in potency or *in actu primo* when at rest, 145.

AFTER-IMAGE. Continued experience of a sense-impression after the outward stimulus has ceased. 367.

AGENT INTELLECT. Faculty which makes phantasms intelligible by divesting them of, or abstracting them from, their material characteristics. 403 f.

AGENT, principal. That which acts in virtue of its own power; an instrumental agent acts by the power of the principal agent. The effect is due in its totality to both of them. 192 f.

ALTERATION. Accidental change in a thing's quantity, quality or place. 220.

ANALOGY. Partial resemblance of things which differ in certain aspects. 132 f.

ANALYSIS, logical. Resolution of a concept into the more simple, that is, into the more universal concepts actually contained in its comprehension, and which are none other than the elements or essential parts of a definition, 24, 41. It differs from logical division which is the resolution of a concept into the less universal concepts contained potentially in its extension.

ANALYTIC proposition. Which has a predicate necessarily belonging to it or included in the logical analysis of its subject. 113 f.

ANGELS. Spiritual substances whose essence is not composed like that of material things. 143, 237, 260, 270, 429, 520 f.

ANIMALS. Living beings possessed of organic and sensory faculties but deprived of intellectual and will power. 326 f.

ANNIHILATION. Reduction of a thing to nothing. 474 f.

ANTECEDENT. Member of a proposition which expresses the condition on which the other member or consequent depends. 42.

A POSTERIORI, argument. Argument called *quia*, used in Induction to establish the existence and the nature of a cause from a careful study of its effects. 116, 117.

APPETENCY. From the Latin *appetitus*, meaning the tendency of a thing towards its end. Instinct and the human will are called appetencies.

APPREHENSION. Act by which the intellect conceives an idea without forming a judgement about it. 104.

A PRIORI, argument. Argument called *propter quid* used in Deduction to prove that a conclusion is contained in the general principles affirmed in the premisses. 116, 117.

ASSENT. Intellectual acquiescence in truth. 94 f.

B

BEING. Transcendental concept which can be affirmed by analogy of all that is or exists. 125 f.

BELIEF. Assent of the mind based on trustworthy testimony. 120 f.

C

CARDINAL, number. Quantity with discontinuous parts, or parts which have no essential and fixed order. 238 f.

CATEGORIES. The ten supreme modes or classes of being, also called predicaments. They are logical or metaphysical according to whether they refer to logical or metaphysical beings. 36, 160.

CATEGORICAL. Predicamental, included in, or belonging to, one of the categories. Opposed to transcendental, to conditional 42.

CAUSE. That which directly contributes to the production of a thing. There are four kinds of causes, the material, formal, efficient and final cause. 192, 195 f., 204.

CHANCE. That to which are sometimes attributed unpredictable or unexplainable events. 208, 209.

CHANGE. Passage from one state to another. There are substantial and accidental changes. 197, 220.

CIRCUMSCRIPTION. Limitation of matter by quantitative dimensions which earmark and individuate matter. 257.

CO-EXISTENCE. Shared existence of things which have no proper existence of their own, but exist in and by something else. Thus matter and form share the existence of the suppositum, accidents that of substance. 176, 231, 476.

COGITATIVE. Human faculty which corresponds to the *Aestimativa* or power of estimation called instinct in animals. It collaborates very intimately with the intellect and is therefore called particular reason. 376 f, 444 f.

COGNITION. Act of acquiring knowledge by sense-perception or by intellectual abstraction. It is performed by a vital representation of an object in the cognizing faculty. 333 f.

COMMANDED ACT. That by which the will makes the other faculties accomplish what it has itself, by an elicited act, decided should be done. 487 f, 514 f.

COMMON SENSE. Spontaneous adhesion of the mind to that which is true and reasonable. 72, 83, 97.

COMPREHENSION. Sum of the essential elements of a concept expressed by a definition. 24 f.

CONCEPT. Intellectual representation of the nature of a thing abstracted from the individual characteristics of matter. Also called idea, thought and impressed species. 78, 363, 403 f, 414.

CONCRETE. Individual, not universal. Concrete is a synonym of material only in material things, the individuality of which is tied up with their materiality. Spiritual things are concrete natures unless they are considered in the abstract, because they are individual and not universal. So also the individual nature of material things is a concrete one even when considered as distinct from the suppositum. 170, 436.

CONDITION. That which is required for the production of an effect, but which does not contribute directly towards it.

CONDITIONAL propositions. Those which assert the dependence of one of their members upon the other. They are purely conditional, conjunctive or disjunctive. 42 f.

CONSCIOUSNESS. Internal sense, also called *sensus communis* or fundamental sense. There is also an intellectual consciousness which is not a special faculty but only a special function of the intellect: it is direct or reflex. 350 f.

CONSEQUENCE. Logical inferential connection between the members of a conditional or disjunctive proposition, or between a conclusion and the premisses of a syllogism. 53.

CONSEQUENT. Member of a proposition which depends on a condition expressed in the other member, or conclusion of an argument. 42, 53.

CONTINGENT. That which might not have existed or could cease to exist. It is opposed to necessary. 52, 115.

CONTINUUM. Quantity the internal parts of which have no distinct or separate extremities and follow each other in an immutable order. It is an ordinal quantity and thus differs from a cardinal or discrete one. 238.

CONTRADICTORY proposition. That which denies exactly what another affirms, or affirms what another denies. 46 f.

CONTRARY proposition. One which is incompatible with another. 49 f.

CONVERSION. Transposition of the terms of a proposition, namely of its subject and predicate, according to certain rules, in such a manner that **the converted proposition follows** as a consequence from the first one. 63 f.

CREATION. Production of something out of absolutely nothing. God
alone can create. Each human soul is created. 310, 312.

CRITERION, of truth. Ultimate motive of assent, or, according to others,
supreme test of truth. 124.

D

DEDUCTION. Method of reasoning from general principles to particular
conclusions, opposed to Induction, and generally expressed by a
syllogism. 167.

DEFINITION. Proposition which states the next higher genus and the
last specific difference of a thing. 41, 88.

DELIBERATION. Act by which the intellect judges whether an object is
suitable to be accepted by the will. 49 f. (49 f.)

DIFFERENCE. That by which one species is not another. Strictly speaking a difference is always specific and is thus not a synonym of
distinction. 19.

DILEMMA. Argument that concludes against an opponent from both the
members of a disjunctive proposition called the horns of the dilemma.
51.

DIMENSION. Linear measurement of a continuous quantity in length,
breadth or depth. 241.

DIRECT knowledge. Intellectual knowledge which does not require a
return upon our own mind or on our intellectual acts. 425 f.

DISCRETE. Discontinuous quantity the parts of which have distinct
extremities. 238 f.

DISCURSIVE knowledge. Knowledge acquired by mental discourse,
namely by reasoning. 426.

DISJUNCTIVE proposition. Conditional proposition with two contradictory members. 45.

DISPUTATION, scholastic. Discussion of a thesis in strict syllogistic
form, in which the first figure of syllogisms ought to be used to make
it easier for the defender to distinguish the middle term and for the
opponent to follow up his objections by denying the minor premiss.
The second figure may be used for the last objection.

DISTINCTION. Non-identity of two things. It is logical or real according to whether it is made between two aspects of the same thing, or
between two existing things, even if these are not separable.
151, 166, 167.

DISTRIBUTIVE term. Which is common to all the individuals of a species.
Propositions are called distributive or universal if they have a distributive subject. 30 f.

DIVISION, logical. Enumeration of the inferior concepts contained in the
extension of a logical universal as in a potential whole, such as rational
and irrational in *animal*. 19.

DIVISIBILITY of matter. Separability of the potential parts of a continuum. 244, 253, 259, 325. Of form. 258 f.

DOUBT. State of mind in which assent is suspended through fear of
error. 108.

DURATION. Continued existence of a thing. There are three kinds of
duration: time, eviternity and eternity. 296 f.

E

EFFECT. Change or alteration produced by an agent. It can be proximate of remote; the proximate effect is called passion and only differs mentally from the agent's action. 202, 337.

EFFICIENT cause. Active power which produces a substantial or accidental change. Its existence cannot be denied. 201, 205 f.

EGO. Modern term which designates the suppositum or person. 457.

ELEMENTS. Physical component parts which remain virtually in the compound. 224. We also talk of logical and metaphysical elements. 24.

ELICITED ACT. Act by which the will elects to follow the last practical judgement of the mind and rejoices in this election. 485 f, 507.

EMINENTLY. In a superior and more perfect manner.

EMOTION. Adaptation of the organism to a conscious physical reaction. 382 f.

ENS. Latin equivalent of the term being. 140.

ENTITATIVE potency. The essence considered as needing to be perfected, whilst entitative act is existence considered as giving perfection, in the order of being or existence, *in linea existentiae*. Accidents are entitative potencies, since their particular manner of determining a substance needs to be actuated by the existence of the substance. 140, 177 f.

EQUIVOCAL TERMS. Words which are written or pronounced in the same way, but which have an entirely different meaning. 10, 129.

ERROR. Absence of logical truth. It must be carefully distinguished from ignorance and falsehood. 82, 103 f, 347.

ESSENCE. That which makes a thing what it is, in opposition to existence. 17, 141, 146 f.

ESSENTIAL. Which belongs to, or is inseparable from, the essence or nature of a thing. It is opposed to accidental.

ESTIMATIVA. See Cogitative. 376, 444 f.

ETERNITY. Perpetual and immutable existence of God. In a loose sense Angels and the human soul are called eternal because they will never cease to exist although they have had a beginning and are subject to change. 298 f.

EVITERNITY. Duration or enduring existence of created spirits. 297.

EXERCITO, in actu. Expression which means that an action is to be considered purely in the light of its execution, not in that of the agent's intention in which case it would be said to be *in actu signato*. 358.

EXISTENCE. That which makes a thing be, as distinct from the term *essence*. 140, 153 f.

EXTENSION, logical. Universality or distribution of a term or of a concept which makes it common to several species or individuals. 25 f.

EXTENSION, physical. Synonym of continuous quantity or dimension.

EXTRINSICALLY. With regard to external and accidental qualities or circumstances; in opposition to intrinsically, namely with regard to the essence or to the essential components and properties. 463.

EVIDENCE. Undeniable agreement of subject and predicate. This is objective evidence. Subjective evidence is the clear vision of this agreement. 98 f, 109 f, 118 f.

EVIL. Absence of an actuality of being. It can be divided into evil of nature, of pain and of sin. 215 f., 509.

EVOLUTION. Theory of the origination of one species from another. Inorganic evolution is usually termed Transformism. Organic evolution deals with the origin of living species. 308 f.

EXPRESSED SPECIES. Appearance assumed by the mind when it is modified by the impressed species or concept. It is a perfect resemblance or expression of an object as *cognized* and understood by the mind. 420 f.

F

FACULTIES. Immediate and proximate principles of vital acts. The nature or essence of a thing is the remote and mediate principle, the suppositum or person is the subject which as a whole accomplishes those acts. 340 f, 439, 451, 452.

FAITH. Assent of the mind based on authority; it is a firmer assent than simple belief, 120 f.

FALLACY. Erroneous argument with the appearance of truth. 66.

FIGURE. Form given to a syllogism by the position of its middle term. There are four figures. 55.

FINAL CAUSE. Purpose. There is a purpose in every event, but only intellectual beings are able to know this purpose. The doctrine of the final cause is also called Teleology or Entelechia. 199, 208, 331, 491, 504.

FORM. Determining and specifying principle of things. It is either substantial or accidental. 227, 258, 448 f., 258 f.

FORMALLY. Considered from the point of view of the specific form. This term can be used in opposition to *materially*, i.e. from the point of view of the material or common element of a thing; to *accidentally*, i.e. with regard to an accidental property; to *radically*, namely with regard to the suppositum considered without its subsistence, and finally to *fundamentally* when speaking of the universal as it exists outside the mind. 80, 145, 159, 162.

FREE-WILL. Man's freedom of choice in selecting the means he prefers to attain an end. 123, 491 f.

FRUITION. Relief of the will when, after deliberation, the mind arrives at a final judgement. 513.

FUNDAMENTALLY. Not formally or actually universal as the concept is, but only potentially so, the same specific nature of several things being the foundation of the universality of the concept. 80, 145, 159.

G

GENERATION. Scholastic term used for the general idea of production. Opposed to corruption which means destruction. 222.

GENUS. Common nature or essence of several species. 18 f., 131.

GOODNESS. Transcendental property of being, meaning its actuality or perfection. 214, 492.

H

HABIT. predicamental. One of the ten Categories. 37.

HABITS. Acquired reflexes performed easily and often unconsciously. 391 f.

HUMAN SOUL. Substantial, spiritual and immortal form of man. 448 f.

HYLOMORPHISM. Theory of primary matter and substantial form. 219 f.

HYPOSTASIS. Term used in theology to designate the suppositum or person.

I

IDEA. Concept. Strictly it would mean only an archetype idea, but it is used as a synonym of concept and even of mental images or phantasms. This term must be used with care to avoid equivocation. 404.

ILLUSION. Erroneous sense-perception. It does not really occur in the sense, but in the interpretation of sensation. 90 f. 347.

IMAGE, mental. See Phantasm.

IMAGINATION. Internal sense by which we perceive absent objects. 360 f.

IGNORANCE. Absence of knowledge. 104.

IMMANENT ACT. Which perfects the actual agent performing it. Opposed to transient act, the scope of which is to perfect an object distinct from the agent. 300 f, 421, 422.

IMMATERIAL. Spiritual or not material, that is, not measurable by quantitative dimensions. 257, 448 f.

IMMEDIATE action. Which follows without an appreciable lapse of time. A cause is immediate when it acts without an intermediary cause or medium; thus instruments are immediate causes, the principal agent is a mediate or remote one. The intellect is the immediate cause of cognition because the concept is not a medium *by* which but *in* which we know directly the object as in or through a mirror. 174, 205, 420.

IMMORTALITY. Indestructibility of the human soul. 468 f.

IMPENETRABILITY. Exclusion of two material substances from the same place at the same time. It can be suspended by divine power. 251 f., 401.

IMPRESSED SPECIES. Spiritual representation of an object abstracted from all material characteristics and impressed on the intellect. 339, 413 f.

INBORN ideas. Which the mind would have been endowed with from birth. Also called innate. That we have such ideas contradicts facts. 366, 426, 460, 469, 523.

INDIVIDUAL. Not shared by another. The existing substance is individual, and also its nature or its essence considered apart from its existence. 168 f.

INDIVIDUAL CONCEPT. That of a particular object. 435 f.

INDIVIDUATION, principle of. Which makes an individual numerically distinct from another. 246, 247, 255 f.

INDIVISIBLE. That cannot be divided. Simple concepts such as being, are logically indivisible. The point and the instant are physical indivisibles. Substantial form is also indivisible. 242 f., 258, 282 f.

INDUCTION. Inference from particular facts to general conclusions. 67 f.

INFERENCE, principle of. On which all reasoning is based, namely that two things equal to a third are equal to each other. 84 f. 112. Conditional inference. 43.

INFERIOR, logical. A less universal term or concept when compared to another superior one. 26 f.

INFINITE. Without limits to its perfection or else to its need and deficiency. 265 f, 276.

INFINITE series. Series of things every one of which would depend on still another one, which is impossible. 163, 456.

INNATE ideas. See Inborn.

INSTANT. The indivisible and continually flowing reality of motion and time. 282 f, 293.

INSTINCT. Animal faculty, of estimation. 326, 376 f., 444 f.

INSTRUMENTAL cause. That which acts in virtue of the power of another cause, namely of the principal cause. 192 f.

INTELLECT. Spiritual faculty capable of knowing the nature of things. 394 f.

INTENTION. Elicited act of the will. 485, 502 f.

INTENTION, first and second. Synonyms for direct and reflex concepts. 417 f. 431.

INTENTIONAL. Spiritual mode of being proper to abstract concepts, and, in a certain degree, to the sense-impressed species. 339, 405, 417 f.

INTERACTION. Reciprocal influence of the body and soul. 464 f.

INTERNAL QUANTITY. Internal order of the parts in the whole without respect to the place they occupy, 240, 249 f.

INTRINSICALLY. See extrinsically.

INTUITION. Mode of knowing which enables the mind to understand as soon as it grasps the meaning of the terms. 110, 428, 523.

J

JUDGEMENT. Affirmation or negation of the identity between a subject and predicate. Judgements are true or false, self-evident or not, analytic or synthetic. 38 f, 109.

L

LIFE. Existence of a being able to perform immanent or self-perfecting actions. 300 f.

LINEA existentiae, in. With regard to the existence of the thing in question, in opposition to *in linea essentiae*, with regard to the essence. 177, 178.

M

MAJOR, MINOR. First and second premiss of a syllogism. The major and minor terms are those of the conclusion which are contained respectively in the major and in the minor premiss. 54.

MATERIAL. Composed of, or dependent on, matter. The proof of the materiality of a thing is its measurability by quantitative dimensions. 245, 448.

MATERIALLY. With respect to the material or generic part of a thing.

MATTER, primary. Subjective potency which, united to the quidditative act or substantial form, constitutes a material essence. Secondary matter is the complete material essence with its accidents. 225 f, 228 f, 257.

MEASURABILITY. Relationship between the quantitative parts of a thing and those of another taken as unities. 252.

MEMORY. Internal faculty of recalling past events and of recognizing them. 370 f.

MIDDLE TERM. Term common to both premisses of a syllogism. 54

MIND. Faculty of forming either mental images or abstract concepts. To avoid equivocation, the context must make it clear whether this term is meant to designate the imagination or the intellect. 360, 395.

MENTAL IMAGES. Internal representations of material objects after the sense-stimulus has ceased. 360, 369. Not to be confused with after-images or concepts. 78, 367, 404.

MNEMONIC. That helps the memory. Logic makes use of the mnemonic letters A. E. I. O. to designate propositions, 34, 56; and of the mnemonic words Barbara, Celarent, Cesare, Camestres and Camenes and others, to facilitate the construction of syllogisms. 59, 373.

MODAL ACCIDENT. Relation, which has no other reality than to be a mode. 182.

MODAL DISTINCTION. That which exists between two things, one of which belongs to the other. 151, 167, 168.

MODAL PROPOSITION. That in which the predicate is referred to the subject in a similar manner. 52.

MODE. Configuration given to a syllogism by quantity and quality. 57. Supreme mode of being. 37, 135. Relative mode. 185.

MOTION. Actuality of a thing which is still receding from its state of potentiality. 281 f.

MULTITUDE. Discrete or discontinuous quantity. It is cardinal, its units having no fixed order. It can be conceived as being negatively infinite. 240, 268 f.

N

NATURE. Essence considered as the remote principle of action rather than as an intrinsic constituent of being. 158. The nature of a thing is universal or common to all the individuals of the same species. 79.

NUMBER. Ratio or proportion between the units of a discrete quantity. 261 f, 330.

O

OBEDIENTIAL potency. Capacity of being modified directly by the First Cause. 144.

OBJECTIVE. Real, in opposition to subjective which means existing only in the mind. With regard to potency, however, the meaning of these terms is reversed: objective potency meaning something conceived by the mind as possible, subjective potency meaning the subject which forms one of the real constituents of being, namely the essence, or, in material things, the primary matter. 144, 148, 229.

OBJECT. The primary objects of intellectual knowledge are material things. The secondary ones are spiritual objects. 431.

OPPOSITION. Contradiction or contrariety of propositions. 42, 50.

ORDER. Invariable sequence of the parts of a continuum. 239 f.

ORGANICITY. Characteristic of living bodies which consists in the special design and co-ordination of their parts in view of the perfection of the whole. 324 f, 451.

P

PART. That into which a whole can be divided. 238.

PARTICULAR TERM. Term which is not meant to designate all the individuals contained in its extension. 9, 30.

PARTICULAR REASON. See Cogitative.

PASSION. Action considered as being submitted to. 190 f.

PASSIONS. Emotions.

PASSIVE FACULTY. That is set in motion and stirred to action by the object it knows. 336, 412, 413 f.

PERCEPTION. Special function of consciousness. Often used as a synonym of cognition in general. 355 f.

PERFECTION. Completion or actuation given to a thing by its act. Some accidental perfections are absolute, such as to be able to see; others are relative such as to be able to bark. 214

PER SE, PER ACCIDENS. Absolutely, in a straightforward meaning, or relatively namely under a particular point of view or according to some casual perfection or circumstance.

PERSON. Existing individual or suppositum endowed with the power of intellection. 164 f.

PHANTASM. Mental image of a thing or of a sensation previously experienced; it always presupposes sense-experience. See Imagination. 360 f, 440 f, 463.

PLACE. Surface surrounding a body considered as immovable. 270 f.

PORPHYRIAN TREE. Diagram of logical universals. 29.

POTENCY. That which can be or act. Active potency is a vital or non vital energy. Objective potency is possibility. Subjective potency is a subject in need of completion namely primary matter which is a quidditative potency, and essence which is an entitative potency. Accidents are entitative potencies. 144 f, 148, 177 f, 229.

POTENCY OF MATTER. Forms inferior to the human soul are said to return to the potency of matter when the individual ceases to exist because, under appropriate conditions, that individual could be made to exist again with its previous form which would thus be drawn out of the potency of matter. 233, 235, 332.

PREDICABLE. That which can be predicated univocally of a subject. There are five kinds of predicables. 16 f, 180.

PREDICAMENTS. See Categories.

PREDICAMENTAL. Categorical, belonging to a category, as opposed to transcendental or metaphysical. 22, 180, 184, 257.

PRINCIPLES. Propositions needing no demonstration. First or primary principles are self-evident; secondary principles are taken for granted, having been proved elsewhere. 109 f.

PRIORITY OF TIME. Antecedence of that which precedes by a measurable duration of time. Priority of nature is that of a thing upon which the existence of something else depends, even though it has no precedence in time; thus we talk of primary and secondary acts or forms of primary matter, of a cause being prior to its effect. 174, 202.

PROPOSITION. Verbal expression of a judgement. 38 f.

PURPOSE. Final cause or design. Only intellectual beings can be conscious of the purpose of their own actions and of that of other things. See Final Cause. Purpose constitutes the object of the will's intention. 68, 331, 481, 491, 502 f.

Q

QUALITY, logical. Affirmative or negative quality of a proposition. 34, 56.

QUALITY, metaphysical. One of the nine accidents, divided into habits, power, physical attributes and figures. 161.

QUANTITY, logical. Distribution or non-distribution of the subject of a proposition. 34, 56.

QUANTITY, metaphysical. Accident which is the cause of a plurality of distinct material parts. 238 f., 398.

QUIDDITATIVE potency. Primary matter, which is wanting in perfection in the order of essence, *in linea essentiae*, until it has been united to the quidditative act, namely substantial form. 141 f, 148, 178, 229.

R

RADICAL suppositum. Individual nature which is not actually a suppositum by itself, but which is the basis or root from which the suppositum derives by the addition of subsistence. 162, 170.

REAL. Not produced by our minds and existing outside them. The component elements of things are real, such as essence and existence; primary matter and form; the nature or substance of things is hidden by their outward appearances; accidents or qualities which are sense-perceived, such as colour, sound and so forth are all also real, and are not mere subjective creations of the mind. 127 f, 153 f, 179, 231 f, 448.

REASON. Discursive intellect. 427.

REDUCTION. Transformation of a syllogism of another figure into the first one. 62.

REFLEX KNOWLEDGE. Indirect cognition of abstract or spiritual things which form the secondary object of our intellect. 431 f.

REFLEXES. Unconscious automatic movements, and also muscular habits acquired unconsciously, called respectively unconditioned and conditioned reflexes. 387 f.

RELATION. Respect or towardness, existing, or conceived as existing, between two things. 137, 183 f, 257.

RELATIVE. See Absolute.

S

SECUNDUM QUID. See *simpliciter*.

SENSES. Material faculties of cognition, exterior and interior. 346. f.

SENSUS COMMUNIS. Scholastic term for consciousness. 354. See Common Sense.

SEPARATION. Disjunction or division of two things previously joined together. Separable things are distinct, but distinct things are not always separable, such as essence and existence. 151, 168.

SIGNATO. See *exercito*.

SIGNS of distribution. Adjectival particles which serve to determine whether a term is distributive or not, such as none, a few, many, some, all. They are also called sycategorematic signs. 2, 30.

SIMPLE. Not composed of parts. All forms are simple. Physical simple elements are not metaphysically simple.

SIMPLICITER, SECUNDUM QUID. Scholastic expressions used in order to show whether a term is to be taken in its straightforward and obvious meaning or rather in a restricted one, under some particular aspect or point of view. They are more or less synonyms of *absolué* and *relative*, which however usually imply that a term is to be considered without or with regard to something else.

SINGULAR TERM. Which designates only one thing. 5, 33, 58.

SORITES. Special kind of polysyllogism, namely of a syllogism with more than two premisses. 65.

SOUL. Substantial form of living beings. 317 f.

SPACE. Distance between the opposite surfaces of place. 275 f.

SPEECH. Vocal expression of our intellectual acts. Even mental reading is accompanied by incipient movements of the larynx and other muscles of speech. 369.

SPECIES, intentional. See expressed, impressed species.

SPECIES, logical. Predicable which is common to several individuals. 17 f.

SPIRITUAL. That which is not united to, or is not intrinsically dependent on, matter.

SPIRITUALITY of the human soul. 397, 448 f.

SQUARE OF OPPOSITION. Scheme showing how contrary and contradictory propositions are opposed 50.

SUBJECTIVE. See Objective.

SUBJECTIVISM. Theory of those who deny the objectivity of our knowledge. 71 f.

SUBSISTENCE. Ultimate terminus of an individual nature by which this becomes an incommunicable suppositum. 172 f.

SUBSTANCE. That which exists by itself without a supporting subject. This term can be taken in various meanings. 160 f.

SUPERIOR, logical. Term or concept which has more extension and less comprehension than another. 26 f.

SUPPOSITION. Meaning given to a term by the context. 11 f.

SUPPOSITUM. Complete, subsisting and incommunicable nature. Synonym of person. 164 f, 172 f.

SYLLOGISM. Verbal expression of a strict logical deduction from general principles. 53 f. Its reliability. 82 f.

SYNCATEGOREMATIC sign. See Signs.

SYNTHETIC proposition. Proposition with a predicate which could be conceived as not belonging to the subject, and which is known to belong to it only by experimental observation. It is said to be *in materia contingenti*. 115.

T

TELEOLOGY. Doctrine of final causes which teaches that there is a design or purpose in every event. Also called entelechia. 199, 208.

THOUGHT. Synonym of idea. As with the terms idea and mind, the context must show clearly whether thought refers to a mental image or to an abstract concept. 404.

TERMS. Words used as subject or predicate. Any substantive, even when not actually used in a proposition, is sometimes called a term. 1 f.

TIME. Measure of motion conceived as having preceding and following parts. 291 f.

TRADUCIANISM. Theory which maintains that the human soul is transmitted to the child by its parents and not by creation. 312.

TRANSCENDENTAL. Not predicamental, namely not contained in any single category. 135, 212.

TRANSCENDENTAL RELATION. An essential one, without which a thing cannot be conceived, such as that of potency to act, of matter to form. 184, 257.

TRANSIENT ACT. See Immanent.

TRUTH. Logical truth is the correspondence of mind to fact; metaphysical truth is the correspondence of fact to the mind of the Creator. 39, 101 f.

U

UNIFORMITY of nature. Self-evident fact by which nature is known not to vary in its manifestations, unless prevented to perform them on account of some exterior agent. 68.

UNITY. Transcendental property of being which makes each individual whole and undivided. Predicamental unity is the continuity of the quantitative parts of matter. 213.

UNIVERSAL. Common to many. In Logic a distributive term is called universal. Predicables are universal. Concepts are also universal because they abstract from the material individuality of things. We can however know indirectly the individual. 23, 435 f.

UNIVERSALS, problem of. Epistemological question regarding the truth and objectivity of universal terms and concepts. 75 f.

UNIVOCAL TERM. That which has always the same meaning. 10, 130.

V

VOID. Relative void is an empty space, absolute void is the negation of all matter, place and space. 278 f.

VIRTUALLY. Term generally used in opposition to formally, to signify that a thing is not actually present, or is not actually doing something by itself, but that it makes its presence or influence felt by means of someone or something else.

W

WILL. Rational impulse of an intellectual being towards that which is good, capable of freely choosing the means to attain its purpose. 106, 123, 393, 481 f, 491, 502 f.

TRANSCENDENTALISM. Not a philosophical doctrine so much as any single system, *c. g.* 872.

TRANSCENDENTAL RELATION. An ens rationis whose subject cannot be represented as that of power, *such as* matter-form. 784.

TRANSCENDENTAL ALS. See Immanent.

TRUTH. Logical truth is the correspondence of mind to objects; ontological, the correspondence of object to the mind of the Creator. 80, 331 ff.

U

UNIFORMITY of nature. Self-evident truth by which nature is known never to vary, the uniformity of nature prevents it to perform its act. Account of some circumstances, 66.

UNITY. Transcendental property of being which makes each individuality whole and indivisible. Pre-eminent unity is the preliminary for the community. See of nature. 312.

UNIVERSAL. Common to many. In Logic a distributive term. Logical universal. Predicates are analyzed. Principles are also universal premises. The abstract from the singular in such kind of things. We can know both only the individual. 69.

(1) UNIVERSAL S. problem of. Rational or real question regarding the truth and objectivity of mental terms and concepts. 75 f.

(2) UNIVOCAL TERM. That which has always the same meaning for. 179.

V

VOID. Relative void is an empty space; absolute void is the negation of all matter, place and motion. 328 f.

VIRTUALLY. Term generally used in opposition to formally or actually, that a thing is not actually present, nor is not a really being, something. The itself has that it makes its presence or influence felt by means of something or something else.

W

WILL. Rational appetite of animal desire; being towards that which is good; capable of freely choosing the means to attain its purpose. 700. 114, 393, 341 ff. 363 f.

A SHORT BIBLIOGRAPHY

I.—DICTIONARIES AND ENCYCLOPEDIAS

Dictionnaire de Théologie catholique. 15 vol. Paris. 1909-1947.
SIGNORIELLO, NUNTIUS. Lexicon peripatecicum philosophics-Theologicum in quo Scholasticorum distinctiones et effata praecipua explicantur. 5th ed. Rome, Pustet. 1931.
The Catholic Encyclopedia. 16 vol. New York. New ed. 1936-1941.
RUNES, DAGOBERT D. The Dictionary of Philosophy. 4th ed. New York, Philosophical Library. 1944.
LALANDE, ANDRÉ. Vocabulaire technique et critique de la Philosophie. 6th ed. 2 vol. Paris, Presses Universitaires de France, 1951.
BRUGGER. WALTER. Philosophisches Wörterbuch. 5th ed. Fribourg, Herder. 1953.
WUELLNER, BERNARD, S.J. Dictionary of Scholastic Philosophy. Milwaukee, Bruce Publ. Co. 1956.
Enciclopedia filosofica. 4 vol. Venezia, Centro di Studi Filosofici di Gallarate. 1957-1958.

II.—INTRODUCTIONS

JAMES, WILLIAM. Some problems of Philosophy. A beginning of an Introduction to Philosophy. London, Longmans and Green. 1911.
RYAN, JAMES H. An Introduction to Philosophy. New York, Macmillan. 1932.
JOAD, C. E. M. Guide to Philosophy. London, V. Gallanez. 1938.
MURPHY, GARDNER. An Historical Introduction to Modern Psychology. London, Kegan Paul. 1938.
GLENN, PAUL J. An Introduction to Philosophy. St. Louis, Herder. 1944.
GILSON, ETIENNE. Le Thomisme. Introduction à la Philosophie de Saint Thomas d'Aquin. 5th ed. Paris, J. Vrin. 1945.
MARITAIN, JACQUES. Eléments de Philosophie. I. Introduction à la Philosophie. 20th ed. Paris, P. Tequi. 1946.
DE WULF, MAURICE. Initiation à l'étude de S. Thomas d'Aquin. Montreal, Institut d'Etudes Médiévales. 1950.
DE RAEYMAEKER, LOUIS. Introduction à la Philosophie. 4th ed. Louvain, Publications Universitaires. 1956.

III.—PHILOSOPHICAL WORKS AND MANUALS

Stonyhurst Philosophical Series. 10 vol. London, Longmans, Green. 1888. seq.

HUGON, ED. Cursus Philosophiae thomisticae, ad Theologiam Doctoris Angelici propaedeuticus. 3 vol. Paris, Lethielleux. 1907.

Cours de Philosophie. (Mercier, de Wulf, Nys D.) Bibliothèque de l'Institut Supérieur de Philosophie. 12 vol. Louvain, Inst. Sup. de Philosophie. 1892-1947.

ZIGLIARA, TH. M. Summa philosophica. 3 vol. 17th ed. Paris, Beauchesne, 1926.

REMER, VINC. Summa Philosophiae Scholasticae. 6 vol. 7th ed. by Paul Gény, S.J. Rome, Univ. Gregor. 1927-1936.

DE MANDATO, PIO. Institutiones philosophicae, ad normam doctrinae Aristotelis et S. Thomae Aquinatis. 5th ed. Rome, Univ. Gregor. 1929-1930.

MARIANI, BERN. O.S.M. Philosophiae christianae Institutiones in usum adolescentium. 3 vol. Turin-Rome, Marietti. 1932-1936.

FARGES, A. ET BERBADETTE. D. Cours de Philosophie scholastique. 16th ed. Paris, Berche et Pagis. 1934.

GLENN, PAUL J. Scholastic Philosophy. 10 vol. St. Louis, Herder. 1929-1944.

PHILLIPS, R. P. Modern Thomistic Philosophy. 2 vol. London, Burns, Oates and Washbourne. 1934-1948.

IV.—WORKS ON SPECIAL SUBJECTS

WOODWORTH, ROBERT, Psychology. rev. ed. New York, Henry Holl and Co. 1929.

MOORE, THOMAS VERNER. Cognitive Psychology. Chicago, The Lippincott Co. 1939.

BRENNAN, ROBERT E. Thomistic Psychology. A Philosophical Analysis of the nature of man. New York, The Macmillan Co. 1941. General Psychology. An Interpretation of the Science of Mind based on Thomas Aquinas. New York, The Macmillan Co. 1841.

DEZZA, PAULUS, S.J. Metaphysica Generalis. 2nd ed. Rome, Univ. Gregor. 1948.

HOENEN, PETRUS, S.J. Cosmologia.—4th ed. Rome. Univ. Gregor. 1948.

SMITH, VINCENT E. The Elements of Logic. Milwaukee, Bruce Publ. Co. 1957.

V.—HISTORIES OF PHILOSOPHY

TURNER, WILLIAM. History of Philosophy. Boston, The Athenaeum Press. 1903.

Everyman's Library. 700 vol. London, Dent. 1906 seq.

MUIRHEAD, J. H. Contemporary British Philosophy. 2 vol. New York. 1924.

UEBERWEG, FRIEDRICK. Grundriss der Geschichte der Philosophie. 13th ed. 5 vol. Berlin, E. S. Mittler und Sohn. 1926-1953.

RUNES, DAGOBERT D. Twentieth Century Philosophy. Living schools of thought. New York, Philosophical Library. 1944.

COPLESTON, FREDERICK, S.J. A History of Philosophy. (The Bellarmine Series). (Heythrop). 3 vol. London, Burns, Oates and Washbourne. 1946-1953.
DE WULF, MAURICE. Histoire de la philosophie médiévale. 6th ed. 3 vol. Louvain, Inst. Super. de Philosophie. 1947. English translation of 5th ed. by Ernest Messenger, London.
SCHNEIDER, HERBERT W. A History of American Philosophy. New York, 1949.
GILSON, ETIENNE. A History of Christian Philosophy in the Middle Ages. New York, Random House. 1954.
COLLINS, JAMES. A History of Modern European Philosophy. Milwaukee, Bruce Publ. Co. 1954.
GLENN, PAUL J. The History of Philosophy. St. Louis (Missouri). 13th reprint. Herder. 1948.